FROM MARX TO MAO AND MARCHAIS

FROM MARX TO MAO AND MARCHAIS

DOCUMENTS ON THE DEVELOPMENT OF COMMUNIST VARIATIONS

Edited by
DAN N. JACOBS

LONGMAN
New York and London

FROM MARX TO MAO AND MARCHAIS
Documents on the Development of Communist Variations

Longman Inc., New York
Associated companies, branches, and representatives throughout the world.

Developmental Editor: Edward Artinian
Editorial and Design Supervisor: Linda Salmonson
Design: Tim McKeen
Manufacturing and Production Supervisor: Louis Gaber
Composition: Maryland Linotype Composition Co., Inc.
Printing and Binding: The Murray Printing Company

Library of Congress Cataloging in Publication Data

Main entry under title:
From Marx to Mao and Marchais.
Includes index.
1. Communism—History—Sources. I. Jacobs, Daniel Norman, 1925–
HX40.F74 335.43'09 78–13764
ISBN 0–528–28062–1

Manufactured in the United States of America

CONTENTS

PREFACE

From Marx to Mao and Marchais is intended principally as a useful adjunct for classroom teaching.

The shorter documents have been reproduced in full; the longer ones have been excerpted with the aim of preserving and highlighting those points that the teacher is most likely to want the student to grasp.

The Introduction is meant to put the documents collectively in historical and political focus. Of course, the instructor can do this in the classroom in greater detail and to better effect, but the Introduction is included should the instructor wish to make use of it in connection with the documents.

The translations of the interview with Togliatti, the speech by Marchais, and the excerpts from *Eurocommunism and the State* were done, respectively, by Peter N. Pedroni, Jane Jackson, and Robert Phillips, all of the faculty of Miami University.

Permission to excerpt from *Eurocommunism and the State* has been received from Lawrence Hill and Co., which controls the English-language rights and has published the entire work.

INTRODUCTION

In one form or another, in one way or another, everything that Marx wrote has been under attack from the day it first appeared in print. This has been so, even—especially—among those who have considered themselves to be "Marxists." Marx himself cautioned that his theory was not a "dogma," and those who have considered themselves to be his followers, in every generation, have taken him at his word and have interpreted and reinterpreted him according to what they have considered the needs of their time and situation. They have sought constantly to bring Marx "up to date." But not all "Marxists" have seen current needs in the same way—and thus there have developed a variety of "authentic" renderings of "Marx in our time." Such was the case eight decades ago—and such is the case today.

When Marx described the disintegration of capitalism, he pictured its total collapse occurring in one of the countries of the highest development of capitalism—in Britain, in Germany, in France. He thought that the revolution which would then take place would be bloody (or perhaps not) and that it would spread from one country to another, until all of mankind was enveloped by it. Many of those who differed with Marx while he still lived, or shortly after he died, disagreed over whether the revolution had to be bloody. They felt that changes that had taken place in capitalism indicated increased possibilities of a "peaceful" transition to socialism.

Lenin did not disagree with Marx essentially over whether the revolution was or was not going to be bloody, but he did "contemporize" him about how and where the revolution would break out. It was to occur not primarily as the result of the progressive deterioration of capitalism, the immiserization, or impoverishment, of the masses, and so forth—but because of the efforts of a small, dedicated corps of full-time, professional revolutionaries. And it was to occur not in the country of the highest development of capitalism but in that of the "weakest link" of capitalism—Russia, whose revolutionizing, despite his obeisance in the direction of the "international" revolution, chiefly interested Lenin.

However, when the revolution actually did break out in Russia, Lenin was convinced that it could not survive there unless it quickly spread to the more highly developed countries of the West. In 1918 and 1919, he waited anxiously on the latest reports from Berlin, Paris, and London to determine if, indeed, the revolution was spreading. When the reports were favorable, he was elated; when they told of working-class defeat or disinterest, he was depressed. In 1919, he created the Communist International (Comintern; CI) to help hasten the spread of revolution abroad.

By 1920, Lenin had reached two conclusions about the revolution: it was not going to spread; nevertheless, it had the possibility for survival in Russia. But, if it was to survive, it had to be nourished. The capitalist regimes in the West, which did not seem in imminent danger of collapse, should not be further antagonized and motivated against Russia by the overt threat of revolutions that were without hope of success. Soviet efforts and resources should, for the time being, be concentrated on building up Russia, not on creating external revolutions.

In the mid-1920s, with Lenin dead, Stalin, who was now

in the driver's seat or rapidly climbing into that perch, despite the warnings against such a development that Lenin left behind, went a step beyond his predecessor to speak of "socialism in one country." At first he thought only in terms of the "possibility" of achieving "socialism in one country," but, shortly, under the force of the popularity of the idea, he began referring to the "necessity" of achieving "socialism in one country" and seemed to be indefinitely postponing, if not dropping, the idea of international revolution.

"Socialism in one country" seemed a reasonable concept, given the isolated situation in which the Soviet regime found itself. But some Bolsheviks, who had come to Marx and the revolution through idealism, with the determination to liberate not only Russians but all humanity, found the direction in which the revolution was moving in Russia to be the antithesis of liberation and the antithesis of internationalism. Their internationalist position, however, was not the popular one in exhausted, chauvinistic Russia. For this and other reasons they lost out, and "socialism in one country" survived as a major pillar of Stalin's establishment position.

The enthronement of "socialism in one country" did not mean that Stalin's regime eliminated the international revolution from its ideology. It continued to speak highly of internationalism, steadfastly expressing its expectation of the latter's ultimate realization; but in practice it sat on it, insisting not only that it be kept under control but that whatever aspects of it were allowed to function be completely at the service of Soviet interests.

The reverse side of "socialism in one country" was that "what is good for the Soviet Union is good for the international movement." It meant that Russian interests always had to come first, before the interests of any other country. Repeatedly in the 1920s and 1930s there was evidence that the Russian nationalism of Stalin's party was unacceptable to some non-Russian communists. But they were a small minority who either voluntarily left the ranks of the Stalin-dominated movement or were forced from them. Opposition to "socialism in one country" was rather easily discouraged or dispatched so long as there was only a single successful revolution and a single socialist regime. The emergence of that regime as the fulcrum of the struggle against fascism—even though it briefly surrendered that role from August 1939 through June 1941, with disastrous results for the membership rolls of the international movement—only strengthened acceptance of "socialism in one country."

But in the wake of World War II, new socialist regimes emerged in Poland, Rumania, Bulgaria, Hungary, Yugoslavia, Albania, and later Czechoslovakia and East Germany. In most instances these regimes were led by domestic communists of long standing who had spent the war years in Moscow, had been installed in power by the Red Army, and were largely without authority in their own countries, except for that imparted by Soviet military might. Such leaders were in no position to contest Soviet appropriation of their railroad rolling stock, bridges, and factories, in order to more speedily build up a war-ravaged Russia, nor to complain about Soviet domination of their bureaucracies and attempts to Russianize and Sovietize their educational systems and national life.

Only in Yugoslavia—where Tito, who had established and led an effective partisan force against the Nazis during World War II, had a strong popular following, and had established his own communist regime—was there the possibility of opposition. And while Tito and his comrades were not oblivious to Soviet communist discipline, and were used to and expected to take Stalin's orders, they were finally moved to protest. When they did, Stalin ousted them from the movement.

The Yugoslavs were shocked—and frightened—at being cast adrift, which Stalin had certainly contemplated. They were not used to standing outside the communist pale. The isolation, the loneliness, was in itself frightening. Even more so were the prospects of domestic anarchy, spurred on among Yugoslavia's numerous minorities by the Soviet Union, or of Russian invasion—or even an attempt by the capitalist world to regain a lost outpost.

In time, however, the Yugoslavs realized that none of these was going to happen, that they were going to have the possibility of their own "socialism in one country," just as the opportunity had been afforded Soviet Russia a quarter of a century earlier. But it would not do for the People's Republic of Yugoslavia simply to repeat Soviet Russian experience. Pride in self and "Yugoslav" distinctiveness and independence, the need to justify their own defiance of Soviet leadership, required altering—improving—the Soviet model. Tito and many of those close to him had spent long periods in the USSR. They knew what its problems had been and were. As loyal partisans of the only revolution and the system that had resulted from it, they had for years blinded themselves to its shortcomings. But having been driven from the Soviet camp, there was no longer reason to hide its errors. The Yugoslavs began to criticize the Russians, and to develop their own *Yugoslav* road to socialism.

Although other Eastern European leaders observed the Yugoslav experience, they were not of a mind, or able if they had been so motivated, to move in similar directions; they were held firmly in the grip of Soviet domination. The Yugoslav aberration, the evidence of support among Soviet Jews for the new state of Israel when its first ambassador to the USSR appeared in Moscow, and, particularly, the victory of the Chinese communists and the establishment of the People's Republic of China, gravely disquieted Stalin. In the last case he was faced not with another small, client state, beholden to him, and subject to his power—even one of these was troubling him—but with the most populous state in the world, possessed of an ancient civilization and headed by an able and determined leader who had exasperated the Kremlin because of his independence for over two decades. By 1948, Stalin already knew that there was also a *Chinese* road to socialism. There wasn't much he could do about it, but he could admonish those, whether in the USSR or in Eastern Europe, who might have ideas suggestive of independence, that he would not put up with any nationalist nonsense from them. He embarked upon a bloody campaign against cosmopolitan, international-style communists to blacken Titoism and to warn of what would happen to those who embraced it—or even gave evidence of thinking about it.

As long as Stalin remained alive, no additional roads to socialism appeared. But his death in 1953 ushered in a gradually and intermittently appearing "thaw" in the Soviet Union that served to further undermine "socialism in one country." Khrushchev, who was engaged in the struggle to succeed Stalin, visited Yugoslavia on his initial trip abroad and tried to win the renewed adherence of Tito to the Soviet camp. He only partially succeeded, and in a continuing attempt to placate particularly the Yugoslav leadership, in February 1956, in his "Report to Party Congress XX," he endorsed the concept of *many roads* to socialism. He noted that already there were a number of different forms of "reorganization of society on socialist foundations," and indicated that it "is quite probable that the forms of transition to socialism will become more and more varied."

Despite such assurance from the Soviet source, there remained strong objection to the concept of many roads to socialism among communists both inside and outside the USSR. In Eastern Europe, the abrogation of "socialism in one country" was seen as a direct threat to those local leaders who had come to power under Stalin and had carried out his instructions often at the expense of their own people. They felt that they were being abandoned to the whim of domestic popularity. Such local leadership was placed under additional pressure by Khrushchev's revelations about Stalin at Party Congress XX. The great man whom all had worshipped as a "genius," a courageous lover of humanity, was revealed to be a scheming, murderous misanthrope. All that he and his followers represented was disclosed to have been a snare and a delusion. The survivors were deprived of their authority.

Out of the confusion created by Stalin's death, the gradually developing "thaw," Khrushchev's "Secret Speech," and the resultant damage to Soviet and communist authority, came the aborted revolution in Poland in October 1956, and the bloody Hungarian revolution of late October–early November of the same year.

Though Soviet armed intervention prevented Hungary from pulling out of the Warsaw Pact and kept the Eastern

European bloc intact, it did not solve the crisis of Soviet leadership, either inside the Soviet Union or with respect to the international movement. The Soviet Union had the raw power to dominate, but could it only dominate by armed might? What was to be its role in those countries and among those parties where the threat posed by the Red Army was not decisive; in places like Yugoslavia, China, France, and Italy?

Gradually, the Soviet leadership was able to abate the disintegration of the movement which threatened in late 1956. It did this through the warning issued by its move into Hungary, through limited concessions, and by the realization of other communists that although they disliked Soviet domination, they did not necessarily dislike the Soviet model and they needed its presence. Without it, their own power was threatened.

It had gradually been recognized by individual communist regimes that the disintegration of Soviet authority was not only an opportunity but also a danger to communism everywhere. Both aspects were particularly evident to the Chinese, who welcomed the weakening of the Russian position among the communist parties of the world because it strengthened their own, but did not want to see the movement disintegrate, because it was a source of psychological and physical support for them. Moreover, they wished to see the movement remain intact, because they hoped to take an increasingly significant role in leading it.

Accordingly, in late 1956 and early 1957, the Chinese communists sought to strengthen the standing of the Soviet Union in the movement. They maintained the correctness of the Soviet position: *against* Stalin, and *in favor of* many paths to socialism and the Soviet intervention in Hungary. And they involved themselves on the Soviet behalf in negotiations with Eastern European and other communist parties.

But, in exchange for their support, the Chinese expected certain quid pro quos from the Soviets: a sharing of the leadership role in the movement; economic aid on a greatly increased scale; and strong pressures, not excluding the threat of nuclear war, against the United States, to secure the takeover of Taiwan by the mainland government. By the end of 1957, however, the situation in the communist world had stabilized: the danger of its imminent dissolution had dissipated; Khrushchev had emerged victorious over his Stalinist opposition at home—and "Sputnik" had been launched. The world looked like a much more pleasant place to Khrushchev, and he was not about to share the leadership of his part of it with the Chinese, nor, as he saw it, to risk its survival for the sake of Chinese military objectives that were less than prime to him.

Beginning in 1958, the Chinese grew disenchanted with the Russians, with their new "liberalism," and with Khrushchev. It became increasingly clear that Russian and Chinese objectives were not the same: that the two countries were at different stages of development and had different perspectives on the matters of war and peace, conflicting aspirations to dominate the international movement, long-standing territorial disputes, and well-established suspicions of each other's leaders and peoples.

Out of these differences came the increasingly vituperative attacks that characterized Sino-Russian relations beginning in the late 1950s. At times, the recriminations were soft-pedaled, as when Khrushchev was removed from office in 1964 and following Mao's death in 1976. But the respites were only temporary. In 1969, the differences resulted in pitched battles along the Ussuri River involving hundreds of men. The Russians and Chinese argued over numerous subjects—over Stalin, Tito, Khrushchev, Mao; over the Chinese way to socialism versus the Soviet way ("one-pot communism" versus "goulash communism"); over which was the greater friend of peace, the stauncher defender of proletarian interests, the truer follower of Lenin. But whatever form the argument took, its primary concern was: who is going to dominate the movement?

The Chinese road to socialism took on different complexions at different times. Sometimes it was more agricultural-based, sometimes less; sometimes it was characterized by a pursuit of the classic model of modernization, sometimes it was not; sometimes it seemed to run off after purely ideological objectives, sometimes it was rigidly pragmatic. But, whatever the case, it was always distinctively pro-Chinese, as seen by its leadership, just as "socialism in one country" had been distinctively pro-Russian.

Although Sino–Soviet differences largely dominated the landscape of international communism during the 1960s, they did not blot out developments elsewhere. Soviet intervention in Hungary in 1956 had served as a warning to other Eastern European countries that they would not be permitted to break off membership in the Soviet bloc. But the push for liberalization within the Soviet Union, Khrushchev's desire to appear reasonable, and the Russians' apparent determination to avoid a repetition of the Hungarian experience all indicated that there was still the possibility of local variation, if it was wished, and if the approval—or at least indifference—of the Kremlin could be guaranteed. This meant that in the various Eastern European countries, different patterns developed: Hungary strayed from the Soviet path domestically, allowing a considerable assortment of lower-level experiments, but moved hardly at all from the Soviet line in foreign policy. Rumania's economy was developed strictly according to Soviet doctrine, but in foreign policy that country repeatedly indicated independence of the USSR. Such departures were abided by the Soviet Union, in the name of peace and stability. But, in 1968, Czechoslovakia, which had departed scarcely at all from the course indicated by Soviet leadership, began to veer strongly in new directions. Not only did Czechoslovakia move to decentralize her economy, making it more responsive to popular demand (thus in two ways breaking from the Soviet model), but—more alarmingly, to Russian eyes—she also began to speak of the need for democratic reforms and to carry out such changes, laying out a distinctive Czech road to socialism.

The Czech road, particularly its democratic impulses, was highly threatening to the USSR, which feared that once innovations had been installed in Prague, it would be difficult to keep them away from Berlin, Warsaw, and Moscow, too.

Though the Soviet leaders had many doubts, were cautioned from many sides against taking action, and proscratinated for weeks, they finally gave the order to move the Red Army and token Warsaw Pact forces against the Prague reformers. They quickly crushed the Czech road to socialism.

Brezhnev justified Soviet intervention in Czechoslovakia by reaffirming Stalin's "socialism in one country," which journalists in the West named the "Brezhnev Doctrine." In it, the Soviet party chief declared that whenever socialism was threatened (only the Soviet leaders could say when that would be) in a country where it already existed, the Soviet regime had the responsibility to intervene to protect it. The disappearance of socialist regimes from countries where they were in power was not good for the Soviet Union; therefore it could not be good for the people of those countries either, regardless of what they themselves thought.

There were few protests in Eastern Europe to the Soviet move into Czechoslovakia. The Yugoslavs didn't like it, and in Red Square a few forlorn dissenters briefly voiced their disapproval. But to an overwhelming degree the bloc took heed of what Russian leadership was saying: we will not, in Eastern Europe, where our military might allows us to control the situation, abide any changes that we consider inimical to Soviet interests. For the next decade and beyond there were few attempts at instituting economic, not to mention political, changes in the socialist countries of the Eastern bloc.

But while there were few protests against the Soviet invasion of Czechoslovakia in the Eastern bloc, shock—though not action—was the almost universal response beyond it. Many parties in the West castigated the Soviet leadership for what was described as its Stalinist conduct; in some communist circles, Soviet behavior was even described as fascist. In instance after instance, Western communist parties disassociated themselves from the Soviet invasion.

When the Western communist parties upbraided the USSR for its move into Czechoslovakia in the late 1960s, they were still trying to cast off the reputation of Stalinism that hampered their quest for power in their own countries.

They had till that time continued, for the most part, to be tightly bound up with the Soviet Union, and they were not prone to gratuitously attack the USSR. But the Czech invasion seemed to Western communists to be particularly loutish and injurious to the image they were trying to develop, and they let their objections be known. However, despite the tongue-lashings directed toward Moscow, they remained closely tied to the Soviet Union. After all, the USSR was, for communist parties not in power, the homeland of the Revolution, the source of ideological certitude, their international security blanket.

For communist parties that had survived in the West, this was the way things had been since their founding. Although Soviet authority had been undermined on more than one occasion—1939, 1956, 1968, to mention three—it still remained strong among parties who were not in power, had seemingly little chance of soon coming to power, and felt alone and isolated in their own countries. But in the 1970s, communist parties in the West, particularly those in Italy and in France, saw what they believed was the development of circumstances that had great potential for catapulting them into power. The economic boom that had carried Western Europe along for more than two decades was coming to an end. Prosperity and a rapidly rising standard of living for many of the working class were replaced by unemployment and inflation. During the affluence of the '50s, '60s, and early '70s, the need for social, political, and economic reform had been obscured. Things were working well —not perfectly, but good enough. There was no push for change. But when things ceased working well, the errors, insufficiencies, and inequities of the system came to the fore. The communists—the traditional party in opposition—saw the opportunity to profit from the accelerating disenchantment with the present.

But the communist parties of Western Europe had two strikes against them. They were believed to be under foreign —Soviet—control. And communist regimes in practice had the reputation of being repressive, undemocratic, and impossible to dislodge once in power. As much as a quarter of a century earlier, Palmiro Togliatti, the Italian party boss at the time, had indicated the necessity for the communist movement in Italy to shed the totalitarian image imparted to it by the Soviet experience. Togliatti wrote of *polycentric* communism and the Italian road to socialism. No one paid much attention to his words at the time or for twenty years after. But now, in the 1970s, Togliatti's strategy took on a new life. Under the leadership of Berlinguer, the CPI vigorously sought to disassociate itself from the Soviet Union, even intimated that in power, having NATO protection *against* the USSR would not be a bad idea. The CPI attacked the repression identified with the Soviet Union, its persecution of minorities, and its lack of democracy. It emphasized a firm belief in democratic procedures, declared devotion to electoral pluralism, and conceived of the possibility that just as it could be voted into power, it could be voted out of power. It espoused what came to be known as *Eurocommunism*.

The French party, encountering the possibility of being elected to power as part of a left coalition in alliance with the socialists, went even beyond the Italian position, and discarded the treasured Marxist principle of the dictatorship of the proletariat. "Dictatorship" was not acceptable under any circumstances. There had already been too many bitter experiences with it. The CPF was more interested in securing electoral support than in maintaining Marxist orthodoxy.

And in 1977, Santiago Carrillo, the secretary general of the recently legalized Communist Party of Spain, also involved in an election, embraced both the Italian and French positions and went still further, to intimate doubt that the USSR was even a socialist state.

In 1977, in the face of almost certain electoral victory, the Communist Party of France began to have second thoughts about the position it had taken. Long a Stalinist-conservative party, strong elements within it opposed criticism of the Soviet Union and the embracing of "bourgeois" democratic values. And when it became apparent that the communists—whose popularity was not really growing, certainly not in comparison with the mushrooming support the socialists were receiving—could not control the left alliance, which would take power, they apparently preferred to break it rather than play second fiddle to the socialists. Although they did not withdraw their recently stated positions on the Soviet Union and democracy, they soft-pedaled them.

But in Spain and Italy, both parties continued full support of Eurocommunism. In both countries, as in France, as wherever such things were discussed, the question arose and was endlessly discussed as to how serious the Western communist parties were in their denunciation of the Soviet Union and their championing of democratic rights. Particularly in the case of Italy and Spain, there seemed reason to *believe* that the party leadership *believed* it was sincere in its criticism of the USSR and its espousal of democracy. But what would happen once communist parties were in power and crisis situations arose? Would a communist Italy, as a member of NATO, take up arms against a rogue Soviet Union? If the communist leadership did not satisfy popular demands, would it permit riots against itself? Would it permit itself to be replaced, if the majority wished such? Out of power, it might sincerely believe so. But when actually confronted, would it? Really?

The international movement has moved far from "socialism in one country," from the time when it was accepted throughout the movement that what was good for the Soviet Union was good for communists everywhere. Today large parts of the movement thrive on attacking the USSR; they take pains to indicate how the Soviet Union has gone wrong and how they differ from it. Many roads to socialism have appeared: Yugoslav, Chinese, Polish, Rumanian, Cuban, Vietnamese—some with significant departures from the Soviet model, some distinguished from it more in that they are non-Russian than in any substantive way. Recently there has appeared still another road, that of Eurocommunism. And even the Soviet model is not what it was under Stalin. Though still rigid and often harsh, it has become somewhat more humane. Under the unabating pressures of modernization, it is likely to become further modified.

The varieties of socialism in the world will doubtless continue to proliferate. The world is, for better or worse, moving steadily away from private ownership, the United States included. The next step—to government ownership—may be a long or a short one, but it is in sequence. While this may in the United States be considered a frightening development, and therefore widely opposed, it is not so in much of the rest of the world.

In its simplest terms, as perceived by most of those throughout the world who have any recognition of such terms at all, socialism stands for government ownership and development of the means of production on behalf of the masses. And it is seen as *good*—everywhere except in the United States and a few other spots.

Socialism, in this sense, is a growing phenomenon, widely accepted. As it spreads, it will perforce take on local coloration. Where its past association with the Soviet Union stands in the way, that association will, sooner or later, be broken off, perhaps even vigorously opposed. Where its emphasis on equality comes to be seen as disabling, that will be modified. Where its name hampers its realization, the name will be changed. Thus, a hundred roads to socialism—or whatever else it may be called—will occur.

But to what degree will these new roads to socialism correspond with the ideas of Karl Marx?

1

THE MANIFESTO OF THE COMMUNIST LEAGUE*

Karl Marx and Friedrich Engels
(Published in London, February 1848)

Of all the documents of the modern socialist movement, The Manifesto of the Communist League, *commonly known as* The Communist Manifesto, *has been the most widely read. It has been published in a hundred languages, in thousands of editions, in millions of copies.*

It and Das Kapital, *which appeared almost two decades later, are the two basic classics of the Marxist library. But whereas* Das Kapital *fills volumes, and tends toward being ponderous and overbearing, the* Manifesto *is comparatively brief and fast-paced, filled with passages that generate excitement, hope, and assurance. Its opening statement ("A specter is haunting Europe—the specter of communism") and its closing one ("The proletarians have nothing to lose but their chains. They have a world to win. Workingmen of all countries unite!") have become the clarion calls of the movement for over a century. Not without good reason the Soviets have referred to the* Manifesto *as "the song of songs of Marxism," even as* Das Kapital *is regarded as its "Bible."*

In contrast with its accomplishments, the Manifesto *started out slowly. It had practically no impact on the revolution of 1848. And for a while, Marx seemed to avoid being*

* Complete

identified as its author. But in time he recognized it as one of the principal sources of his reputation.

The Manifesto *contains virtually all of Marx's important ideas. The dialectic, materialism, the class struggle, the acceleration of capitalist disintegration and proletarian misery —all are here. And they are often expressed in language that has for more than a century quickened the pulses of generations of youthful utopians, seeking a better world.*

A specter is haunting Europe—the specter of Communism. All the powers of old Europe have entered into a holy alliance to exorcise this specter; Pope and Czar, Metternich and Guizot, French radicals and German police spies.

Where is the party in opposition that has not been decried as Communistic by its opponents in power? Where the opposition that has not hurled back the branding reproach of Communism, against the more advanced opposition parties, as well as against its reactionary adversaries?

Two things result from this fact.

1. Communism is already acknowledged by all European powers to be in itself a power.

2. It is high time that Communists should openly, in the face of the whole world, publish their views, their aims, their tendencies, and meet this nursery tale of the Specter of Communism with a Manifesto of the party itself.

To this end the Communists of various nationalities have assembled in London, and sketched the following manifesto to be published in the English, French, German, Italian, Flemish, and Danish languages.

I
BOURGEOIS AND PROLETARIANS[1]

The history of all hitherto existing society[2] is the history of class struggles.

[All foonotes are by Engels.]

1. By bourgeoisie is meant the class of modern Capitalists, owners of the means of social production and employers of wage-labor. By proletariat, the class of modern wage-laborers who, having no means of production of their own, are reduced to selling their labor-power in order to live.

2. That is, all written history. In 1847, the pre-history of society, the social

Freeman and slave, patrician and plebeian, lord and serf, guild master[3] and journeyman, in a word, oppressor and oppressed, stood in constant opposition to one another, carried on an uninterrupted, now hidden, now open fight, that each time ended, either in the revolutionary reconstitution of society at large, or in the common ruin of the contending classes.

In the earlier epochs of history we find almost everywhere a complicated arrangement of society into various orders, a manifold gradation of social rank. In ancient Rome we have patricians, knights, plebeians, slaves; in the middle ages, feudal lords, vassals, guild masters, journeymen, apprentices, serfs; in almost all of these classes, again, subordinate gradations.

The modern bourgeois society that has sprouted from the ruins of feudal society has not done away with class antagonisms. It has but established new classes, new conditions of oppression, new forms of struggle in place of the old ones.

Our epoch, the epoch of the bourgeoisie, possesses, however, this distinctive feature: it has simplified the class antagonisms. Society as a whole is more and more splitting up into two great hostile camps, into two great classes directly facing each other: Bourgeoisie and Proletariat.

From the serfs of the middle ages sprang the chartered burghers of the earliest towns. From these burgesses the first elements of the bourgeoisie were developed.

The discovery of America, the rounding of the Cape,

organization existing previous to recorded history, was all but unknown. Since then, Haxthausen discovered common ownership of land in Russia, Maurer proved it to be the social foundation from which all Teutonic races started in history, and by and by village communities were found to be, or to have been the primitive form of society everywhere from India to Ireland. The inner organization of this primitive Communistic society was laid bare, in its typical form, by Morgan's crowning discovery of the true nature of the Gens and its relation to the Tribe. With the dissolution of these primeval communities society begins to be differentiated into separate and finally antagonistic classes. I have attempted to retrace this process of dissolution in The Origin of the Family, Private Property, and the State.

3. Guild master, that is, a full member of a guild, a master within, not a head of a guild.

opened up fresh ground for the rising bourgeoisie. The East Indian and Chinese markets, the colonization of America, trade with the colonies, the increase in the means of exchange and in commodities generally, gave to commerce, to navigation, to industry, an impulse never before known, and thereby, to the revolutionary element in the tottering feudal society, a rapid development.

The feudal system of industry, under which industrial production was monopolized by closed guilds, now no longer sufficed for the growing wants of the new markets. The manufacturing system took its place. The guild masters were pushed on one side by the manufacturing middle class; division of labor between the different corporate guilds vanished in the face of division of labor in each single workshop.

Meantime the markets kept ever growing, the demand ever rising. Even manufacture no longer sufficed. Thereupon steam and machinery revolutionized industrial production. The place of manufacture was taken by the giant, Modern Industry, the place of the industrial middle class, by industrial millionaires, the leaders of whole industrial armies, the modern bourgeois.

Modern industry has established the world-market, for which the discovery of America paved the way. The market has given an immense development to commerce, to navigation, to communication by land. This development has, in its turn, reacted on the extension of industry; and in proportion as industry, commerce, navigation and railways extended, in the same proportion the bourgeoisie developed, increased its capital, and pushed into the background every class handed down from the middle ages.

We see, therefore, how the modern bourgeoisie is itself the product of a long course of development, of a series of revolutions in the modes of production and of exchange.

Each step in the development of the bourgeoisie was accompanied by a corresponding political advance of that class. An oppressed class under the sway of the feudal nobility, an armed and self-governing association in the medieval commune,[4] here independent urban republic (as in Italy and Germany), there taxable "third estate" of the monarchy (as in France), afterwards, in the period of manufacture proper, serving either the semi-feudal or the absolute monarchy as a counterpoise against the nobility, and, in fact, cornerstone of the great monarchies in general, the bourgeoisie has at last, since the establishment of Modern Industry and of the world-market, conquered for itself, in the modern representative State, exclusive political sway. The executive of the modern State is but a committee for managing the common affairs of the whole bourgeoisie.

The bourgeoisie, historically, has played a most revolutionary part.

The bourgeoisie, wherever it has got the upper hand, has put an end to all feudal, patriarchal, idyllic relations. It has pitilessly torn asunder the motley feudal ties that bound man to his "natural superiors," and has left remaining no other nexus between man and man than naked self-interest, callous "cash payment." It has drowned the most heavenly ecstasies of religious fervor, of chivalrous enthusiasm, of philistine sentimentalism, in the icy water of egotistical calculation. It has resolved personal worth into exchange value, and in place of the numberless indefeasible chartered freedoms, has set up that single, unconscionable freedom—Free Trade. In one word, for exploitation, veiled by religious and political illusions, it has substituted naked, shameless, direct, brutal exploitation.

The bourgeoisie has stripped of its halo every occupation hitherto honored and looked up to with reverent awe. It has converted the physician, the lawyer, the priest, the poet, the man of science, into its paid wage-laborers.

The bourgeoisie has torn away from the family its sentimental veil, and has reduced the family relation to a mere money relation.

4. "Commune" was the name taken, in France, by the nascent towns even before they had conquered from their feudal lords and masters, local self-government and political rights as the "Third Estate." Generally speaking, for the economic development of the bourgeoisie, England is here taken as the typical country; for its political development, France.

The bourgeoisie has disclosed how it came to pass that the brutal display of vigor in the middle ages, which Reactionists so much admire, found its fitting complement in the most slothful indolence. It has been the first to show what man's activity can bring about. It has accomplished wonders far surpassing Egyptian pyramids, Roman aqueducts, and Gothic cathedrals; it has conducted expeditions that put in the shade all former Exoduses of nations and crusades.

The bourgeoisie cannot exist without constantly revolutionizing the instruments of production, and thereby the relations of production, and with them the whole relations of society. Conservation of the old modes of production in unaltered forms, was, on the contrary, the first condition of existence for all earlier industrial classes. Constant revolutionizing of production, uninterrupted disturbance of all social conditions, everlasting uncertainty and agitation, distinguish the bourgeois epoch from all earlier ones. All fixed, fast-frozen relations, with their train of ancient and venerable prejudices and opinions, are swept away; all new-formed ones become antiquated before they can ossify. All that is solid melts into air, all that is holy is profaned, and man is at last compelled to face with sober senses his real conditions of life and his relations with his kind.

The need of a constantly expanding market for its products chases the bourgeoisie over the whole surface of the globe. It must nestle everywhere, settle everywhere, establish connections everywhere.

The bourgeoisie has through its exploitation of the world-market given a cosmopolitan character to production and consumption in every country. To the great chagrin of Reactionists, it has drawn from under the feet of industry the national ground on which it stood. All old-established national industries have been destroyed or are daily being destroyed. They are dislodged by new industries, whose introduction becomes a life-and-death question for all civilized nations, by industries that no longer work up indigenous raw material, but raw material drawn from the remotest zones, industries whose products are consumed, not only at home, but in every quarter of the globe. In place of the old wants, satisfied by the productions of the country, we find new wants, requiring for their satisfaction the products of distant lands and climes. In place of the old local and national seclusion and self-sufficiency, we have intercourse in every direction, universal interdependence of nations. And as in material, so also in intellectual production. The intellectual creations of individual nations become common property. National one-sidedness and narrow-mindedness become more and more possible, and from the numerous national and local literatures, there arises a world literature.

The bourgeoisie, by the rapid improvement of all instruments of production, by the immensely facilitated means of communication, draws all, even the most barbarian, nations into civilization. The cheap prices of its commodities are the heavy artillery with which it batters down all Chinese walls, with which it forces the barbarians' intensely obstinate hatred of foreigners to capitulate. It compels all nations, on pain of extinction, to adopt the bourgeois mode of production; it compels them to introduce what it calls civilization into their midst, i.e., to become bourgeois themselves. In one word, it creates a world after its own image.

The bourgeoisie has subjected the country to the rule of the towns. It has created enormous cities, has greatly increased the urban population as compared with the rural, and has thus rescued a considerable part of the population from the idiocy of rural life. Just as it has made the country dependent on the towns, so it has made barbarian and semi-barbarian countries dependent on the civilized ones, nations of peasants on nations of bourgeois, the East on the West.

The bourgeoisie keeps more and more doing away with the scattered state of the population, of the means of production, and of property. It has agglomerated population, centralized means of production, and has concentrated property in a few hands. The necessary consequence of this was political centralization. Independent, or but loosely connected provinces, with separate interests, laws, governments and systems of taxation, became lumped together into one nation, with one government, one code of laws, one national class interest, one frontier, and one customs tariff.

The bourgeoisie, during its rule of scarce one hundred years, has created more massive and more colossal productive forces than have all preceding generations together. Subjection of Nature's forces to man, machinery, application of chemistry to industry and agriculture, steam nagivation, railways, electric telegraphs, clearing of whole continents for cultivation, canalization of rivers, whole populations conjured out of the ground—what earlier century had even a presentiment that such productive forces slumbered in the lap of social labor?

We see then: the means of production and of exchange, on whose foundation the bourgeoisie built itself up, were generated in feudal society. At a certain stage in the development of these means of production and of exchange, the conditions under which feudal society produced and exchanged, the feudal organization of agriculture and manufacturing industry, in one word, the feudal relations of property, became no longer compatible with the already developed productive forces; they became so many fetters. They had to be burst asunder; they were burst asunder.

Into their place stepped free competition, accompanied by a social and political constitution adapted to it, and by the economic and political sway of the bourgeois class.

A similar movement is going on before our own eyes. Modern bourgeois society with its relations of production, of exchange, and of property, a society that has conjured up such gigantic means of production and of exchange, is like the sorcerer, who is no longer able to control the powers of the nether world whom he has called up by his spells. For many a decade past the history of industry and commerce is but the history of the revolt of modern productive forces against modern conditions of production, against the property relations that are the conditions for the existence of the bourgeoisie and of its rule. It is enough to mention the commercial crises that by their periodical return put on its trial, each time more threateningly, the existence of the bourgeois society. In these crises a great part not only of the existing products, but also of the previously created productive forces, is periodically destroyed. In these crises there breaks out an epidemic that, in all earlier epochs, would have seemed an absurdity—the epidemic of overproduction. Society suddenly finds itself put back into a state of momentary barbarism; it appears as if a famine, a universal war of devastation had cut off the supply of every means of subsistence; industry and commerce seem to be destroyed; and why? Because there is too much civilization, too much means of subsistence, too much industry, too much commerce. The productive forces at the disposal of society no longer tend to further the development of the conditions of bourgeois property; on the contrary, they have become too powerful for these conditions, by which they are fettered, and so soon as they overcome these fetters, they bring disorder into the whole of bourgeois society, endanger the existence of bourgeois property. The conditions of bourgeois society are too narrow to comprise the wealth created by them. And how does the bourgeoisie get over these crises? On the one hand, by enforced destruction of a mass of productive forces; on the other, by the conquest of new markets, and by the more thorough exploitation of the old ones. That is to say, by paving the way for more extensive and more destructive crises, and by diminishing the means whereby crises are prevented.

The weapons with which the bourgeoisie felled feudalism to the ground are now turned against the bourgeoisie itself.

But not only has the bourgeoisie forged the weapons that bring death to itself; it has also called into existence the men who are to wield those weapons—the modern working class—the proletarians.

In proportion as the bourgeoisie, i.e., capital, is developed, in the same proportion is the proletariat, the modern working class, developed; a class of laborers, who live only so long as they find work, and who find work only so long as their labor increases capital. These laborers, who must sell themselves piecemeal, are a commodity, like every other article of commerce, and are consequently exposed to all the vicissitudes of competition, to all the fluctuations of the market.

Owing to the extensive use of machinery and to division of labor, the work of the proletarians has lost all individual character, and, consequently, all charm for the workman. He becomes an appendage of the machine, and it is only the most simple, most monotonous, and most easily acquired knack, that is required of him. Hence, the cost of production of a workman is restricted almost entirely to the means of subsistence that he requires for his maintenance, and for the propagation of his race. But the price of a commodity, and therefore also of labor, is equal, in the long run, to its cost of production. In proportion, therefore, as the repulsiveness of the work increases, the wage decreases. Nay, more, in proportion as the use of machinery and division of labor increase, in the same proportion the burden of toil also increases, whether by prolongation of the working hours, by increase of the work exacted in a given time, or by increased speed of the machinery, etc.

Modern industry has converted the little workshop of the patriarchal master into the great factory of the industrial capitalist. Masses of laborers, crowded into the factory, are organized like soldiers. As privates of the industrial army they are placed under the command of a perfect hierarchy of officers and sergeants. Not only are they slaves of the bourgeois class, and of the bourgeois State, they are daily and hourly enslaved by the machine, by the overseer, and, above all, by the individual bourgeois manufacturer himself. The more openly this despotism proclaims gain to be its end and aim, the more petty, the more hateful and the more embittering it is.

The less skill and exertion of strength is implied in manual labor, in other words, the more modern industry becomes developed, the more is the labor of men superseded by that of women. Differences of age and sex have no longer any distinctive social validity for the working class. All are instruments of labor, more or less expensive to use, according to age and sex.

No sooner is the exploitation of the laborer by the manufacturer so far at an end that he receives his wages in cash, than he is set upon by the other portions of the bourgeoisie, the landlord, the shopkeeper, the pawnbroker, etc.

The lower strata of the middle class—the small tradespeople, shopkeepers, and retired tradesmen generally, the handicraftsmen and peasants—all these sink gradually into the proletariat, partly because their diminutive capital does not suffice for the scale on which modern industry is carried on, and is swamped in the competition with the large capitalists, partly because their specialized skill is rendered worthless by new methods of production. Thus the proletariat is recruited from all classes of the population.

The proletariat goes through various stages of development. With its birth begins its struggle with the bourgeoisie. At first the contest is carried on by individual laborers, then by the workpeople of a factory, then by the operatives of one trade, in one locality, against the individual bourgeois who directly exploits them. They direct their attacks not against the bourgeois conditions of production, but against the instruments of production themselves; they destroy imported wares that compete with their labor, they smash to pieces machinery, they set factories ablaze, they seek to restore by force the vanished status of the workman of the middle ages.

At this stage the laborers still form an incoherent mass scattered over the whole country, and broken up by their mutual competition. If anywhere they unite to form more compact bodies, this is not yet the consequence of their own active union, but of the union of the bourgeoisie, which class, in order to attain its own political ends, is compelled to set the whole proletariat in motion, and is moreover yet, for a time, able to do so. At this stage, therefore, the proletarians do not fight their enemies, but the enemies of their enemies, the remnants of absolute monarchy, the land owners, the non-industrial bourgeois, the petty bourgeoisie. Thus the whole historical movement is concentrated in the hands of the bourgeoisie; every victory so obtained is a victory for the bourgeoisie.

But with the development of industry the proletariat not only increases in number; it becomes concentrated in greater masses, its strength grows and it feels that strength more.

The various interests and conditions of life within the ranks of the proletariat are more and more equalized, in proportion as machinery obliterates all distinctions of labor, and nearly everywhere reduces wages to the same low level. The growing competition among the bourgeois, and the resulitng commercial crises, make the wages of the workers ever more fluctuating. The unceasing improvement of machinery, ever more rapidly developing, makes their livelihood more and more precarious; the collisions between individual workman and individual bourgeois take more and more the character of collisions between two classes. Thereupon the workers begin to form combinations (trade unions) against the bourgeois; they club together in order to keep up the rate of wages; they found permanent associations in order to make provision beforehand for these occasional revolts. Here and there the contest breaks out into riots.

Now and then the workers are victorious, but only for a time. The real fruit of their battles lies not in the immediate result but in the ever-expanding union of the workers. This union is helped on by the improved means of communication that are created in modern industry and that place the workers of different localities in contact with one another. It was just this contact that was needed to centralize the numerous local struggles, all of the same character, into one national struggle between classes. But every class struggle is a political struggle. And that union, to attain which the burghers of the middle ages, with their miserable highways, required centuries, the modern proletarians, thanks to railways, achieve in a few years.

This organization of the proletarians into a class and consequently into a political party, is continually being upset again by the competition between the workers themselves. But it ever rises up again; stronger, firmer, mightier. It compels legislative recognition of particular interests of the workers, by taking advantage of the divisions among the bourgeoisie itself. Thus the ten-hours bill in England was carried.

Altogether collisions between the classes of the old society further, in many ways, the course of the developments of the proletariat. The bourgeoisie finds itself involved in a constant battle. At first with the aristocracy; later on, with those portions of the bourgeoisie itself whose interests have become antagonistic to the progrcss of industry; at all times with the bourgeoisie of foreign countries. In all these battles it sees itself compelled to appeal to the proletariat, to ask for its help, and thus to drag it into the political arena. The bourgeoisie itself, therefore, supplics the proletariat with its own elements of political and general education—in other words, it supplies the proletariat with weapons for fighting the bourgeoisie.

Further, as we have already seen, entire sections of the ruling classes are, by the advance of industry, precipitated into the proletariat, or are at least threatened in their conditions of existence. These also supply the proletariat with fresh elements of enlightenment and progress.

Finally, in times when the class struggle nears the decisive hour, the process of dissolution going on within the ruling class, in fact within the whole range of old society, assumes such a violent, glaring character, that a small section of the ruling class cuts itself adrift, and joins the revolutionary class, the class that holds the future in its hands. Just as, therefore, at an earlier period, a section of the nobility went over to the bourgeoisie, so now a portion of the bourgeoisie goes over to the proletariat, and in particular, a portion of the bourgeois ideologists, who have raised themselves to the level of comprehending theoretically the historical movement as a whole.

Of all the classes that stand face to face with the bourgeoisie today, the proletariat alone is a really revolutionary class. The other classes decay and finally disappear in the face of modern industry; the proletariat is its special and essential product.

The lower middle class, the small manufacturer, the shopkeeper, the artisan, the peasant, all these fight against the bourgeoisie to save from extinction their existence as fractions of the middle class. They are therefore not revolutionary, but conservative. Nay, more, they are reactionary, for they try to roll back the wheel of history. If by chance they are revolutionary, they are so only in view of their impending transfer into the proletariat; they thus defend not their present, but their future interests; they desert their own standpoint to place themselves at that of the proletariat.

The "dangerous class," the social scum, that passively rotting mass thrown off by the lowest layers of old society, may, here and there, be swept into the movement by a proletarian revolution; its conditions of life, howvee, prepare it far more for the part of a bribed tool of reactionary intrigue.

In the conditions of the proletariat, those of old society at large are already virtually swamped. The proletarian is without property; his relation to his wife and children has no longer anything in common with the bourgeois family relations; modern industrial labor, modern subjection to capital, the same in England as in France, in America as in Germany, has stripped him of every trace of national character. Law, morality, religion, are to him so many bourgeois prejudices, behind which lurk in ambush just as many bourgeois interests.

All the preceding classes that got the upper hand sought to fortify their already acquired status by subjecting society at large to their conditions of appropriation. The proletarians cannot become masters of the productive forces of society, except by abolishing their own previous mode of appropriation, and thereby also every other previous mode of appropriation. They have nothing of their own to secure and to fortify; their mission is to destroy all previous securities for, and insurances of, individual property.

All previous historical movements were movements of minorities, or in the interest of minorities. The proletarian movement is the self-conscious, independent movement of the immense majority, in the interest of the immense majority. The proletariat, the lowest stratum of our present society, cannot stir, cannot raise itself up, without the whole superincumbent strata of official society being sprung into the air.

Though not in substance, yet in form, the struggle of the proletariat with the bourgeoisie is at first a national struggle.

The proletariat of each country must, of course, first of all settle matters with its own bourgeoisie.

In depicting the most general phases of the development of the proletariat, we traced the more or less veiled civil war, raging within existing society, up to the point where that war breaks out into open revolution, and where the violent overthrow of the bourgeoisie lays the foundation for the sway of the proletariat.

Hitherto every form of society has been based, as we have already seen, on the antagonism of oppressing and oppressed classes. But in order to oppress a class certain conditions must be assured to it under which it can, at least, continue its slavish existence. The serf, in the period of serfdom, raised himself to membership in the commune, just as the petty bourgeois, under the yoke of feudal absolutism, managed to develop into a bourgeois. The modern laborer, on the contrary, instead of rising with the progress of industry, sinks deeper and deeper below the conditions of existence of his own class. He becomes a pauper, and pauperism develops more rapidly than population and wealth. And here it becomes evident that the bourgeoisie is unfit any longer to be the ruling class in society and to impose its conditions of existence upon society as an over-riding law. It is unfit to rule because it is incompetent to assure an existence to its slave within his slavery, because it cannot help letting him sink into such a state that it has to feed him instead of being fed by him. Society can no longer live under this bourgeoisie; in other words, its existence is no longer compatible with society.

The essential condition for the existence, and for the sway of the bourgeois class, is the formation and augmentation of capital; the condition for capital is wage-labor. Wage-labor rests exclusively on competition between the laborers. The advance of industry, whose involuntary promoter is the bourgeoisie, replaces the isolation of the laborers, due to competition, by their revolutionary combination, due to association. The development of modern industry, therefore, cuts from under its feet the very foundation on which the bourgeoisie produces and appropriates products. What the bourgeoisie therefore produces, above all, are its own grave diggers. Its fall and the victory of the proletariat are equally inevitable.

II
PROLETARIANS AND COMMUNISTS

In what relation do the Communists stand to the proletarians as a whole?

The Communists do not form a separate party opposed to other working-class parties.

They have no interests separate and apart from those of the proletariat as a whole.

They do not set up any sectarian principles of their own by which to shape and mould the proletarian movement.

The Communists are distinguished from the other working-class parties by this only: (1) In the national struggles of the proletarians of the different countries, they point out and bring to the front the common interests of the entire proletariat, independently of all nationality. (2) In the various stages of development which the struggle of the working class against the bourgeoisie has to pass through, they always and everywhere represent the interests of the movement as a whole.

The Communists, therefore, are on the one hand, practically, the most advanced and resolute section of the working-class parties of every country, that section which pushes forward all others; on the other hand, theoretically, they have over the great mass of the proletariat the advantage of clearly understanding the line of march, the conditions, and the ultimate general results of the proletarian movement.

The immediate aim of the Communists is the same as that of all the other proletarian parties: formation of the proletariat into a class, overthrow of the bourgeois supremacy, conquest of political power by the proletariat.

The theoretical conclusions of the Communists are in no way based on ideas or principles that have been invented, or discovered, by this or that would-be universal reformer.

They merely express, in general terms, actual relations springing from an existing class struggle, from a historical movement going on under our very eyes. The abolition of existing property relations is not at all a distinctive feature of Communism.

All property relations in the past have continually been subject to historical change, consequent upon the change in historical conditions.

The French Revolution, for example, abolished feudal property in favor of bourgeois property.

The distinguishing feature of Communism is not the abolition of property generally, but the abolition of bourgeois property. But modern bourgeois private property is the final and most complete expression of the system of producing and appropriating products, that is based on class antagonisms, on the exploitation of the many by the few.

In this sense the theory of the Communists may be summed up in the single sentence: Abolition of private property.

We Communists have been reproached with the desire of abolishing the right of personally acquiring property as the fruit of a man's own labor, which property is alleged to be the ground work of all personal freedom, activity and independence.

Hard-won, self-acquired, self-earned property! Do you mean the property of the petty artisan and of the small peasant, a form of property that preceded the bourgeois form? There is no need to abolish that; the development of industry has to a great extent already destroyed it, and is still destroying it daily.

Or do you mean modern bourgeois private property?

But does wage-labor create any property for the laborer? Not a bit. It creates capital, i.e., that kind of property which exploits wage-labor, and which cannot increase except upon condition of begetting a new supply of wage-labor for fresh exploitation. Property, in its present form, is based on the antagonism of capital and wage-labor. Let us examine both sides of this antagonism.

To be a capitalist, is to have not only a purely personal,

but a social *status* in production. Capital is a collective product, and only by the united action of many members, nay, in the last resort, only by the united action of all members of society, can it be set in motion.

Capital is therefore not a personal, it is a social power.

When, therefore, capital is converted into common property, into the property of all members of society, personal property is not thereby transformed into social property. It is only the social character of the property that is changed. It loses its class character.

Let us now take wage-labor.

The average price of wage-labor is the minimum wage, i.e., that quantum of the means of subsistence, which is absolutely requisite to keep the laborer in bare existence as a laborer. What, therefore, the wage-laborer appropriates by means of his labor, merely suffices to prolong and reproduce a bare existence. We by no means intend to abolish this personal appropriation of the products of labor, an appropriation that is made for the maintenance and reproduction of human life, and that leaves no surplus wherewith to command the labor of others. All that we want to do away with, is the miserable character of this appropriation, under which the laborer lives merely to increase capital, and is allowed to live only in so far as the interest of the ruling class requires it.

In bourgeois society living labor is but a means to increase accumulated labor. In Communist society accumulated labor is but a means to widen, to enrich, to promote the existence of the laborer.

In bourgeois society, therefore, the past dominates the present; in Communist society, the present dominates the past. In bourgeois society capital is independent and has individuality, while the living person is dependent and has no individuality.

And the abolition of this state of things is called by the bourgeois: abolition of individuality and freedom! And rightly so. The abolition of bourgeois individuality, bourgeois independence, and bourgeois freedom is undoubtedly aimed at.

By freedom is meant, under the present bourgeois conditions of production, free trade, free selling and buying.

But if selling and buying disappear, free selling and buying disappear also. This talk about free selling and buying, and all the other "brave words" of our bourgeoisie about freedom in general, have a meaning, if any, only in contrast with restricted selling and buying, with the fettered traders of the middle ages, but have no meaning when opposed to the Communistic abolition of buying and selling, of the bourgeois conditions of production, and of the bourgeoisie itself.

You are horrified at our intending to do away with private property. But in your existing society private property is already done away with for nine-tenths of the population; its existence for the few is solely due to its non-existence in the hands of those nine-tenths. You reproach us, therefore, with intending to do away with a form of property, the necessary condition for whose existence is the non-existence of any property for the immense majority of society.

In one word, you reproach us with intending to do away with your property. Precisely so: that is just what we intend.

From the moment when labor can no longer be converted into capital, money, or rent, into a social power capable of being monopolized, i.e., from the moment when individual property can no longer be transformed into bourgeois property, into capital, from that moment, you say, individuality vanishes!

You must, therefore, confess that by "individual" you mean no other person than the bourgeois, than the middle-class owner of property. This person must, indeed, be swept out of the way, and made impossible.

Communism deprives no man of the power to appropriate the products of society: all that it does is to deprive him of the power to subjugate the labor of others by means of such appropriation.

It has been objected that upon the abolition of private property all work will cease, and universal laziness will overtake us.

According to this, bourgeois society ought long ago to

have gone to the dogs through sheer idleness; for those of its members who work acquire nothing, and those who acquire anything do not work. The whole of this objection is but another expression of tautology, that there can no longer be any wage-labor when there is no longer any capital.

All objections against the Communistic mode of producing and appropriating material products, have, in the same way, been urged against the Communistic modes of producing and appropriating intellectual products. Just as, to the bourgeois, the disappearance of class property is the disappearance of production itself, so the disappearance of class culture is to him identical with the disappearance of all culture.

That culture, the loss of which he laments, is, for the enormous majority, a mere training to act as a machine.

But don't wrangle with us so long as you apply to our intended abolition of bourgeois property, the standard of your bourgeois notions of freedom, culture, law, etc. Your very ideas are but the outgrowth of the conditions of your bourgeois production and bourgeois property, just as your jurisprudence is but the will of your class made into a law for all, a will whose essential character and direction are determined by the economic conditions of existence of your class.

The selfish misconception that induces you to transform into eternal laws of nature and of reason the social forms springing from your present mode of production and form of property—historical relations that rise and disappear in the progress of production—this misconception you share with every ruling class that has preceded you. What you see clearly in the case of ancient property, what you admit in the case of feudal property, you are of course forbidden to admit in the case of your own bourgeois form of property.

Abolition of the family! Even the most radical flare up at this infamous proposal of the Communists.

On what foundation is the present family, the bourgeois family, based? On capital, on private gain. In its completely developed form this family exists only among the bourgeoisie. But this state of things finds its complement in the practical absence of the family among the proletarians, and in public prostitution.

The bourgeois family will vanish as a matter of course when its complement vanishes, and both will vanish with the vanishing of capital.

Do you charge us with wanting to stop the exploitation of children by their parents? To this crime we plead guilty.

But, you will say, we destroy the most hallowed of relations, when we replace home education by social.

And your education! Is not that also social, and determined by the social conditions under which you educate, by the intervention, direct or indirect, of society by means of schools, etc? The Communists have not invented the intervention of society in education; they do but seek to alter the character of that intervention, and to rescue education from the influence of the ruling class.

The bourgeois clap-trap about the family and education, about the hallowed co-relation of parent and child becomes all the more disgusting, as, by the action of modern industry, all family ties among the proletarians are torn asunder, and their children transformed into simple articles of commerce and instruments of labor.

But you Communists would introduce community of women, screams the whole bourgeoisie in chorus.

The bourgeois sees in his wife a mere instrument of production. He hears that the instruments of production are to be exploited in common, and, naturally, can come to no other conclusion than that the lot of being common to all will likewise fall to the women.

He has not even a suspicion that the real point aimed at is to do away with the status of women as mere instruments of production.

For the rest nothing is more ridiculous than the virtuous indignation of our bourgeois at the community of women which, they pretend, is to be openly and officially established by the Communists. The Communists have no need to introduce community of women; it has existed almost from time immemorial.

Our bourgeois, not content with having the wives and

daughters of their proletarians at their disposal, not to speak of common prostitutes, take the greatest pleasure in seducing each other's wives.

Bourgeois marriage is in reality a system of wives in common, and thus, at the most, what the Communists might possibly be reproached with is that they desire to introduce, in substitution for a hypocritically concealed, an openly legalized community of women. For the rest it is self-evident that the abolition of the present system of production must bring with it the abolition of the community of women springing from that system, i.e., of prostitution both public and private.

The Communists are further reproached with desiring to abolish countries and nationality.

The workingmen have no country. We cannot take from them what they have not got. Since the proletariat must first of all acquire political supremacy, must rise to be the leading class of the nation, must constitute itself *the* nation, it is, so far, itself national, though not in the bourgeois sense of the word.

National differences and antagonisms between peoples are daily more and more vanishing, owing to the development of the bourgeoisie, to freedom of commerce, to the world-market, to uniformity in the mode of production and in the conditions of life corresponding thereto.

The supremacy of the proletariat will cause them to vanish still faster. United action, of the leading civilized countries at least, is one of the first conditions for the emancipation of the proletariat.

In proportion as the exploitation of one individual by another is put an end to, the exploitation of one nation by another will also be put an end to. In proportion as the antagonism between classes within the nation vanishes, the hostility of one nation to another will come to an end.

The charges against Communism made from a religious, a philosophical, and, generally, from an ideological standpoint are not deserving of serious examination.

Does it require deep intuition to comprehend that man's ideas, views, and conceptions, in one word, man's consciousness, changes with every change in the conditions of his material existence, in his social relations and in his social life?

What else does the history of ideas prove, than that intellectual production changes its character in proportion as material production is changed? The ruling ideas of each age have ever been the ideas of its ruling class.

When people speak of ideas that revolutionize society they do but express the fact that within the old society the elements of a new one have been created, and that the dissolution of the old ideas keeps even pace with the dissolution of the old conditions of existence.

When the ancient world was in its last throes the ancient religions were overcome by Christianity. When Christian ideas succumbed in the eighteenth century to rationalist ideas, feudal society fought its death battle with the then revolutionary bourgeoisie. The ideas of religious liberty and freedom of conscience merely gave expression to the sway of free competition within the domain of knowledge.

"Undoubtedly," it will be said, "religious, moral, philosophical and juridical ideas have been modified in the course of historical development. But religion, morality, philosophy, political science, and law constantly survived this change.

"There are besides, eternal truths, such as Freedom, Justice, etc., that are common to all states of society. But Communism abolishes eternal truths, it abolishes all religion and all morality, instead of constituting them on a new basis; it therefore acts in contradiction to all past historical experience."

What does this accusation reduce itself to? The history of all past society has consisted in the development of class antagonisms, antagonisms that assumed different forms at different epochs.

But whatever form they may have taken, one fact is common to all past ages, viz., the exploitation of one part of society by the other. No wonder, then, that the social consciousness of past ages, despite all the multiplicity and variety it displays, moves within certain common forms, or general ideas, which cannot completely vanish except with the total disappearance of class antagonisms.

The Communist revolution is the most radical rupture with traditional property relations; no wonder that its development involves the most radical rupture with traditional ideas.

But let us have done with the bourgeois objections to Communism.

We have seen above that the first step in the revolution by the working class is to raise the proletariat to the position of the ruling class; to win the battle of democracy.

The proletariat will use its political supremacy to wrest, by degrees, all capital from the bourgeoisie; to centralize all instruments of production in the hands of the State, i.e., of the proletariat organized as the ruling class; and to increase the total of productive forces as rapidly as possible.

Of course, in the beginning this cannot be effected except by means of despotic inroads on the rights of property and on the conditions of bourgeois production; by means of measures, therefore, which appear economically insufficient and untenable, but which in the course of the movement outstrip themselves, necessitate further inroads upon the old social order, and are unavoidable as a means of entirely revolutionizing the mode of production.

These measures will, of course, be different in different countries.

Nevertheless in the most advanced countries the following will be pretty generally applicable:

1. Abolition of property in land and application of all rents of land to public purposes
2. A heavy progressive or graduated income tax
3. Abolition of all right of inheritance
4. Confiscation of the property of all emigrants and rebels
5. Centralization of credit in the hands of the State, by means of a national bank with State capital and an exclusive monopoly
6. Centralization of the means of communication and transport in the hands of the State
7. Extension of factories and instruments of production

owned by the State; the bringing into cultivation of waste lands, and the improvement of the soil generally in accordance with a common plan

8. Equal liability of all to labor. Establishment of industrial armies, especially for agriculture

9. Combination of agriculture with manufacturing industries: gradual abolition of the distinction between town and country, by a more equable distribution of the population over the country

10. Free education for all children in public schools. Abolition of children's factory labor in its present form. Combination of education with industrial production, etc., etc.

When, in the course of development, class distinctions have disappeared and all production has been concentrated in the hands of a vast association of the whole nation, the public power will lose its political character. Political power, properly so called, is merely the organized power of one class for oppressing another. If the proletariat during its contest with the bourgeoisie is compelled, by the force of circumstances, to organize itself as a class, if, by means of a revolution, it makes itself the ruling class, and, as such, sweeps away by force the old conditions of production, then it will, along with these conditions, have swept away the conditions for the existence of class antagonisms, and of classes generally, and will thereby have abolished its own supremacy as a class.

In place of the old bourgeois society with its classes and class antagonisms we shall have an association in which the free development of each is the condition for the free development of all.

III
SOCIALIST AND COMMUNIST LITERATURE

Reactionary Socialism
Feudal Socialism

Owing to their historical position, it became the vocation of the aristocracies of France and England to write pamphlets against modern bourgeois society. In the French revolution of July, 1830, and in the English reform agitation, these aristocracies again succumbed to the hateful upstart. Thenceforth, a serious political contest was altogether out of the question. A literary battle alone remained possible. But even in the domain of literature the old cries of the restoration period[5] had become impossible.

In order to arouse sympathy, the aristocracy were obliged to lose sight, apparently, of their own interests, and to formulate their indictment against the bourgeoisie in the interest of the exploited working class alone. Thus the aristocracy took their revenge by singing lampoons on their new master, and whispering in his ears sinister prophecies of coming catastrophe.

In this way arose feudal socialism; half lamentation, half lampoon; half echo of the past, half menace of the future; at times, by its bitter, witty and incisive criticism, striking the bourgeoisie to the very heart's core, but always ludicrous in its effect, through total incapacity to comprehend the march of modern history.

The aristocracy, in order to rally the people to them, waved the proletarian alms-bag in front for a banner. But the people, so often as it joined them, saw on their hindquarters the old feudal coats of arms, and deserted with loud and irreverent laughter.

One section of the French Legitimists, and "Young England," exhibited this spectacle.

In pointing out that their mode of exploitation was different to that of the bourgeoisie, the feudalists forgot that they exploited under circumstances and conditions that were quite different, and that are now antiquated. In showing that, under their rule, the modern proletariat never existed, they forget that the modern bourgeoisie is the necessary offspring of their own form of society.

For the rest, so little do they conceal the reactionary character of their criticism, that their chief accusation against

5. Not the English Restoration 1660 to 1689, but the French Restoration 1814 to 1830.

the bourgeoisie amounts to this, that under the bourgeois regime a class is being developed which is destined to cut up root and branch the old order of society.

What they upbraid the bourgeoisie with is not so much that it creates a proletariat as that it creates a revolutionary proletariat.

In political practice, therefore, they join in all coercive measures against the working-class; and in ordinary life, despite their highfalutin phrases, they stoop to pick up the golden apples dropped from the tree of industry, and to barter truth, love, and honor for traffic in wool, beetroot sugar and potato spirit.[6]

As the parson has ever gone hand-in-hand with the landlord, so has Clerical Socialism with Feudal Socialism.

Nothing is easier than to give Christian asceticism a Socialist tinge. Has not Christianity declaimed against private property, against marriage, against the State? Has it not preached in the place of these, charity and poverty, celibacy, and mortification of the flesh, monastic life and Mother Church? Christian Socialism is but the Holy Water with which the priest consecrates the heartburnings of the aristocrat.

Petty Bourgeois Socialism

The feudal aristocracy was not the only class that was ruined by the bourgeoisie, not the only class whose conditions of existence pined and perished in the atmosphere of modern bourgeois society. The medieval burgesses and the small peasant bourgeoisie were the precursors of the modern bourgeoisie. In those countries which are but little developed, industrially and commercially, these two classes still vegetate side by side with the rising bourgeoisie.

6. This applies chiefly to Germany where the landed aristocracy and squirearchy have large portions of their estates cultivated for their own account by stewards, and are moreover, extensive beet-root-sugar manufacturers and distillers of potato spirits. The wealthier British aristocracy are, as yet, rather above that; but they, too, know how to make up for declining rents by lending their names to floaters of more or less shady joint-stock companies.

In countries where modern civilization has become fully developed, a new class of petty bourgeois has been formed, fluctuating between proletariat and bourgeoisie, and ever renewing itself as a supplementary part of bourgeois society. The individual members of this class, however, are being constantly hurled down into the proletariat by the action of competition, and, as modern industry develops, they can see the moment approaching when they will completely disappear as an independent section of modern society, to be replaced, in manufacture, agriculture and commerce, by overseers, bailiffs, and shopmen.

In countries like France, where the peasants constitute far more than half of the population, it was natural that writers who sided with the proletariat against the bourgeoisie should use, in their criticism of the bourgeois regime, the standard of the peasant and petty bourgeois, and from the standpoint of these intermediate classes should take up the cudgels for the working class. Thus arose petty bourgeois Socialism. Sismondi was the head of this school, not only in France, but also in England.

This school of Socialism dissected with great acuteness the contradictions in the conditions of modern production. It laid bare the hypocritical apologies of economists. It proved, incontrovertibly, the disastrous effects of machinery and division of labor; the concentration of capital and land in a few hands; overproduction and crises; it pointed out the inevitable ruin of the petty bourgeois and peasant, the misery of the proletariat, the anarchy in production, the crying inequalities in the distribution of wealth, the industrial war of extermination between nations, the dissolution of old moral bonds, of the old family relations, of the old nationalities.

In its positive aims, however, this form of Socialism aspires either to restoring the old means of production and of exchange, and with them the old property relations, and the old society, or to cramping the modern means of production and of exchange, within the framework of the old property relations that have been, and were bound to be exploded by those means. In either case, it is both reactionary and Utopian.

Its last words are: corporate guilds for manufacture; patriarchal relations in agriculture.

Ultimately, when stubborn historical facts had dispersed all intoxicating effects of self-deception, this form of socialism ended in a miserable fit of the blues.

German or "True" Socialism

The Socialist and Communist literature of France, a literature that originated under the pressure of a bourgeoisie in power, and that was the expression of the struggle against this power, was introduced into Germany at a time when the bourgeoisie in that country had just begun its contest with feudal absolutism.

German philosophers, would-be philosophers, and *beaux esprits*, eagerly seized on this literature, only forgetting that when these writings immigrated from France into Germany, French social conditions had not immigrated along with them. In contact with German social conditions, this French literature lost all its immediate practical significance and assumed a purely literary aspect. Thus, to the German philosophers of the Eighteenth Century, the demands of the first French Revolution were nothing more than the demands of "Practical Reason" in general, and the utterance of the will of the revolutionary French bourgeoisie signified in their eyes the laws of pure Will, of Will as it was bound to be, of true human Will generally.

The work of the German literati consisted solely in bringing the new French ideas into harmony with their ancient philosophical conscience, or rather, in annexing the French ideas without deserting their own philosophical point of view.

This annexation took place in the same way in which a foreign language is appropriated, namely by translation.

It is well known how the monks wrote silly lives of Catholic Saints over the manuscripts on which the classical works of ancient heathendom had been written. The German literati reversed this process with the profane French literature. They wrote their philosophical nonsense beneath the French original. For instance, beneath the French criticism of the economic functions of money, they wrote "Alienation of Humanity," and beneath the French criticism of the bourgeois State, they wrote, "Dethronement of the Category of the General," and so forth.

The introduction of these philosophical phrases at the back of the French historical criticisms they dubbed "Philosophy of Action," "True Socialism," "German Science of Socialism," "Philosophical Foundation of Socialism," and so on.

The French Socialist and Communist literature was thus completely emasculated. And, since it ceased in the hands of the German to express the struggle of one class with the other, he felt conscious of having overcome "French onesidedness" and of representing, not true requirements, but the requirements of Truth, not the interests of the proletariat, but the interests of Human Nature, of Man in general, who belongs to no class, has no reality, who exists only in the misty realm of philosophical fantasy.

This German Socialism, which took its school-boy task so seriously and solemnly, and extolled its poor stock-in-trade in such mountebank fashion, meanwhile gradually lost its pedantic innocence.

The fight of the German, and, especially, of the Prussian bourgeoisie, against feudal aristocracy and absolute monarchy, in other words, the liberal movement, became more earnest.

By this the long-wished-for opportunity was offered to "True Socialism" of confronting the political movement with the socialist demands, of hurling the traditional anathemas against liberalism, against representative government, against bourgeois competition, bourgeois freedom of the press, bourgeois legislation, bourgeois liberty and equality, and of preaching to the masses that they had nothing to gain, and everything to lose, by this bourgeois movement. German socialism forgot, in the nick of time, that the French criticism, whose silly echo it was, presupposed the existence of modern bourgeois society, with its corresponding economic conditions, and the political constitution adapted thereto, the very things whose attainment was the object of the pending struggle in Germany.

To the absolute governments, with their following of parsons, professors, country squires and officials, it served as a welcome scarecrow against the threatening bourgeoisie.

It was a sweet finish after the bitter pills of floggings and bullets, with which these same governments, just at that time, dosed the German working-class uprisings.

While this "True" Socialism thus served the government as a weapon for fighting the German bourgeoisie, it, at the same time, directly represented a reactionary interest, the interest of the German Philistines. In Germany the petty bourgeois class, a relic of the sixteenth century, and since then constantly cropping up again under various forms, is the real social basis of the existing state of things.

To preserve this class is to preserve the existing state of things in Germany. The industrial and political supremacy of the bourgeoisie threatens it with certain destruction; on the one hand, from the concentration of capital; on the other, from the rise of a revolutionary proletariat. "True" Socialism appeared to kill these two birds with one stone. It spread like an epidemic.

The robe of speculative cobwebs, embroidered with flowers of rhetoric, steeped in the dew of sickly sentiment, this transcendental robe in which the German Socialists wrapped their sorry "eternal truths," all skin and bone, served to wonderfully increase the sale of their goods amongst such a public.

And on its part, German Socialism recognized, more and more, its own calling as the bombastic representative of the petty bourgeois Philistine.

It proclaimed the German nation to be the model nation and the German petty Philistine to be the typical man. To every villainous meanness of this model man it gave a hidden, higher socialistic interpretation, the exact contrary of its true character. It went to the extreme length of directly opposing the "brutally destructive" tendency of Communism, and of proclaiming its supreme and impartial contempt of all class struggles. With very few exceptions, all the so-called Socialist and Communist publications that now (1847) circulate in Germany belong to the domain of this foul and enervating literature.

Conservative or Bourgeois Socialism

A part of the bourgeoisie is desirous of redressing social grievances, in order to secure the continued existence of bourgeois society.

To this section belong economists, philanthropists, humanitarians, improvers of the condition of the working class, organizers of charity, members of societies for the prevention of cruelty to animals, temperance fanatics, hole-and-corner reformers of every imaginable kind. This form of Socialism has, moreover, been worked out into complete systems.

We may cite Proudhon's *Philosophie de la Misère* as an example of this form.

The socialistic bourgeois want all the advantages of modern social conditions without the struggles and dangers necessarily resulting therefrom. They desire the existing state of society minus its revolutionary and disintegrating elements. They wish for a bourgeoisie without a proletariat. The bourgeoisie naturally conceives the world in which it is supreme to be the best; and bourgeois socialism develops this comfortable conception into various more or less complete systems. In requiring the proletariat to carry out such a system, and thereby to march straightway into the social New Jerusalem, it but requires in reality, that the proletariat should remain within the bounds of existing society, but should cast away all its hateful ideas concerning the bourgeoisie.

A second and more practical, but less systematic, form of this socialism sought to depreciate every revolutionary movement in the eyes of the working class, by showing that no mere political reform, but only a change in the material conditions of existence, in economic relations, could be of any advantage to them. By changes in the material conditions of existence, this form of Socialism, however, by no means understands abolition of the bourgeois relations of production, an abolition that can be effected only by a revolution, but administrative reforms, based on the continued existence of these relations; reforms, therefore, that in no respect affect the relations between capital and labor, but, at the best, lessen the cost, and simplify the administrative work, of bourgeois government.

Bourgeois Socialism attains adequate expression, when, and only when, it becomes a mere figure of speech.

Free trade: for the benefit of the working class. Protective duties: for the benefit of the working class. Prison reform: for the benefit of the working class. This is the last word and the only seriously meant word of bourgeois Socialism.

It is summed up in the phrase: the bourgeois is a bourgeois—for the benefit of the working class.

Critical-Utopian Socialism and Communism

We do not here refer to that literature which, in every great modern revolution, has always given voice to the demands of the proletariat, such as the writings of Babeuf and others.

The first direct attempts of the proletariat to attain its own ends were made in times of universal excitement, when feudal society was being overthrown. These attempts necessarily failed, owing to the then undeveloped state of the proletariat, as well as to the absence of the economic conditions for its emancipation, conditions that had yet to be produced, and could be produced by the impending bourgeois epoch alone. The revolutionary literature that accompanied these first movements of the proletariat had necessarily a reactionary character. It inculcated universal asceticism and social leveling in its crudest form.

The Socialist and Communist systems properly so-called, those of Saint-Simon, Fourier, Owen and others, spring into existence in the early undeveloped period, described above, of the struggle between proletariat and bourgeoisie (see Section I, Bourgeois and Proletarians).

The founders of these systems see, indeed, the class antagonisms, as well as the action of the decomposing elements in the prevailing form of society. But the proletariat, as yet in its infancy, offers to them the spectacle of a class without any historical initiative or any independent political movement.

Since the development of class antagonism keeps even pace with the development of industry, the economic situation, as they find it, does not as yet offer to them the material conditions for the emancipation of the proletariat. They therefore search after a new social science, after new social laws, that are to create these conditions.

Historical action is to yield to their personal inventive action, historically created conditions of emancipation to fantastic ones, and the gradual, spontaneous class-organization of the proletariat to an organization of society specially contrived by these inventors. Future history resolves itself, in their eyes, into the propaganda and the practical carrying out of their social plans.

In the formation of their plans they are conscious of caring chiefly for the interests of the working-class, as being the most suffering class. Only from the point of view of being the most suffering class does the proletariat exist for them.

The undeveloped state of the class struggle, as well as their own surroundings, cause Socialists of this kind to consider themselves far superior to all class antagonisms. They want to improve the condition of every member of society, even that of the most favored. Hence they habitually appeal to society at large, without distinction of class; nay, by preference, to the ruling class. For how can people, when once they understand their system, fail to see in it the best possible plan of the best possible state of society?

Hence, they reject all political, and especially all revolutionary action; they wish to attain their ends by peaceful means, and endeavor, by small experiments, necessarily doomed to failure, and by the force of example, to pave the way for the new social Gospel.

Such fantastic pictures of future society, painted at a time when the proletariat is still in a very undeveloped state, and has but a fantastic conception of its own position, correspond with the first instinctive yearnings of that class for a general reconstruction of society.

But these Socialist and Communist publications also contain a critical element. They attack every principle of existing society. Hence they are full of the most valuable materials for the enlightenment of the working class. The practical measures proposed in them, such as the abolition of the distinction between town and country, of the family, of the carrying on of industries for the account of private individuals, and of the wage system, the proclamation of social harmony, the conversion of the functions of the State into a mere superintendence of production, all these proposals point solely to the disappearance of class antagonisms which were, at that time, only just cropping up, and which, in these publications, are recognized under their earliest, indistinct and undefined forms only. These proposals, therefore, are of a purely Utopian character.

The significance of Critical-Utopian Socialism and Communism bears an inverse relation to historical development. In proportion as the modern class struggle develops and takes definite shape, this fantastic standing apart from the contest, these fantastic attacks on it lose all practical value and all theoretical justification. Therefore, although the originators of these systems were, in many respects, revolutionary, their disciples have, in every case, formed mere reactionary sects. They hold fast by the original views of their masters, in opposition to the progressive historical development of the proletariat. They therefore endeavor, and that consistently, to deaden the class struggle and to reconcile the class antagonisms. They still dream of experimental realization of their social Utopias, of founding isolated "phalanstéres," of establishing "Home Colonies," of setting up a "Little Icaria"[7]—duodecimo editions of the New Jerusalem, and to realize all these castles in the air, they are compelled to appeal to the feelings and purses of the bour-

7. Phalanstéres were socialist colonies on the plan of Charles Fourier. Icaria was the name given by Cabot to his Utopia and, later on, to his American Communist colony.

geois. By degrees they sink into the category of the reactionary conservative Socialists depicted above, differing from these only by more systematic pedantry, and by their fanatical and superstitious belief in the miraculous effects of their social science.

They, therefore, violently oppose all political action on the part of the working class; such action, according to them, can only result from blind unbelief in the new Gospel.

The Owenites in England, and the Fourierists in France, respectively, oppose the Chartists and the "Reformists."

IV
POSITION OF THE COMMUNISTS IN RELATION TO THE VARIOUS EXISTING OPPOSITION PARTIES

Section II has made clear the relations of the Communists to the existing working-class parties, such as the Chartists in England and the Agrarian Reformers in America.

The Communists fight for the attainment of the immediate aims, for the enforcement of the momentary interests of the working class; but in the movement of the present, they also represent and take care of the future of that movement. In France the Communists ally themselves with the Social-Democrats,[8] against the conservative and radical bourgeoisie, reserving, however, the right to take up a critical position in regard to phrases and illusions traditionally handed down from the great Revolution.

In Switzerland they support the Radicals, without losing sight of the fact that this party consists of antagonistic elements, partly of Democratic Socialists, in the French sense, partly of radical bourgeois.

In Poland they support the party that insists on an agrarian revolution as the prime condition for national emancipation, that party which fomented the insurrection of Cracow in 1846.

8. The party then represented in parliament by Ledru-Rollin, in literature by Louis Blanc, in the daily press by the Réforme. The name of Social-Democracy signified, with these its inventors, a section of the Democratic or Republican party more or less tinged with Socialism.

In Germany they fight with the bourgeoisie whenever it acts in a revolutionary way against the absolute monarchy, the feudal squirearchy, and the petty bourgeoisie.

But they never cease, for a single instant, to instill into the working class the clearest possible recognition of the hostile antagonism between bourgeoisie and proletariat, in order that the German workers may straightway use, as so many weapons against the bourgeoisie, the social and political conditions that the bourgeoisie must necessarily introduce along with its supremacy, and in order that, after the fall of the reactionary classes in Germany, the fight against the bourgeoisie itself may immediately begin.

The Communists turn their attention chiefly to Germany, because that country is on the eve of a bourgeois revolution that is bound to be carried out under more advanced conditions of European civilization, and with a much more developed proletariat, than that of England was in the seventeenth, and of France in the eighteenth century, and because the bourgeois revolution in Germany will be but the prelude to an immediately following proletarian revolution.

In short, the Communists everywhere support every revolutionary movement against the existing social and political order of things.

In all these movements they bring to the front, as the leading question in each, the property question, no matter what its degree of development at the time.

Finally, they labor everywhere for the union and agreement of the democratic parties of all countries.

The Communists disdain to conceal their views and aims. They openly declare that their ends can be attained only by the forcible overthrow of all existing social conditions. Let the ruling classes tremble at a Communistic revolution. The proletarians have nothing to lose but their chains. They have a world to win.

Workingmen of all countries unite!

2

WHAT IS TO BE DONE?*

V. I. Lenin
(Published in Stuttgart, March 1902)

What Is to Be Done? *is Lenin's basic statement on organization. In many respects it is his most influential work.*

In Siberian exile, just before the turn of the century, Lenin was frequently in turmoil over what he considered the organizational shortcomings of the Russian revolutionary movement. He formulated plans for a new organization, and after his release he sought to publicize those plans in What Is to Be Done?

In it, he called for the establishment of a corps of full-time, professional revolutionaries, adept at working in secret and completely dedicated to only one goal: the achievement of the revolution. The corps—the party—was to have as its immediate objective the publishing of a newspaper, which would serve to awaken and educate the proletariat and, through the clandestine operations necessary for newsgathering and the distribution of the paper, to fashion the revolutionary apparatus.

As in all his writing, Lenin here too sought justification in

* Excerpts

Marx. But basically his concepts were drawn from Russian experience, not Marxist ideology. Marx had foreseen a party that would be open to everyone and operate openly. But Lenin argued that if such a party were to appear in Russia, all of its members would be arrested. Therefore, he proposed the cellular, conspiratorial, essentially non-Marxist apparatus that was to become the hallmark of Leninist revolutionaries in all countries.

Lenin took the title for What Is to Be Done? *from the novel of the same name by N. G. Chernyshevsky, which had been published in the 1860s and had been a favorite of Lenin's executed brother as it was to become Lenin's own favorite. Chernyshevsky's work told of the need for new men and women, filled with the passion of self-sacrifice for the achievement of the revolution, the same kind of men and women Lenin was seeking.*

* * *

THE SPONTANEITY OF THE MASSES AND THE CONSCIOUSNESS OF THE SOCIAL-DEMOCRATS

We have said that our movement, much more extensive and deep than the movement of the seventies, must be inspired with the same devoted determination and energy that inspired the movement at that time. Indeed, no one, we think, has until now doubted that the strength of the present-day movement lies in the awakening of the masses (principally, the industrial proletariat) and that its weakness lies in the lack of consciousness and initiative among the revolutionary leaders.

* * *

[W]e have become convinced that the fundamental error committed by the "new trend" in Russian Social-Democracy is its bowing to spontaneity and its failure to understand that the spontaneity of the masses demands a high degree of consciousness from us Social-Democrats. The greater the spontaneous upsurge of the masses and the more widespread the movement, the more rapid, incomparably so, the demand for greater consciousness in the theoretical, political, and organizational work of Social-Democracy.

The spontaneous upsurge of the masses in Russia proceeded (and continues) with such rapidity that the young Social-Democrats proved unprepared to meet these gigantic tasks. This unpreparedness is our common misfortune, the misfortune of *all* Russian Social-Democrats. The upsurge of the masses proceeded and spread with uninterrupted continuity; it not only continued in the places where it began, but spread to new localities and to new strata of the population (under the influence of the working-class movement, there was a renewed ferment among the student youth, among the intellectuals generally, and even among the peasantry). Revolutionaries, however, *lagged behind* this upsurge, both in their "theories" and in their activity; they failed to establish a constant and continuous organization capable of *leading* the whole movement.

* * *

POLITICAL EXPOSURES AND "TRAINING IN REVOLUTIONARY ACTIVITY"

* * *

A basic condition for the necessary expansion of political agitation is the organization of *comprehensive* political exposure. *In no way* except by means of such exposures *can* the masses be trained in political consciousness and revolutionary activity.

* * *

Why do the Russian workers still manifest little revolutionary activity in response to the brutal treatment of the people by the police, the persecution of religious sects, the flogging of peasants, the outrageous censorship, the torture of soldiers, the persecution of the most innocent cultural undertakings, etc.? Is it because the "economic struggle" does not "stimulate" them to this, because such activity does not "promise palpable results," because it produces little that is "positive"? To adopt such an opinion, we repeat, is merely to direct the charge where it does not belong, to blame the working masses for one's own philistinism (or Bernsteinism). We must blame ourselves, our lagging behind the mass movement, for still being unable to organize sufficiently wide, striking, and rapid exposures of all the shameful outrages. When we do that (and we must and can do it), the most backward worker will understand, *or will feel,* that the students and religious sects, the peasants and the authors are being abused and outraged by those same dark forces that are oppressing and crushing him at every step of his life. Feeling that, he himself will be filled with an irresistible desire to react, and he will know how to hoot the censors one day, on another day to demonstrate outside the house of a governor who has brutally suppressed a peasant uprising, on still another day to teach a lesson to the gendarmes in surplices who are doing the work of the Holy Inquisition, etc.

* * *

THE WORKING CLASS AS A VANGUARD FIGHTER FOR DEMOCRACY

* * *

We must train our Social-Democratic practical workers to become political leaders, able to guide all the manifestations of this all-round struggle, able at the right time to "dictate a positive program of action" for the aroused students, the discontented Zemstvo people, the incensed religious sects, the offended elementary schoolteachers, etc., etc.

* * *

Everywhere in the provinces there are people, resident there by dint of circumstance, who have taken part in the movement in the past or who desire to do so now and who are gravitating toward Social-Democracy (whereas in 1894 one could count the Social-Democrats on the fingers of one hand). A basic political and organizational shortcoming of our movement is our *inability* to utilize all these forces and give them appropriate work. . . . The overwhelming majority of these forces entirely lack the opportunity of "going among the workers," so that there are no grounds for fearing that we shall divert forces from our main work. In order to be able to provide the workers with real, comprehensive, and live political knowledge, we must have "our own people," Social-Democrats, everywhere, among all social strata, and in all positions from which we can learn the inner springs of our state mechanism. Such people are required, not only for propaganda and agitation, but in a still larger measure for organization.

* * *

In our time only a party that will *organize* really *nationwide* exposures can become the vanguard of the revolutionary forces. The word "nationwide" has a very profound meaning. The overwhelming majority of the non-working-class exposers (be it remembered that in order to become the vanguard, we must attract other classes) are sober politicians and level-headed men of affairs. They know perfectly well how dangerous it is to "complain" even against a minor official, let alone against the "omnipotent" Russian Government. And they will come *to us* with their complaints only when they see that these complaints can really have effect, and that we represent *a political force*. In order to become such a force in the eyes of outsiders, much persistent and stubborn work is required *to raise* our own consciousness, initiative, and energy. To accomplish this it is not enough to attach a "vanguard" label to rearguard theory and practice.

But if we have to undertake the organization of a really nationwide exposure of the government, in what way will then the class character of our movement be expressed?—the overzealous advocate of "close organic contact with the proletarian struggle" will ask us, as indeed he does. The reply is manifold: we Social-Democrats will organize these nationwide exposures; all questions raised by the agitation will be explained in a consistently Social-Democratic spirit, without any concessions to deliberate or undeliberate distortions of Marxism; the all-round political agitation will be conducted by a party which unites into one inseparable whole the assault on the government in the name of the entire people, the revolutionary training of the proletariat, and the safeguarding of its political independence, the guidance of the economic struggle of the working class, and the utilization of all its spontaneous conflicts with its exploiters which rouse and bring into our camp increasing numbers of the proletariat.

* * *

ORGANIZATION OF WORKERS AND ORGANIZATION OF REVOLUTIONARIES

It is only natural to expect that for a Social-Democrat whose conception of the political struggle coincides with the conception of the "economic struggle against the employers and the government," the "organization of revolutionaries" will more or less coincide with the "organization of workers." This, in fact, is what actually happens; so that when we speak of organization, we literally speak in different tongues. I vividly recall, for example, a conversation I once had with a fairly consistent Economist, with whom I had not been previously acquainted. We were discussing the pamphlet, *Who Will Bring About the Political Revolution?* and were soon of a mind that its principal defect was its ignoring of the question of organization. We had begun to assume full agreement between us; but, as the conversation proceeded, it became evident that we were talking of different things. My interlocutor accused the author of ignoring strike funds, mutual benefit societies, etc., whereas I had in mind an organization of revolutionaries as an essential factor in "bringing about" the political revolution. As soon as the disagreement became clear, there was hardly, as I remember, a single question of principle upon which I was in agreement with the Economist!

* * *

[T]he organization of the revolutionary Social-Democratic Party must inevitably be of *a kind different* from the organization of the workers designed for this struggle. The workers' organization must in the first place be a trade-union organization; secondly, it must be as broad as possible; and thirdly, it must be as public as conditions will allow (here, and further on, of course, I refer only to absolutist Russia). On the other hand, the organization of the revolutionaries must consist first and foremost of people who make revolutionary activity their profession (for which reason I speak of the organization of *revolutionaries*, meaning revolutionary Social-Democrats). In view of this common characteristic of the members of such an organization, *all distinctions as between workers and intellectuals*, not to speak of distinctions of trade and profession, in both categories, *must be effaced.* Such an organization must perforce not be very extensive and must be as secret as possible.

* * *

A small, compact core of the most reliable, experienced, and hardened workers, with responsible representatives in the principal districts and connected by all the rules of strict secrecy with the organization of revolutionaries, can, with the widest support of the masses and without any formal organization, perform *all* the functions of a trade-union organization, in a manner, moreover, desirable to Social-Democracy. Only in this way can we secure the *consolidation* and development of a *Social-Democratic* trade-union movement, despite all the gendarmes.

It may be objected that an organization which is so *loose* that it is not even definitely formed, and which has not even an enrolled and registered membership, cannot be called an organization at all. Perhaps so. Not the name is important. What is important is that this "organization without members" shall do everything that is required, and from the very outset ensure a solid connection between our future trade unions and socialism. Only an incorrigible utopian would have a *broad* organization of workers, with elections, reports, universal suffrage, etc., under the autocracy.

The moral to be drawn from this is simple. If we begin with the solid foundation of a strong organization of revolutionaries, we can ensure the stability of the movement as a whole and carry out the aims both of Social-Democracy and of trade unions proper. If, however, we begin with a broad workers' organization, which is supposedly most "accessible" to the masses (but which is actually most accessible to the gendarmes and makes revolutionaries most accessible to the police), we shall achieve neither the one aim nor the other[.]

* * *

I assert: (1) that no revolutionary movement can endure without a stable organization of leaders maintaining continuity; (2) that the broader the popular mass drawn spontaneously into the struggle, which forms the basis of the movement and participates in it, the more urgent the need for such an organization, and the more solid this organization must be (for it is much easier for all sorts of demagogues to sidetrack the more backward sections of the masses); (3) that such an organization must consist chiefly of people professionally engaged in revolutionary activity; (4) that in an autocratic state, the more we *confine* the membership of such an organization to people who are professionally engaged in revolutionary activity and who have been professionally trained in the art of combating the political police, the more difficult will it be to unearth the organization; and (5) the *greater* will be the number of people from the working class and from the other social classes who will be able to join the movement and perform active work in it.

* * *

At the moment, I shall deal only with the last two points. The question as to whether it is easier to wipe out "a dozen wise men" or "a hundred fools" reduces itself to the question, above considered, whether it is possible to have a mass *organization* when the maintenance of strict secrecy is essential. We can never give a mass organization that degree of secrecy without which there can be no question of persistent and continuous struggle against the government. To concentrate all secret functions in the hands of as small a number of professional revolutionaries as possible does not mean that the latter will "do the thinking for all" and that the rank and file will not take an active part in the *movement*. On the contrary, the membership will promote increasing numbers of the professional revolutionaries from its ranks; for it will know that it is not enough for a few students and for a few workingmen waging the economic struggle to gather in order to form a "committee," but that it takes years to train oneself to be a professional revolutionary; and the rank and file will "think," not only of amateurish methods, but of such training. Centralization of the secret functions of the *organization* by no means implies centralization of all the functions of the *movement*. Active participation of the widest masses in the illegal press will not diminish because a "dozen" professional revolutionaries centralize the secret functions connected with this work; on the contrary, it will *increase* tenfold. In this way, and in this way alone, shall we ensure that reading the illegal press, writing for it, and to some extent even distributing it, will *almost cease to be secret work,* for the police will soon come to realize the folly and impossibility of judicial and administrative red-tape procedure over every copy of a publication that is being distributed in the thousands. This holds not only for the press, but for every function of the movement, even for demonstrations. The active and widespread participation of the masses will not suffer; on the contrary, it will benefit by the fact that a "dozen" experienced revolutionaries, trained professionally no less than the police, will centralize all the secret aspects of the work—the drawing up of leaflets, the working out of approximate plans; and the appointing of bodies of leaders for each urban district, for each factory district, and for each educational institution, etc. (I know that exception will be taken to my "undemocratic" views, but I shall reply below fully to this anything but intelligent objection.) Centralization of the most secret functions in an organization of revolutionaries will not diminish, but rather increase the extent and enhance the quality of the activity of a large number of other organizations that are intended for a broad public and are therefore as loose and as non-secret as possible, such as workers' trade unions; workers' self-education circles and circles for reading illegal literature; and socialist, as well as democratic, circles among *all* other sections of the population; etc., etc. We must have such circles, trade unions, and organizations everywhere in *as large a number as possible* and with the widest variety of functions; but it would be absurd and harmful *to confound* them with the organization of *revolutionaries*, to efface the borderline between them, to make still more hazy the all too faint recognition of the fact that in order to "serve" the mass movement we must have people who will devote themselves exclusively to Social-Democratic activities, and that such people must *train* themselves patiently and steadfastly to be professional revolutionaries.

Yes, this recognition is incredibly dim. Our worst sin with regard to organization consists in the fact that *by our primitiveness we have lowered the prestige of revolutionaries in Russia.* A person who is flabby and shaky on questions of theory, who has a narrow outlook, who pleads the spontaneity of the masses as an excuse for his own sluggishness, who resembles a trade-union secretary more than a spokesman of the people, who is unable to conceive of a broad and bold plan that would command the respect even of opponents, and who is inexperienced and clumsy in his own professional art—the art of combating the political police—such a man is not a revolutionary, but a wretched amateur!

Let no active worker take offense at these frank remarks, for as far as insufficient training is concerned, I apply them first and foremost to myself. I used to work in a study circle that set itself very broad, all-embracing tasks; and all of us, members of that circle, suffered painfully and acutely from the realization that we were acting as amateurs at a moment in history when we might have been able to say, varying a well-known statement: "Give us an organization of revolutionaries, and we will overturn Russia!" The more I recall the burning sense of shame I then experienced, the bitterer become my feelings toward those pseudo-Social-Democrats whose preachings "bring disgrace on the calling of a revolutionary," who fail to understand that our task is not to champion the degrading of the revolutionary to the level of an amateur, but *to raise* the amateurs to the level of revolutionaries.

THE SCOPE OF ORGANIZATIONAL WORK

* * *

To be fully prepared for his task, the worker-revolutionary must likewise become a professional revolutionary . . . [It is wrong to say] that since the worker spends eleven and a half hours in the factory, the brunt of all other revolutionary functions (apart from agitation) "*must necessarily* fall mainly upon the shoulders of an extremely small force of intellectuals." But this condition does not obtain out of sheer "necessity." It obtains because we are backward, because we do not recognize our duty to assist every capable worker to become a *professional* agitator, organizer, propagandist, literature distributor, etc., etc. In this respect, we waste our strength in a positively shameful manner; we lack the ability to husband that which should be tended and reared with special care. Look at the Germans: their forces are a hundredfold greater than ours. But they understand perfectly well that really capable agitators, etc., are not often promoted from the ranks of the "average." For this reason they immediately try to place every capable working man in conditions that will enable him to develop and apply his abilities to the fullest: he is made a professional agitator; he is encouraged to widen the field of his activity, to spread it from one factory to the whole of the industry, from a single locality to the whole country. He acquires experience and dexterity in his profession; he broadens his outlook and increases his knowledge; he observes at close quarters the prominent political leaders from other localities and of other parties; he strives to rise to their level and combine in himself the knowledge of the working-class environment and the freshness of socialist convictions with professional skill, without which the proletariat *cannot* wage a stubborn struggle against its excellently trained enemies. In this way alone do the working masses produce men of the stamp of Bebel and Auer. But what is to a great extent automatic in a politically free country must in Russia be done deliberately and systematically by our organizations. A worker-agitator who is at all gifted and "promising" *must not be left* to work eleven hours a day in a factory. We must arrange that he be maintained by the Party; that he may go underground in good time; that he change the place of his activity, if he is to enlarge his experience, widen his outlook, and be able to hold out for at least a few years in the struggle against the gendarmes. As the spontaneous rise of their movement becomes broader and deeper, the working-class masses promote from their ranks not only an increasing number of talented agitators, but also talented organizers, propagandists, and "practical workers" in the best sense of the term (of whom there are so few among our intellectuals who, for the most part, in the Russian manner, are somewhat careless and sluggish in their habits). When we have forces of specially trained worker-revolutionaries who have gone through extensive preparation (and, of course, revolutionaries "of all arms of the service"), no political police in the world will then be able to contend with them, for these forces, boundlessly devoted to the revolution, will enjoy the boundless confidence of the widest masses of the workers. We are directly *to blame* for doing too little to "stimulate" the workers to take this path, common to them and to the "intellectuals," of professional revolutionary training, and for all too often dragging them back by our silly speeches about what is "accessible" to the masses of the workers, to the "average workers," etc.

In this, as in other respects, the narrow scope of our organizational work is without a doubt due directly to the fact . . . that we restrict our theories and our political tasks to a narrow field. Subservience to spontaneity seems to inspire a fear of taking even one step away from what is "accessible" to the masses, a fear of rising too high above mere attendance on the immediate and direct requirements of the masses. Have no fear, gentlemen! Remember that we stand so low on the plane of organization that the very idea that we *could* rise *too* high is absurd!

"CONSPIRATORIAL ORGANIZATION" AND "DEMOCRATISM"

* * *

Is it conceivable in Russia for all "who accept the principles of the Party program and render the Party all possible support" to control every action of the revolutionary working in secret? Is it possible for all to elect one of these revolutionaries to any particular office, when, in the very interests of the work, the revolutionary *must* conceal his identity from nine out of ten of these "all"? Reflect somewhat, . . . and you will realize that "broad democracy" in Party organization, amidst the gloom of the autocracy and the domination of gendarmerie, is nothing more than a *useless and harmful toy*. It is a useless toy because, in point of fact, no revolutionary organization has ever practiced, or could practice, *broad* democracy, however much it may have desired to do so. It is a harmful toy because any attempt to practice "the broad democratic principle" will simply facilitate the work of the police in carrying out large-scale raids, will perpetuate the prevailing primitiveness, and will divert the thoughts of the practical workers from the serious and pressing task of training themselves to become professional revolutionaries to that of drawing up detailed "paper" rules for election systems. Only abroad, where very often people with no opportunity for conducting really active work gather, could this "playing at democracy" develop here and there, especially in small groups.

* * *

The only serious organizational principle for the active workers of our movement should be the strictest secrecy, the strictest selection of members, and the training of professional revolutionaries. Given these qualities, something even more than "democratism" would be guaranteed to us, namely, complete, comradely, mutual confidence among revolutionaries. This is absolutely essential for us, because there can be no question of replacing it by general democratic control in Russia. It would be a great mistake to believe that the impossibility of establishing real "democratic" control renders the members of the revolutionary organization beyond control altogether. They have not the time to think about toy forms of democratism (democratism within a close and compact body of comrades in which complete, mutual confidence prevails), but they have a lively sense of their *responsibility*, knowing as they do from experience that an organization of real revolutionaries will stop at nothing to rid itself of an unworthy member. Moreover, there is a fairly well-developed public opinion in Russian (and international) revolutionary circles which has a long history behind it, and which sternly and ruthlessly punishes every departure from the duties of comradeship (and "democratism", real and not toy democratism, certainly forms a component part of the conception of comradeship). Take all this into consideration and you will realize that this talk and these resolutions about "anti-democratic tendencies" have the musty odor of the playing at generals which is indulged in abroad.

* * *

THE "PLAN" FOR AN ALL-RUSSIAN POLITICAL NEWSPAPER

* * *

The mere function of distributing a newspaper would help to establish *actual* contacts (if it is a newspaper worthy of the name, i.e., if it is issued regularly, not once a month like a magazine, but at least four times a month). At the present time, communication between towns on revolutionary business is an extreme rarity, and, at all events, is the exception rather than the rule. If we had a newspaper, however, such communication would become the rule and would secure, not only the distribution of the newspaper, of course, but (what is more important) an exchange of experience, of material, of forces, and of resources. Organizational work would immediately acquire much greater scope, and the success of one locality would serve as a standing encouragement to further perfection; it would arouse the desire to utilize the experience gained by comrades working in other parts of the country. Local work would become far richer and more varied than it is at present. Political and economic exposures gathered from all over Russia would provide mental food for workers of all trades and *all stages of development*; they would provide material and occasion for talks and readings on the most divers subjects, which would, in addition, be suggested by hints in the legal press, by talk among the people, and by "shamefaced" government statements. Every outbreak, every demonstration, would be weighed and discussed in its every aspect in all parts of Russia and would thus stimulate a desire to keep up with, and even surpass, the others (we socialists do not by any means flatly reject all emulation or all "competition"!) and consciously prepare that which at first, as it were, sprang up spontaneously, a desire to take advantage of the favorable conditions in a given district or at a given moment for modifying the plan of attack, etc. At the same time, this revival of local work would obviate that desperate, "convulsive" exertion of *all* efforts and risking of *all* forces which every single demonstration or the publication of every single issue of a local newspaper now frequently entails. On the one hand, the police would find it much more difficult to get at the "roots," if they did not know in what district to dig down for them. On the other hand, regular common work would train our people to adjust the force of a *given* attack to the strength of the given contingent of the common army (at the present time hardly anyone ever thinks of doing that, because in nine cases out of ten these attacks occur spontaneously); such regular common work would facilitate the "transportation" from one place to another, not only of literature, but also of revolutionary forces.

In a great many cases these forces are now being bled white on restricted local work, but under the circumstances we are discussing it would be possible to transfer a capable agitator or organizer from one end of the country to the other, and the occasion for doing this would constantly arise. Beginning with short journeys on Party business at the Party's expense, the comrades would become accustomed to being maintained by the Party, to becoming professional revolutionaries, and to training themselves as real political leaders.

And if indeed we succeeded in reaching the point when all, or at least a considerable majority, of the local committees, local groups, and study circles took up active work for the common cause, we could, in the not distant future, establish a weekly newspaper for regular distribution in tens of thousands of copies throughout Russia. This newspaper would become part of an enormous pair of smith's bellows that would fan every spark of the class struggle and of popular indignation into a general conflagration. Around what is in itself still a very innocuous and very small, but regular and *common* effort, in the full sense of the word, a regular army of tried fighters would systematically gather and receive their training. On the ladders and scaffolding of this general organizational structure there would soon develop and come to the fore Social-Democratic Zhelyabovs from among our revolutionaries and Russian Bebels from among our workers, who would take their place at the head of the mobilized army and rouse the whole people to settle accounts with the shame and the curse of Russia.

That is what we should dream of!

* * *

It would be a grievous error indeed to build the Party organization in anticipation only of outbreaks and street fighting, or only upon the "forward march of the drab everyday struggle." We must *always* conduct our everyday work and always be prepared for every situation, because very frequently it is almost impossible to foresee when a period of outbreak will give way to a period of calm. In the instances, however, when it is possible to do so, we could not turn this foresight to account for the purpose of reconstructing our organization; for in an autocratic country these changes take place with astonishing rapidity, being sometimes connected with a single night raid by the tsarist janizaries. And the revolution itself must not by any means be regarded as a single act . . . but as a series of more or less powerful outbreaks rapidly alternating with periods of more or less complete calm. For that reason, the principal content of the activity of our Party organization, the focus of this activity, should be work that is both possible and essential in the period of a most powerful outbreak as well as in the period of complete calm, namely, work of political agitation, connected throughout Russia, illuminating all aspects of life, and conducted among the broadest possible strata of the masses. But this work is *unthinkable* in present-day Russia without an All-Russian newspaper, issued very frequently. The organization, which will form round this newspaper, the organization of its *collaborators* (in the broad sense of the word, i.e., all those working for it), will be ready *for everything*, from upholding the honor, the prestige, and the continuity of the Party in periods of acute revolutionary "depression" to preparing for, appointing the time for, and carrying out the *nationwide armed uprising*.

Indeed, picture to yourselves a very ordinary occurrence in Russia—the total round-up of our comrades in one or several localities. In the absence of a *single*, common, regular activity that combines *all* the local organizations, such round-ups frequently result in the interruption of the work for many months. If, however, all the local organizations had one common activity, then, even in the event of a very serious round-up, two or three energetic persons could in the course of a few weeks establish contact between the common center and new youth circles, which, as we know, spring up very quickly even now. And when the common activity, hampered by the arrests, is apparent to all, new circles will be able to come into being and make connections with the center even more rapidly.

On the other hand, picture to yourselves a popular uprising. Probably everyone will now agree that we must think of this and prepare for it. But *how*? Surely the Central Committee cannot appoint agents to all localities for the purpose of preparing the uprising. Even if we had a Central Committee, it could achieve absolutely nothing by such appointments under present-day Russian conditions. But a network of agents[1] that would form in the course of establishing and distributing the common newspaper would not have to "sit about and wait" for the call for an uprising, but could carry on the regular activity that would guarantee the highest probability of success in the event of an uprising. Such activity would strengthen our contacts with the broadest strata of the working masses and with all social strata that are discontented with the autocracy, which is of such importance for an uprising. Precisely such activity would serve to cultivate the ability to estimate correctly the general political situation and, consequently, the ability to select the proper moment for an uprising. Precisely such activity would train *all* local organizations to respond simultaneously to the same political questions, incidents, and events that agitate the whole of Russia and to react to such "incidents" in the most vigorous, uniform, and expedient manner possible; for an uprising is in essence the most vigorous, most uniform, and

1. Alas, alas! Again I have let slip that awful word "agents", which jars so much on the democratic ears of the Martynovs! I wonder why this word did not offend the heroes of the seventies and yet offends the amateurs of the nineties? I like the word, because it clearly and trenchantly indicates the common cause to which all the agents bend their thoughts and actions, and if I had to replace this word by another, the only word I might select would be the word "collaborator," if it did not suggest a certain bookishness and vagueness. The thing we need is a military organization of agents. However, the numerous Martynovs (particularly abroad), whose favorite pastime is "mutual grants of generalships to one another", may instead of saying "passport agent" prefer to say, "Chief of the Special Department for Supplying Revolutionaries with Passports," etc.

most expedient "answer" of the entire people to the government. Lastly, it is precisely such activity that would train all revolutionary organizations throughout Russia to maintain the most continuous, and at the same time the most secret, contacts with one another, thus creating *real* Party unity; for without such contacts it will be impossible collectively to discuss the plan for the uprising and to take the necessary preparatory measures on the eve, measures that must be kept in the strictest secrecy.

In a word, the "plan for an All-Russian political newspaper," far from representing the fruits of the labor of armchair workers, infected with dogmatism and bookishness (as it seemed to those who gave but little thought to it), is the most practical plan for immediate and all-around preparation of the uprising, with, at the same time, no loss of sight for a moment of the pressing day-to-day work.

THE STATE AND REVOLUTION*

V. I. Lenin
(Written in Finland, August–September 1917)

Lenin, whose guiding passion was achieving the revolution, rarely thought of what would happen afterward. But in mid-1917, for the only time in his life, he seems to have concentrated his attention on the shape of the future, which he describes in The State and Revolution, *though his reasons for doing so were not disassociated from the realization of the revolution.*

In August–September 1917, when Lenin wrote The State and Revolution, *he was in hiding. Despite the setback suf-*

* Excerpts

fered during the July Days, a successful seizure of power by his Bolsheviks still seemed imminently possible. Yet, at the same time, as a fugitive, he feared arrest and execution. And so, while eagerly waiting for the next stage of the revolution to unfold, Lenin put to paper his vision of the post-revolutionary future. In part, he did it because possibly that future was at hand and it was necessary to think about it. In part, because he feared that death might appear on the scene at any moment to snatch him away, and he desperately wanted to participate, if only on paper, in the revolution, which seemed so close. But perhaps most important, Lenin wrote The State and Revolution *to justify non-Marxist elements of the seizure of power that he hoped to bring off.*

For Marx, the purpose of the revolution was to liberate the proletariat. Once the revolution was accomplished there would be little further need of a party to lead, guide, and train the, by definition, fully developed working class. But in Russia, where the revolution was about to occur, the working class had not even begun to approach full development. In The State and Revolution *Lenin indicates that the party in Russia will continue to be necessary after the revolution in order to organize the proletariat—that, in effect, it, not the proletariat, will take power. The immediate post-revolutionary stage was, whatever it might be called, not to be Marx's dictatorship of the proletariat, but the dictatorship of Lenin and the Bolshevik party, acting for the good of the proletariat.*

PREFACE TO THE FIRST EDITION

The question of the state is now acquiring particular importance both in theory and in practical politics. The imperialist war has immensely accelerated and intensified the process of transformation of monopoly capitalism into state-monopoly capitalism. The monstrous oppression of the working people by the state, which is merging more and more with the all-powerful capitalist associations, is becoming increasingly monstrous. The advanced countries—we mean their hinterland—are becoming military convict prisons for the workers.

The unprecedented horrors and miseries of the protracted war are making the people's position unbearable and increasing their anger. The world proletarian revolution is clearly maturing. The question of its relation to the state is acquiring practical importance.

The elements of opportunism that accumulated over the decades of comparatively peaceful development have given rise to the trend of social-chauvinism which dominates the official socialist parties throughout the world. This trend—socialism in words and chauvinism in deeds (Plekhanov, Potresov, Breshkovskaya, Rubanovich, and, in a slightly veiled form, Tsereteli, Chernov and Co. in Russia; Scheidemann, Legien, David, and others in Germany; Renaudel, Guesde, and Vandervelde in France and Belgium; Hyndman and the Fabians in England, etc., etc.)—is conspicuous for the base, servile adaptation of the "leaders of socialism" to the interests not only of "their" national bourgeoisie, but of "their" state, for the majority of the so-called Great Powers have long been exploiting and enslaving a whole number of small and weak nations. And the imperialist war is a war for the division and redivision of this kind of booty. The struggle to free the working people from the influence of the bourgeoisie in general, and of the imperialist bourgeoisie in particular, is impossible without a struggle against opportunist prejudices concerning the "state."

First of all we examine the theory of Marx and Engels of the state, and dwell in particular detail on those aspects of this theory which are ignored or have been distorted by the opportunists. Then we deal specially with the one who is chiefly responsible for these distortions, Karl Kautsky, the best-known leader of the Second International (1889–1914), which has met with such miserable bankruptcy in the present war. Lastly, we sum up the main results of the experience of the Russian revolutions of 1905 and, particularly, of 1917. Apparently, the latter is now (early August 1917) completing the first stage of its development; but this revolution as a whole can only be understood as a link in a chain of socialist proletarian revolutions being caused by the imperialist war. The question of the relation of the socialist proletarian revolution to the state, therefore, is acquiring not only practical political importance, but also the significance of a most urgent problem of the day, the problem of explaining to the masses what they will have to do before long to free themselves from capitalist tyranny.

The Author

August 1917

* * *

THE PROLETARIAT AND THE STATE

[W]e have a formulation of one of the most remarkable and most important ideas of Marxism on the subject of the state, namely, the idea of the "dictatorship of the proletariat" (as Marx and Engels began to call it after the Paris Commune); and also, a highly interesting definition of the state, which is also one of the "forgotten words" of Marxism: *"the state, i.e., the proletariat organized as the ruling class"*.

This definition of the state has never been explained in the prevailing propaganda and agitation literature of the official Social-Democratic parties. More than that, it has been deliberately ignored, for it is absolutely irreconcilable with reformism, and is a slap in the face for the common opportunist prejudices and philistine illusions about the "peaceful development of democracy."

The proletariat needs the state—this is repeated by all the opportunists, social-chauvinists and Kautskyites, who assure us that this is what Marx taught. But they "*forget*" to add that, in the first place, according to Marx, the proletariat needs only a state which is withering away, i.e., a state so constituted that it begins to wither away immediately, and cannot but wither away. And, secondly, the working people need a "state, i.e., the proletariat organized as the ruling class."

The state is a special organization of force: it is an organization of violence for the suppression of some class. What class must the proletariat suppress? Naturally, only the exploiting class, i.e., the bourgeoisie. The working people need the state only to suppress the resistance of the exploiters, and only the proletariat can direct this suppression, can carry it out. For the proletariat is the only class that is consistently revolutionary, the only class that can unite all the working and exploited people in the struggle against the bourgeoisie, in completely removing it.

The exploiting classes need political rule to maintain exploitation, i.e., in the selfish interests of an insignificant minority against the vast majority of the people. The exploited classes need political rule in order to completely abolish all exploitation, i.e., in the interests of the vast majority of the people, and against the insignificant minority consisting of the modern slave-owners—the landowners and capitalists.

The petty-bourgeois democrats, those sham socialists who replaced the class struggle by dreams of class harmony, even pictured the socialist transformation in a dreamy fashion—not as the overthrow of the rule of the exploiting class, but as the peaceful submission of the minority to the majority which has become aware of its aims. This petty-bourgeois utopia, which is inseparable from the idea of the state being above classes, led in practice to the betrayal of the interests of the working classes, as was shown, for example, by the history of the French revolutions of 1848 and 1871, and by the experience of "socialist" participation in bourgeois Cabinets in Britain, France, Italy and other countries at the turn of the century.

All his life Marx fought against this petty-bourgeois socialism, now revived in Russia by the Socialist-Revolutionary and Menshevik parties. He developed his theory of the class struggle consistently, down to the theory of political power, of the state.

The overthrow of bourgeois rule can be accomplished only by the proletariat, the particular class whose economic conditions of existence prepare it for this task and provide it with the possibility and the power to perform it. While the bourgeoisie break up and disintegrate the peasantry and all the petty-bourgeois groups, they weld together, unite, and organize the proletariat. Only the proletariat—by virtue of the economic role it plays in large-scale production—is capable of being the leader of *all* the working and exploited people, whom the bourgeoisie exploit, oppress and crush, often not less but more than they do the proletarians, but who are incapable of waging an *independent* struggle for their emancipation.

The theory of the class struggle, applied by Marx to the question of the state and the socialist revolution, leads as a matter of course to the recognition of the *political rule* of the proletariat, of its dictatorship, i.e., of undivided power directly backed by the armed force of the people. The overthrow of the bourgeoisie can be achieved only by the proletariat becoming the *ruling class*, capable of crushing the inevitable and desperate resistance of the bourgeoisie, and of organizing *all* the working and exploited people for the new economic system.

The proletariat needs state power, a centralized organization of force, an organization of violence, both to crush the resistance of the exploiters and to *lead* the enormous mass of the population—the peasants, the petty bourgeoisie, and semi-proletarians—in the work of organizing a socialist economy.

By educating the workers' party, Marxism educates the vanguard of the proletariat, capable of assuming power and leading the whole people to socialism, of directing and organizing the new system, of being the teacher, the guide, the leader of all the working and exploited people in organizing their social life without the bourgeoisie and against the bourgeoisie. By contrast, the opportunism now prevailing trains the members of the workers' party to be the representatives of the better-paid workers, who lose touch with the masses, "get along" fairly well under capitalism, and sell their birthright for a mess of pottage, i.e., renounce their role as revolutionary leaders of the people against the bourgeoisie.

Marx's theory of "the state, i.e., the proletariat organized as the ruling class," is inseparably bound up with the whole of his doctrine of the revolutionary role of the proletariat in history. The culmination of this role is the proletarian dictatorship, the political rule of the proletariat.

But since the proletariat needs the state as a *special* form of organization of violence *against* the bourgeoisie, the following conclusion suggests itself: is it conceivable that such an organization can be created without first abolishing, destroying the state machine created by the bourgeoisie *for themselves*? The *Communist Manifesto* leads straight to this conclusion[.]

* * *

ADMINISTRATION AFTER THE REVOLUTION

We are not utopians, we do not "dream" of dispensing *at once* with all administration, with all subordination. These anarchist dreams, based upon incomprehension of the tasks of the proletarian dictatorship, are totally alien to Marxism, and, as a matter of fact, serve only to postpone the socialist revolution until people are different. No, we want the socialist revolution with people as they are now, with people who cannot dispense with subordination, control, and "foremen and accountants."

The subordination, however, must be to the armed vanguard of all the exploited and working people, i.e., to the proletariat. A beginning can and must be made at once, overnight, to replace the specific "bossing" of state officials by the simple functions of "foremen and accountants," functions which are already fully within the ability of the average town dweller and can well be performed for "workmen's wages."

We, the workers, shall organize large-scale production on the basis of what capitalism has already created, relying on our own experience as workers, establishing strict, iron discipline backed up by the state power of the armed workers. We shall reduce the role of state officials to that of simply carrying out our instructions as responsible, revocable, modestly paid "foremen and accountants" (of course, with the aid of technicians of all sorts, types, and degrees). This is *our* proletarian task, this is what we can and must *start* with in accomplishing the proletarian revolution. Such a beginning, on the basis of large-scale production, will of itself lead to the gradual "withering away" of all bureaucracy, to the gradual creation of an order—an order without inverted commas, an order bearing no similarity to wage slavery—an order under which the functions of control and accounting, becoming more and more simple, will be performed by each in turn, will then become a habit and will finally die out as the *special* functions of a special section of the population.

A witty German Social-Democrat of the seventies of the last century called the *postal service* an example of the socialist economic system. This is very true. At present the postal service is a business organized on the lines of a state-*capitalist* monopoly. Imperialism is gradually transforming all trusts into organizations of a similar type, in which, standing over the "common" people, who are overworked and starved, one has the same bourgeois bureaucracy. But the mechanism of social management is here already to hand. Once we have overthrown the capitalists, crushed the resistance of these exploiters with the iron hand of the armed workers, and smashed the bureaucratic machine of the modern state, we shall have a splendidly equipped mechanism, freed from the "parasite," a mechanism which can very well be set going by the united workers themselves, who will hire technicians, foremen, and accountants, and pay them *all*, as indeed *all* "state" officials in general, workmen's wages. Here is a concrete, practical task which can immediately be fulfilled in relation to all trusts, a task whose fulfilment will rid the working people of exploitation, a task which takes account of what the Commune had already begun to practice (particularly in building up the state).

To organize the *whole* economy on the lines of the postal service so that the technicians, foremen, and accountants, as well as *all* officials, shall receive salaries no higher than "a workman's wage," all under the control and leadership of the armed proletariat—this is our immediate aim. This is the state and this is the economic foundation we need. This is what will bring about the abolition of parliamentarism and the preservation of representative institutions. This is what will rid the laboring classes of the bourgeoisie's prostitution of these institutions.

* * *

THE TRANSITION FROM CAPITALISM TO COMMUNISM

* * *

[T]he transition from capitalist society—which is developing toward communism—to communist society is impossible without a "political transition period," and the state in this period can only be the revolutionary dictatorship of the proletariat.

What, then, is the relation of this dictatorship to democracy?

We have seen that the *Communist Manifesto* simply places side by side the two concepts: "to raise the proletariat to the position of the ruling class" and "to win the battle of democracy." On the basis of all that has been said above, it is possible to determine more precisely how democracy changes in the transition from capitalism to communism.

In capitalist society, providing it develops under the most favorable conditions, we have a more or less complete democracy in the democratic republic. But this democracy is always hemmed in by the narrow limits set by capitalist exploitation, and consequently always remains, in effect, a democracy for the minority, only for the propertied classes, only for the rich. Freedom in capitalist society always remains about the same as it was in the ancient Greek republics: freedom for the slave-owners. Owing to the conditions of capitalist exploitation, the modern wage slaves are so crushed by want and poverty that "they cannot be bothered with democracy," "cannot be bothered with politics"; in the ordinary, peaceful course of events, the majority of the population is debarred from participation in public and political life.

* * *

Democracy for an insignificant minority, democracy for the rich—that is the democracy of capitalist society. If we look more closely into the machinery of capitalist democracy, we see everywhere, in the "petty"—supposedly petty—details of the suffrage (residential qualification, exclusion of women, etc.), in the technique of the representative institutions, in the actual obstacles to the right of assembly (public buildings are not for "paupers"!), in the purely capitalist organization of the daily press, etc., etc.—we see restriction after restriction upon democracy. These restrictions, exceptions, exclusions, obstacles for the poor seem slight, especially in the eyes of one who has never known want himself and has never been in close contact with the oppressed classes in their mass life (and nine out of ten, if not ninety-nine out of a hundred, bourgeois publicists and politicians come under this category); but in their sum total these restrictions exclude and squeeze out the poor from politics, from active participation in democracy.

Marx grasped this *essence* of capitalist democracy splendidly when, in analyzing the experience of the Commune, he said that the oppressed are allowed once every few years to decide which particular representatives of the oppressing class shall represent and repress them in parliament!

But from this capitalist democracy—that is inevitably narrow and stealthily pushes aside the poor, and is therefore hypocritical and false through and through—forward development does not proceed simply, directly, and smoothly, toward "greater and greater democracy," as the liberal professors and petty-bourgeois opportunists would have us believe. No, forward development, i.e., development toward communism, proceeds through the dictatorship of the proletariat, and cannot do otherwise, for the *resistance* of the capitalist exploiters cannot be *broken* by anyone else or in any other way.

And the dictatorship of the proletariat, i.e., the organization of the vanguard of the oppressed as the ruling class for the purpose of suppressing the oppressors, cannot result merely in an expansion of democracy. *Simultaneously* with an immense expansion of democracy, which *for the first time* becomes democracy for the poor, democracy for the people, and not democracy for the money-bags, the dictatorship of the proletariat imposes a series of restrictions on the freedom of the oppressors, the exploiters, the capitalists. We must suppress them in order to free humanity from wage slavery, their resistance must be crushed by force; it is clear that there is no freedom and no democracy where there is suppression and where there is violence.

Engels expressed this splendidly in his letter to Bebel when he said, as the reader will remember, that "the proletariat needs the state, not in the interests of freedom but in order to hold down its adversaries, and as soon as it becomes possible to speak of freedom the state as such ceases to exist."

Democracy for the vast majority of the people, and suppression by force, i.e., exclusion from democracy, of the exploiters and oppressors of the people—this is the change democracy undergoes during the *transition* from capitalism to communism.

Only in communist society, when the resistance of the capitalists has been completely crushed, when the capitalists have disappeared, when there are no classes (i.e., when there is no distinction between the members of society as regards their relation to the social means of production), *only* then "the state . . . ceases to exist," and "*it becomes possible to speak of freedom.*" Only then will a truly complete democracy become possible and be realized, a democracy without any exceptions whatever. And only then will democracy begin to *wither away*, owing to the simple fact that, freed from capitalist slavery, from the untold horrors, savagery, absurdities and infamies of capitalist exploitation, people will gradually *become accustomed* to observing the elementary rules of social intercourse that have been known for centuries and repeated for thousands of years in all copy-book maxims. They will become accustomed to observing them without force, without coercion, without subordination, *without the special apparatus* for coercion called the state.

The expression "the state *withers away*" is very well chosen, for it indicates both the gradual and the spontaneous nature of the process. Only habit can, and undoubtedly will, have such an effect; for we see around us on millions of occasions how readily people become accustomed to observing the necessary rules of social intercourse when there is no exploitation, when there is nothing that arouses indignation, evokes protest and revolt, and creates the need for *suppression*.

And so in capitalist society we have a democracy that is curtailed, wretched, false, a democracy only for the rich, for the minority. The dictatorship of the proletariat, the period of transition to communism, will for the first time create democracy for the people, for the majority, along with the necessary suppression of the exploiters, of the minority. Communism alone is capable of providing really complete democracy, and the more complete it is, the sooner it will become unnecessary and wither away of its own accord.

In other words, under capitalism we have the state in the proper sense of the word, that is, a special machine for the suppression of one class by another, and, what is more, of the majority by the minority. Naturally, to be successful, such an undertaking as the systematic suppression of the exploited majority by the exploiting minority calls for the utmost ferocity and savagery in the matter of suppressing, it calls for seas of blood, through which mankind is actually wading its way in slavery, serfdom, and wage labor.

Furthermore, during the *transition* from capitalism to communism suppression is *still* necessary, but it is now the suppression of the exploiting minority by the exploited majority. A special apparatus, a special machine for suppression, the "state", is *still* necessary, but this is now a transitional state. It is no longer a state in the proper sense of the word; for the suppression of the minority of exploiters by the majority of the wage slaves of *yesterday* is comparatively so easy, simple, and natural a task that it will entail far less bloodshed than the suppression of the risings of slaves, serfs, or wage-laborers, and it will cost mankind far less. And it is compatible with the extension of democracy to such an overwhelming majority of the population that the need for a *special machine* of suppression will begin to disappear. Naturally, the exploiters are unable to suppress the people without a highly complex machine for performing this task, but *the people* can suppress the exploiters even with a very simple "machine," almost without a "machine," without a special apparatus, by the simple *organization of the armed people* (such as the Soviets of Workers' and Soldiers' Deputies, we would remark, running ahead).

Lastly, only communism makes the state absolutely unnecessary, for there is *nobody* to be suppressed—"nobody" in the sense of a *class*, of a systematic struggle against a definite section of the population. We are not utopians, and do not in the least deny the possibility and inevitability of excesses on the part of *individual persons*, or the need to stop *such* excesses. In the first place, however, no special machine, no special apparatus of suppression, is needed for this; this will be done by the armed people themselves, as simply and as readily as any crowd of civilized people, even in modern society, interferes to put a stop to a scuffle or to prevent a woman from being assaulted. And, secondly, we know that the fundamental social cause of excesses, which consist in the violation of the rules of social intercourse, is the exploitation of the people, their want, and their poverty. With the removal of this chief cause, excesses will inevitably begin to "*wither away*." We do not know how quickly and in what succession, but we do know they will wither away. With their withering away, the state will also *wither away*.

Without building utopias, Marx defined more fully what can be defined *now* regarding this future, namely, the difference between the lower and higher phases (levels, stages) of communist society.

THE FIRST PHASE OF COMMUNIST SOCIETY

* * *

Marx makes a sober estimate of exactly how socialist society will have to manage its affairs. Marx proceeds to make a *concrete* analysis of the conditions of life of a society in which there will be no capitalism, and says:

What we have to deal with here [in analyzing the program of the workers' party] is a communist society, not as it has *developed* on its own foundations, but, on the contrary, just as it *emerges* from capitalist society; which is, therefore, in every respect, economically, morally, and intellectually, still stamped with the birthmarks of the old society from whose womb it comes.

It is this communist society, which has just emerged into the light of day out of the womb of capitalism and which is in every respect stamped with the birthmarks of the old society, that Marx terms the "first," or lower, phase of communist society.

The means of production are no longer the private property of individuals. The means of production belong to the whole of society. Every member of society, performing a certain part of the socially necessary work, receives a certificate from society to the effect that he has done a certain amount of work. And with this certificate he receives from the public store of consumer goods a corresponding quantity of products. After a deduction is made of the amount of labor which goes to the public fund, every worker, therefore, receives from society as much as he has given to it.

"Equality" apparently reigns supreme.

But when Lassalle, having in view such a social order (usually called socialism, but termed by Marx the first phase of communism), says that this is "equitable distribution," that this is "the equal right of all to an equal product of labor," Lassalle is mistaken and Marx exposes the mistake.

"Equal right," says Marx, we certainly do have here; but it is *still* a "bourgeois right," which, like every right, *implies inequality*. Every right is an application of an *equal* measure to *different* people who in fact are not alike, are not equal to one another. That is why "equal right" is a violation of equality and an injustice. In fact, everyone, having performed as much social labor as another, receives an equal share of the social product (after the above-mentioned deductions).

But people are not alike: one is strong, another is weak; one is married, another is not; one has more children, another has less, and so on. And the conclusion Marx draws is:

> With an equal performance of labor, and hence an equal share in the social consumption fund, one will in fact receive more than another, one will be richer than another, and so on. To avoid all these defects, right would have to be unequal rather than equal.

The first phase of communism, therefore, cannot yet provide justice and equality: differences, and unjust differences, in wealth will still persist, but the *exploitation* of man by man will have become impossible because it will be impossible to seize the *means of production*—the factories, machines, land, etc.—and make them private property. In smashing Lassalle's petty-bourgeois, vague phrases about "equality" and "justice" *in general*, Marx shows the *course of development* of communist society, which is *compelled* to abolish at first *only* the "injustice" of the means of production seized by individuals, and which is *unable* at once to eliminate the other injustice, which consists in the distribution of consumer goods "according to the amount of labor performed" (and not according to needs).

* * *

Marx not only most scrupulously takes account of the inevitable inequality of men, but he also takes into account the fact that the mere conversion of the means of production into the common property of the whole of society (commonly called "socialism") *does not remove* the defects of distribution and the inequality of "bourgeois right," which *continues to prevail* so long as products are divided "according to the amount of labor performed." Continuing, Marx says:

But these defects are inevitable in the first phase of communist society as it is when it has just emerged, after prolonged birth pangs, from capitalist society. Right can never be higher than the economic structure of society and its cultural development conditioned thereby.

And so, in the first phase of communist society (usually called socialism) "bourgeois right" is *not* abolished in its entirety, but only in part, only in proportion to the economic revolution so far attained, i.e., only in respect of the means of production. "Bourgeois right" recognizes them as the private property of individuals. Socialism converts them into *common* property. *To that extent*—and to that extent alone—"bourgeois right" disappears.

However, it persists as far as its other part is concerned; it persists in the capacity of regulator (determining factor) in the distribution of products and the allotment of labor among the members of society. The socialist principle, "He who does not work shall not eat," is *already* realized; the other socialist principle, "An equal amount of products for an equal amount of labor," is also *already* realized. But this is not yet communism, and it does not yet abolish "bourgeois right," which gives unequal individuals, in return for unequal (really unequal) amounts of labor, equal amounts of products.

This is a "defect," says Marx, but it is unavoidable in the first phase of communism; for if we are not to indulge in utopianism, we must not think that having overthrown capitalism people will at once learn to work for society *without any standard of right*. Besides, the abolition of capitalism *does not immediately create* the economic prerequisites for *such* a change.

Now, there is no other standard than that of "bourgeois right." To this extent, therefore, there still remains the need for a state, which, while safeguarding the common ownership of the means of production, would safeguard equality in labor and in the distribution of products.

The state withers away insofar as there are no longer any capitalists, any classes, and, consequently, no *class* can be *suppressed*.

But the state has not yet completely withered away, since there still remains the safeguarding of "bourgeois right," which sanctifies actual inequality. For the state to wither away completely, complete communism is necessary.

THE HIGHER PHASE OF COMMUNIST SOCIETY

Marx continues:

> In a higher phase of communist society, after the enslaving subordination of the individual to the division of labor and with it also the antithesis between mental and physical labor has vanished, after labor has become not only a livelihood but life's prime want, after the productive forces have increased with the all-around development of the individual, and all the springs of cooperative wealth flow more abundantly—only then can the narrow horizon of bourgeois right be crossed in its entirety and society inscribe on its banners: From each according to his ability, to each according to his needs!

Only now can we fully appreciate the correctness of Engels's remarks mercilessly ridiculing the absurdity of combining the words "freedom" and "state." So long as the state exists there is no freedom. When there is freedom, there will be no state.

The economic basis for the complete withering away of the state is such a high stage of development of communism at which the antithesis between mental and physical labor disappears, at which there consequently disappears one of the principal sources of modern *social* inequality—a source, moreover, which cannot on any account be removed immediately by the mere conversion of the means of production into public property, by the mere expropriation of the capitalists.

This expropriation will make it *possible* for the productive forces to develop to a tremendous extent. And when we see how incredibly capitalism is already *retarding* this development, when we see how much progress could be achieved on the basis of the level of technique already attained, we are entitled to say with the fullest confidence that the expropriation of the capitalists will inevitably result in an enormous development of the productive forces of human society. But how rapidly this development will proceed, how soon it will reach the point of breaking away from the division of labor, of doing away with the antithesis between mental and physical labor, of transforming labor into "life's prime want"—we do not and *cannot* know.

That is why we are entitled to speak only of the inevitable withering away of the state, emphasizing the protracted nature of this process and its dependence upon the rapidity of development of the *higher phase* of communism, and leaving the question of the time required for, or the concrete forms of, the withering away quite open, because there is *no* material for answering these questions.

The state will be able to wither away completely when society adopts the rule: "From each according to his ability, to each according to his needs," i.e., when people have become so accustomed to observing the fundamental rules of social intercourse and when their labor has become so productive that they will voluntarily work *according to their ability*. "The narrow horizon of bourgeois right," which compels one to calculate with the heartlessness of a Shylock whether one has not worked half an hour more than somebody else, whether one is not getting less pay than somebody else—this narrow horizon will then be crossed. There will then be no need for society, in distributing products, to regulate the quantity to be received by each; each will take freely "according to his needs."

From the bourgeois point of view, it is easy to declare that such a social order is "sheer utopia" and to sneer at the socialists for promising everyone the right to receive from society, without any control over the labor of the individual citizen, any quantity of truffles, cars, pianos, etc. Even to this day, most bourgeois "savants" confine themselves to sneering in this way, thereby betraying both their ignorance and their selfish defence of capitalism.

Ignorance—for it has never entered the head of any socialist to "promise" that the higher phase of the development of communism will arrive; as for the great socialists' *forecast* that it will arrive, it presupposes not the present productivity of labor and *not the present* ordinary run of people, who, like the seminary students in Pomyalovsky's stories, are capable of damaging the stocks of public wealth "just for fun," and of demanding the impossible.

Until the "higher" phase of communism arrives, the socialists demand the *strictest* control by society *and by the state* over the measure of labor and the measure of consumption; but this control must *start* with the expropriation of the capitalists, with the establishment of workers' control over the capitalists, and must be exercised not by a state of bureaucrats, but by a state of *armed workers*.

* * *

And this brings us to the question of the scientific distinction between socialism and communism which Engels touched on in his above-quoted argument about the incorrectness of the name "Social-Democrat." Politically, the distinction between the first, or lower, and the higher phase of communism will in time, probably, be tremendous. But it would be ridiculous to recognize this distinction now, under capitalism, and only individual anarchists, perhaps, could invest it with primary importance[.]

* * *

But the scientific distinction between socialism and communism is clear. What is usually called socialism was termed by Marx the "first," or lower, phrase of communist society. Insofar as the means of production become *common* property, the word "communism" is also applicable here, providing we do not forget that this is *not* complete communism. The great significance of Marx's explanations is that here, too, he consistently applies materialist dialectics, the theory of development, and regards communism as something which develops *out of* capitalism. Instead of scholastically invented, "concocted" definitions and fruitless disputes over words (What is socialism? What is communism?), Marx gives an analysis of what might be called the stages of the economic maturity of communism.

In its first phase, or first stage, communism *cannot* as yet be fully mature economically and entirely free from traditions or vestiges of capitalism. Hence the interesting phenomenon that communism in its first phase retains "the narrow horizon of *bourgeois* right." Of course, bourgeois right in regard to the distribution of *consumer* goods inevitably presupposes the existence of the *bourgeois state*, for right is nothing without an apparatus capable of *enforcing* the observance of the standards of right.

It follows that under communism there remains for a time not only bourgeois right, but even the bourgeois state, without the bourgeoisie!

This may sound like a paradox or simply a dialectical conundrum, of which Marxism is often accused by people who have not taken the slightest trouble to study its extraordinarily profound content.

But in fact, remnants of the old, surviving in the new, confront us in life at every step, both in nature and in society. And Marx did not arbitrarily insert a scrap of "bourgeois" right into communism, but indicated what is economically and politically inevitable in a society emerging *out of the womb* of capitalism.

Democracy is of enormous importance to the working class in its struggle against the capitalists for its emancipation. But democracy is by no means a boundary not to be overstepped; it is only one of the stages on the road from feudalism to capitalism, and from capitalism to communism.

Democracy means equality. The great significance of the proletariat's struggle for equality and of equality as a slogan will be clear if we correctly interpret it as meaning the abolition of *classes*. But democracy means only *formal* equality. And as soon as equality is achieved for all members of society *in relation* to ownership of the means of production, that is, equality of labor and wages, humanity will inevitably be confronted with the question of advancing farther, from formal equality to actual equality, i.e., to the operation of the rule "from each according to his ability, to each according to his needs." By what stages, by means of what practical measures humanity will proceed to this supreme aim we do not and cannot know. But it is important to realize how infinitely mendacious is the ordinary bourgeois conception of socialism as something lifeless, rigid, fixed once and for all, whereas in reality *only* socialism will be the beginning of a rapid, genuine, truly mass forward movement, embracing first the *majority* and then the whole of the population, in all spheres of public and private life.

Democracy is a form of the state, one of its varieties. Consequently, it, like every state, represents, on the one hand, the organized, systematic use of force against persons; but, on the other hand, it signifies the formal recognition of equality of citizens, the equal right of all to determine the structure of, and to administer, the state. This, in turn, results in the fact that, at a certain stage in the development of democracy, it first welds together the class that wages a revolutionary struggle against capitalism—the proletariat, and enables it to crush, smash to atoms, wipe off the face of the earth the bourgeois, even the republican-bourgeois, state machine, the standing army, the police and the bureaucracy and to substitute for them a *more* democratic state machine, but a state machine nevertheless, in the shape of armed workers who proceed to form a militia involving the entire population.

Here "quantity turns into quality": *such* a degree of democracy implies overstepping the boundaries of bourgeois society and beginning its socialist reorganization. If really *all* take part in the administration of the state, capitalism cannot retain its hold. The development of capitalism, in turn, creates the *preconditions* that *enable* really "all" to take part in the administration of the state. Some of these preconditions are: universal literacy, which has already been achieved in a number of the most advanced capitalist countries; then the "training and disciplining" of millions of workers by the huge, complex, socialized apparatus of the postal service, railways, big factories, large-scale commerce, banking, etc., etc.

Given these *economic* preconditions, it is quite possible, after the overthrow of the capitalists and the bureaucrats, to proceed immediately, overnight, to replace them in the *control* over production and distribution, in the work of *keeping account* of labor and products, by the armed workers, by the whole of the armed population. (The question of control and accounting should not be confused with the question of the scientifically trained staff of engineers, agronomists and so on. These gentlemen are working today in obedience to the wishes of the capitalists, and will work even better tomorrow in obedience to the wishes of the armed workers.)

Accounting and control—that is *mainly* what is needed for the "smooth working," for the proper functioning, of the *first phase* of communist society. *All* citizens are transformed into hired employees of the state, which consists of the armed workers. *All* citizens become employees and workers of a *single* countrywide state "syndicate." All that is required is that they should work equally, do their proper share of work, and get equal pay. The accounting and control necessary for this have been *simplified* by capitalism to the utmost and reduced to the extraordinarily simple operations—which any literate person can perform—of supervising and recording, knowledge of the four rules of arithmetic, and issuing appropriate receipts.[1]

When the *majority* of the people begin independently and everywhere to keep such accounts and exercise such control over the capitalists (now converted into employees) and over the intellectual gentry who preserve their capitalist habits, this control will really become universal, general and popular; and there will be no getting away from it, there will be "nowhere to go."

The whole of society will have become a single office and a single factory, with equality of labor and pay.

But this "factory" discipline, which the proletariat, after defeating the capitalists, after overthrowing the exploiters, will extend to the whole of society, is by no means our ideal, or our ultimate goal. It is only a necessary *step* for thoroughly cleaning society of all the infamies and abominations of capitalist exploitation, *and for further* progress.

1. When the more important functions of the state are reduced to such accounting and control by the workers themselves, it will cease to be a "political state" and "public functions will lose their political character and become mere administrative functions." . . .

From the moment all members of society, or at least the vast majority, have learned to administer the state *themselves*, have taken this work into their own hands, have organised control over the insignificant capitalist minority, over the gentry who wish to preserve their capitalist habits and over the workers who have been thoroughly corrupted by capitalism—from this moment the need for government of any kind begins to disappear altogether. The more complete the democracy, the nearer the moment when it becomes unnecessary. The more democratic the "state" which consists of the armed workers, and which is "no longer a state in the proper sense of the word," the more rapidly *every form* of state begins to wither away.

For when *all* have learned to administer and actually do independently administer social production, independently keep accounts and exercise control over the parasites, the sons of the wealthy, the swindlers and other "guardians of capitalist traditions," the escape from this popular accounting and control will inevitably become so incredibly difficult, such a rare exception, and will probably be accompanied by such swift and severe punishment (for the armed workers are practical men and not sentimental intellectuals, and they will scarcely allow anyone to trifle with them), that the *necessity* of observing the simple, fundamental rules of the community will very soon become a *habit*.

Then the door will be thrown wide open for the transition from the first phase of communist society to its higher phase, and with it to the complete withering away of the state.

* * *

POSTSCRIPT TO THE FIRST EDITION

This pamphlet was written in August and September 1917. I had already drawn up the plan for the next, the seventh, chapter, "The Experience of the Russian Revolutions of 1905 and 1917." Apart from the title, however, I had no time to write a single line of the chapter; I was "interrupted" by a political crisis—the eve of the October revolution of 1917. Such an "interruption" can only be welcomed; but the writing of the second part of the pamphlet ("The Experience of the Russian Revolutions of 1905 and 1917") will probably have to be put off for a long time. It is more pleasant and useful to go through the "experience of the revolution" than to write about it.

The Author

Petrograd
November 30, 1917

"LEFT-WING" COMMUNISM—AN INFANTILE DISEASE*

V. I. Lenin
(Published in Moscow, June 1920)

Lenin wrote "Left-wing" Communism *for Comintern Congress II.*† *He sought through it to establish the authority of the Russian Revolution and thereby the authority of the Russian party within the international movement. As he proclaims at the beginning of the pamphlet, Russia is now the "model." Her experience "reveals to* all *countries* something—and something highly significant—of their near and inevitable future."

Russia, says Lenin, is the only country, and the RKP (B) the only party, to have successfully had a revolution. You have tried and failed, he tells the Germans and British in particular. We have succeeded. Listen to what we say!

Having thus presumably established the right of the Rus-

* Excerpts

† In Soviet language, such words as "Left," "Left-wing," etc., are enclosed in quotation marks because, by definition, no one can be more left (radical) than the Russian communists. Others who are left are the so-called left. But sometimes Lenin became tired of always enclosing the word left in quotation marks and conveniently forgot about it.

sian party to give advice, Lenin proceeds to set the line for the period immediately ahead. The revolutionary tide has passed for now, Lenin tells the Comintern delegates. Now we must learn to survive in a situation of retreat from revolution.

How do we survive?

By compromise, by concession, by accommodation. It is necessary to cooperate with the most reactionary trade-union and parliamentary organizations to be accepted by them. We must get inside such groups so that we will be in a position to influence them when revolutionary situations again appear. This is what we did in Russia, Lenin incorrectly states, and this is what the international movement must now do.

However, almost as soon as "Left-wing" Communism *was written, Lenin disregarded his own advice about retreat. He sent the Red Army into Poland, hoping that a communist regime established there would lead to revolutions further west. But, by mid-August, the defeat of the Red Army caused Lenin to return to the* "Left-wing" Communism *line, in practice as in word.*

IN WHAT SENSE WE CAN SPEAK OF THE INTERNATIONAL SIGNIFICANCE OF THE RUSSIAN REVOLUTION?

In the first months after the proletariat in Russia had won political power (October 25 [November 7], 1917), it might have seemed that the enormous difference between backward Russia and the advanced countries of Western Europe would lead to the proletarian revolution in the latter countries bearing very little resemblance to ours. We now possess quite considerable international experience, which shows very definitely that certain fundamental features of our revolution have a significance that is not local, or peculiarly national, or Russian alone, but international. I am not speaking here of international significance in the broad sense of the term: not merely several but all the primary features of our revolution, and many of its secondary features, are of international significance in the meaning of its effect on all countries. I am speaking of it in the narrowest sense of the word, taking international significance to mean the international validity or the historical inevitability of a repetition, on an international scale, of what has taken place in our country. It must be admitted that certain fundamental features of our revolution do possess that significance.

It would, of course, be grossly erroneous to exaggerate this truth and to extend it beyond certain fundamental features of our revolution. It would also be erroneous to lose sight of the fact that, soon after the victory of the proletarian revolution in at least one of the advanced countries, a sharp change will probably come about: Russia will cease to be the model and will once again become a backward country (in the "Soviet" and the socialist sense).

At the present moment in history, however, it is the Russian model that reveals to *all* countries something—and something highly significant—of their near and inevitable future. Advanced workers in all lands have long realized this; more often than not, they have grasped it with their revolutionary class instinct rather than realized it. Herein lies the international "significance" (in the narrow sense of the word) of Soviet power, and of the fundamentals of Bolshevik theory and tactics.

* * *

AN ESSENTIAL CONDITION OF THE BOLSHEVIKS' SUCCESS

It is, I think, almost universally realized at present that the Bolsheviks could not have retained power for two and a half months, let alone two and a half years, without the most rigorous and truly iron discipline in our Party, or without the fullest and unreserved support from the entire mass of the working class, that is, from all thinking, honest, devoted and influential elements in it, capable of leading the backward strata or carrying the latter along with them.

The dictatorship of the proletariat means a most determined and most ruthless war waged by the new class against a *more powerful* enemy, the bourgeoisie, whose resistance is increased *tenfold* by their overthrow (even if only in a single country), and whose power lies, not only in the strength of international capital, the strength and durability of their international connections, but also in the *force of habit*, in the strength of *small-scale production*. Unfortunately, small-scale production is still widespread in the world, and small-scale production *engenders* capitalism and the bourgeoisie continuously, daily, hourly, spontaneously, and on a mass scale. All these reasons make the dictatorship of the proletariat necessary, and victory over the bourgeoisie is impossible without a long, stubborn, and desperate life-and-death struggle which calls for tenacity, discipline, and a single and inflexible will.

I repeat: the experience of the victorious dictatorship of the proletariat in Russia has clearly shown even to those who are incapable of thinking or have had no occasion to give thought to the matter that absolute centralization and rigorous discipline in the proletariat are an essential condition of victory over the bourgeoisie.

This is often dwelt on. However, not nearly enough thought is given to what it means, and under what conditions it is possible. Would it not be better if the salutations addressed to the Soviets and the Bolsheviks were *more frequently* accompanied by a *profound analysis* of the reasons *why* the Bolsheviks have been able to build up the discipline needed by the revolutionary proletariat?

As a current of political thought and as a political party, Bolshevism has existed since 1903. Only the history of Bolshevism during the *entire* period of its existence can satisfactorily explain why it has been able to build up and maintain, under most difficult conditions, the iron discipline needed for the victory of the proletariat.

The first questions to arise are: How is the discipline of the proletariat's revolutionary party maintained? How is it tested? How is it reinforced? First, by the class-consciousness of the proletarian vanguard and by its devotion to the revolution, by its tenacity, self-sacrifice, and heroism. Second, by its ability to link up, maintain the closest contact, and—if you wish—merge, in certain measure, with the broadest masses of the working people—primarily with the proletariat, *but also with the non-proletarian* masses of working people. Third, by the correctness of the political leadership exercised by this vanguard, by the correctness of its political strategy and tactics, provided the broad masses have seen, *from their own experience,* that they are correct. Without these conditions, discipline in a revolutionary party really capable of being the party of the advanced class, whose mission it is to overthrow the bourgeoisie and transform the whole of society, cannot be achieved. Without these conditions, all attempts to establish discipline inevitably fall flat and end up in phrase-mongering and clowning. On the other hand, these conditions cannot emerge at once. They are created only by prolonged effort and hard-won experience. Their creation is facilitated by a correct revolutionary theory, which, in its turn, is not a dogma, but assumes final shape only in close connection with the practical activity of a truly mass and truly revolutionary movement.

The fact that, in 1917–20, Bolshevism was able, under unprecedentedly difficult conditions, to build up and successfully maintain the strictest centralization and iron discipline was due simply to a number of historical peculiarities of Russia.

On the one hand, Bolshevism arose in 1903 on a very firm foundation of Marxist theory. The correctness of this revolutionary theory, and of it alone, has been proved, not only by world experience throughout the nineteenth century, but especially by the experience of the seekings and vacillations, the errors and disappointments of revolutionary thought in Russia. For about half a century—approximately from the forties to the nineties of the last century—progressive thought in Russia, oppressed by a most brutal and reactionary tsarism, sought eagerly for a correct revolutionary theory, and followed with the utmost diligence and thoroughness each and every "last word" in this sphere in Europe and America. Russia achieved Marxism—the only correct revolutionary theory—through the *agony* she experienced in the course of half a century of unparalleled torment and sacrifice, of unparalleled revolutionary heroism, incredible energy, devoted searching, study, practical trial, disappointment, verification, and comparison with European experience. Thanks to the political emigration caused by tsarism, revolutionary Russia, in the second half of the nineteenth century, acquired a wealth of international links and excellent information on the forms and theories of the world revolutionary movement, such as no other country possessed.

On the other hand, Bolshevism, which had arisen on this granite foundation of theory, went through fifteen years of practical history (1903–17) unequaled anywhere in the world in its wealth of experience. During those fifteen years, no other country knew anything even approximating that revolutionary experience, that rapid and varied succession of different forms of the movement—legal and illegal, peaceful and stormy, underground and open, local circles and mass movements, and parliamentary and terrorist forms. In no other country has there been concentrated, in so brief a period, such a wealth of forms, shades, and methods of struggle of *all* classes of modern society, a struggle which, owing to the backwardness of the country and the severity of the tsarist yoke, matured with exceptional rapidity, and assimilated most eagerly and successfully the appropriate "last word" of American and European political experience.

THE PRINCIPAL STAGES IN THE HISTORY OF BOLSHEVISM

* * *

Despite views that are today often to be met with in Europe and America, the Bolsheviks began their victorious struggle against the parliamentary and (in fact) bourgeois republic and against the Mensheviks in a very cautious manner, and the preparations they made for it were by no means simple. At the beginning of the period mentioned, we did *not* call for the overthrow of the government but explained that it was impossible to overthrow it *without* first changing the composition and the temper of the Soviets. We did not proclaim a boycott of the bourgeois parliament, the Constituent Assembly, but said—and following the April (1917) Conference of our Party began to state officially in the name of the Party—that a bourgeois republic with a Constituent Assembly would be better than a bourgeois republic without a Constituent Assembly, but that a "workers' and peasants'" republic, a Soviet republic, would be better than any bourgeois-democratic, parliamentary republic. Without such thorough, circumspect, and long preparations, we could not have achieved victory in October 1917, or have consolidated that victory.

THE STRUGGLE AGAINST WHICH ENEMIES WITHIN THE WORKING-CLASS MOVEMENT HELPED BOLSHEVISM DEVELOP, GAIN STRENGTH, AND BECOME STEELED

* * *

The struggle that Bolshevism waged against "Left" deviations within its own Party assumed particularly large proportions on two occasions: in 1908, on the question of whether or not to participate in a most reactionary "parliament" and in the legal workers' societies, which were being restricted by most reactionary laws; and again in 1918 (the Treaty of Brest-Litovsk), on the question of whether one "compromise" or another was permissible.

In 1908 the "Left" Bolsheviks were expelled from our Party for stubbornly refusing to understand the necessity of participating in a most reactionary "parliament." The "Lefts" —among whom there were many splendid revolutionaries who subsequently were (and still are) commendable members of the Communist Party—based themselves particularly on the successful experience of the 1905 boycott. When, in August 1905, the tsar proclaimed the convocation of a consultative "parliament," the Bolsheviks called for its boycott, in the teeth of all the opposition parties and the Mensheviks, and the "parliament" was in fact swept by the revolution of October 1905. The boycott proved correct at the time, not because non-participation in reactionary parliaments is correct in general, but because we accurately appraised the objective situation, which was leading to the rapid development of the mass strikes first into a political strike, then into a revolutionary strike, and finally into an uprising. Moreover, the struggle centered at that time on the question of whether the convocation of the first representative assembly should be left to the tsar, or an attempt should be made to wrest its convocation from the old regime. When there was not, and could not be, any certainty that the objective situation was of a similar kind, and when there was no certainty of a similar trend and the same rate of development, the boycott was no longer correct.

The Bolsheviks' boycott of "parliament" in 1905 enriched the revolutionary proletariat with highly valuable political experience and showed that, when legal and illegal, parliamentary and non-parliamentary forms of struggle are combined, it is sometimes useful and even essential to reject parliamentary forms. It would, however, be highly erroneous to apply this experience blindly, imitatively and uncritically to *other* conditions and *other* situations. The Bolsheviks' boycott of the Duma in 1906 was a mistake, although a minor and easily remediable one.[1] The boycott of the Duma in 1907, 1908 and subsequent years was a most serious error and difficult to remedy, because, on the one hand, a very rapid rise of the revolutionary tide and its conversion into an uprising was not to be expected, and, on the other hand, the entire historical situation attendant upon the renovation of the bourgeois monarchy called for legal and illegal activities being combined. Today, when we look back at this fully completed historical period, whose connection with subsequent periods has now become quite clear, it becomes most obvious that in 1908–14 the Bolsheviks *could not have* preserved (let alone strengthened and developed) the core of

1. What applies to individuals also applies—with necessary modifications—to politics and parties. It is not he who makes no mistakes that is intelligent. There are no such men, nor can there be. It is he whose errors are not very grave and who is able to rectify them easily and quickly that is intelligent.

the revolutionary party of the proletariat, had they not upheld, in a most strenuous struggle, the viewpoint that it was *obligatory* to combine legal and illegal forms of struggle, and that it was *obligatory* to participate even in a most reactionary parliament and in a number of other institutions hemmed in by reactionary laws (sick-benefit societies, etc.).

In 1918 things did not reach a split. At that time the "Left" Communists formed only a separate group or "faction" within our Party, and that not for long. In the same year, 1918, the most prominent representatives of "Left Communism," for example, Comrades Radek and Bukharin, openly acknowledged their error. It had seemed to them that the Treaty of Brest-Litovsk was a compromise with the imperialists, which was inexcusable on principle and harmful to the party of the revolutionary proletariat. It was indeed a compromise with the imperialists, but it was a compromise which, under the circumstances, *had to be made.*

Today, when I hear our tactics in signing the Brest-Litovsk Treaty being attacked by the Socialist-Revolutionaries, for instance, or when I hear Comrade Lansbury say, in a conversation with me, "Our British trade union leaders say that if it was permissible for the Bolsheviks to compromise, it is permissible for them to compromise too," I usually reply by first of all giving a simple and "popular" example:

Imagine that your car is held up by armed bandits. You hand them over your money, passport, revolver, and car. In return you are rid of the pleasant company of the bandits. That is unquestionably a compromise. "*Do ut des*" (I "give" you money, firearms and a car "so that you give" me the opportunity to get away from you with a whole skin). It would, however, be difficult to find a sane man who would declare such a compromise to be "inadmissible on principle," or who would call the compromiser an accomplice of the bandits (even though the bandits might use the car and the firearms for further robberies). Our compromise with the bandits of German imperialism was just that kind of compromise.

But when, in 1914–18 and then in 1918–20, the Mensheviks and Socialist-Revolutionaries in Russia, the Scheidemannites (and to a large extent the Kautskyites) in Germany, Otto Bauer and Friedrich Adler (to say nothing of the Renners and Co.) in Austria, the Renaudels and Longuets and Co. in France, the Fabians, the Independents and the Labourites in Britain entered into *compromises* with the bandits of their own bourgeoisie, and sometimes of the "Allied" bourgeoisie, and *against* the revolutionary proletariat of their own countries, all these gentlemen were actually acting as *accomplices in banditry.*

The conclusion is clear: to reject compromises "on principle," to reject the permissibility of compromises in general, no matter of what kind, is childishness, which it is difficult even to consider seriously. A political leader who desires to be useful to the revolutionary proletariat must be able to distinguish *concrete* cases of compromises that are inexcusable and are an expression of opportunism and *treachery*; he must direct all the force of criticism, the full intensity of merciless exposure and relentless war, against *these concrete* compromises, and not allow the past masters of "practical" socialism and the the parliamentary Jesuits to dodge and wriggle out of responsibility by means of disquisitions on "compromises in general." It is in this way that the "leaders" of the British trade unions, as well as of the Fabian society and the "Independent" Labour Party, dodge responsibility *for the treachery they have perpetrated*, for having made *a compromise* that is really tantamount to the worst kind of opportunism, treachery, and betrayal.

There are different kinds of compromises. One must be able to analyze the situation and the concrete conditions of each compromise, or of each variety of compromise. One must learn to distinguish between a man who has given up his money and firearms to bandits so as to lessen the evil they can do and to facilitate their capture and execution, and a man who gives his money and firearms to bandits so as to share in the loot. In politics this is by no means always as elementary as it is in this childishly simple example. However, anyone who is out to think up for the workers some kind of recipe that will provide them with cut-and-dried solutions for all contingencies, or promises that the policy of the revolutionary proletariat will never come up against difficult or complex situations, is simply a charlatan.

To leave no room for misinterpretation, I shall attempt to outline, if only very briefly, several fundamental rules for the analysis of concrete compromises.

The party which entered into a compromise with the German imperialists by signing the Treaty of Brest-Litovsk had been evolving its internationalism in practice ever since the end of 1914. It was not afraid to call for the defeat of the tsarist monarchy and to condemn "defense of country" in a war between two imperialist robbers. The parliamentary representatives of this party preferred exile in Siberia to taking a road leading to ministerial portfolios in a bourgeois government. The revolution that overthrew tsarism and established a democratic republic put this party to a new and tremendous test—it did not enter into any agreements with its "own" imperialists, but prepared and brought about their overthrow. When it had assumed political power, this party did not leave a vestige of either landed or capitalist ownership. After making public and repudiating the imperialists' secret treaties, this party proposed peace to *all* nations, and yielded to the violence of the Brest-Litovsk robbers only after the Anglo-French imperialists had torpedoed the conclusion of a peace, and after the Bolsheviks had done everything humanly possible to hasten the revolution in Germany and other countries. The absolute correctness of this compromise, entered into by such a party in such a situation, is becoming ever clearer and more obvious with every day.

The Mensheviks and the Socialist-Revolutionaries in Russia (like all the leaders of the Second International throughout the world, in 1914–20) began with treachery—by directly or indirectly justifying "defense of country," i.e., the defense of *their own* predatory bourgeoisie. They continued their treachery by entering into a coalition with the bourgeoisie of *their own* country, and fighting, together with *their own* bourgeoisie, against the revolutionary proletariat of their own country. Their bloc, first with Kerensky and the Cadets, and then with Kolchak and Denikin in Russia—like the bloc of their *confrères* abroad with the bourgeoisie of *their* respective countries—was in fact desertion to the side of the bourgeoisie, against the proletariat. From beginning to end, *their* compromise with the bandits of imperialism meant their becoming *accomplices* in imperialist banditry.

* * *

SHOULD REVOLUTIONARIES WORK IN REACTIONARY TRADE UNIONS?

The German "Lefts" consider that, as far as they are concerned, the reply to this question is an unqualified negative. In their opinion, declamations and angry outcries . . . against "reactionary" and "counter-revolutionary" trade unions are sufficient "proof" that it is unnecessary and even inexcusable for revolutionaries and Communists to work in yellow, social-chauvinist, compromising, and counter-revolutionary trade unions.

* * *

However firmly the German "Lefts" may be convinced of the revolutionism of such tactics, the latter are in fact fundamentally wrong, and contain nothing but empty phrases.

* * *

This ridiculous "theory" that Communists should not work in reactionary trade unions reveals with the utmost clarity the frivolous attitude of the "Left" Communists toward the question of influencing the "masses," and their misuse of clamor about the "masses." If you want to help the "masses" and win the sympathy and support of the "masses," you should not fear difficulties, or pinpricks, chicanery, insults, and persecution from the "leaders" (who, being opportunists and social-chauvinists, are in most cases directly or indirectly connected with the bourgeoisie and the police), but must absolutely *work wherever the masses are to be found.* You must be capable of any sacrifice, of overcoming the greatest obstacles, in order to carry on agitation and propaganda systematically, perseveringly, persistently, and patiently in those institutions, societies and associations—even the most reactionary—in which proletarian or semi-proletarian masses are to be found.

* * *

SHOULD WE PARTICIPATE IN BOURGEOIS PARLIAMENTS?

It is with the utmost contempt—and the utmost levity—that the German "Left" Communists reply to this question in the negative.

* * *

In Western Europe and America, parliament has become most odious to the revolutionary vanguard of the working class. That cannot be denied. It can readily be understood, for it is difficult to imagine anything more infamous, vilc or treacherous than the behavior of the vast majority of Socialist and Social-Democratic parliamentary deputies during and after the war. It would, however, be not only unreasonable but actually criminal to yield to this mood when deciding *how* this generally recognized evil should be fought. In many countries of Western Europe, the revolutionary mood, we might say, is at present a "novelty," or a "rarity," which has all too long been vainly and impatiently awaited; perhaps that is why people so easily yield to that mood. Certainly, without a revolutionary mood among the masses, and without conditions facilitating the growth of this mood, revolutionary tactics will never develop into action. In Russia, however, lengthy, painful, and sanguinary experience has taught us the truth that revolutionary tactics cannot be built on a revolutionary mood alone. Tactics must be based on a sober and strictly objective appraisal of *all* the class forces in a particular state (and of the states that surround it, and of all states the world over) as well as of the experience of revolutionary movements. It is very easy to show one's "revolutionary" temper merely by hurling abuse at parliamentary opportunism, or merely by repudiating participation in parliaments; its very ease, however, cannot turn this into a solution of a difficult, a very difficult, problem.

* * *

The German "Lefts" complain of bad "leaders" in their party, give way to despair, and even arrive at a ridiculous "negation" of "leaders." But in conditions in which it is often necessary to hide "leaders" underground, the *evolution* of good "leaders," reliable, tested, and authoritative, is a very difficult matter; these difficulties *cannot* be successfully overcome without combining legal and illegal work, and *without testing the "leaders," among other ways*, in parliaments. Criticism—the most keen, ruthless and uncompromising criticism—should be directed, not against parliamentarianism or parliamentary activities, but against those leaders who are unable—and still more against those who are *unwilling*—to utilize parliamentary elections and the parliamentary rostrum in a revolutionary and communist manner. Only such criticism—combined, of course, with the dismissal of incapable leaders and their replacement by capable ones—will constitute useful and fruitful revolutionary work that will simultaneously train the "leaders" to be worthy of the working class and of all working people, and train the masses to be able properly to understand the political situation and the often very complicated and intricate tasks that spring from that situation.

* * *

NO COMPROMISES?

* * *

Naïve and quite inexperienced people imagine that the permissibility of compromise *in general* is sufficient to obliterate any distinction between opportunism, against which we are waging, and must wage, an unremitting struggle, and revolutionary Marxism, or communism. But if such people do not yet know that in nature and in society *all* distinctions are fluid and up to a certain point conventional, nothing can help them but lengthy training, education, enlightenment, and political and everyday experience. In the practical questions that arise in the politics of any particular or specific historical moment, it is important to single out those which display the principal type of intolerable and treacherous compromises, such as embody an opportunism that is fatal to the revolutionary class, and to exert all efforts to explain them and combat them.

* * *

"All compromise with other parties . . . any policy of maneuvering and compromise must be emphatically rejected," the German Lefts write in the Frankfurt pamphlet.

It is surprising that, with such views, these Lefts do not emphatically condemn Bolshevism! After all, the German Lefts cannot but know that the entire history of Bolshevism, both before and after the October Revolution, is *full* of instances of changes of tack, conciliatory tactics, and compromises with other parties, including bourgeois parties!

To carry on a war for the overthrow of the international bourgeoisie, a war which is a hundred times more difficult, protracted, and complex than the most stubborn of ordinary wars between states, and to renounce in advance any change of tack, or any utilization of a conflict of interests (even if temporary) among one's enemies, or any conciliation or compromise with possible allies (even if they are temporary, unstable, vacillating, or conditional allies)—is that not ridiculous in the extreme? Is it not like making a difficult ascent of an unexplored and hitherto inaccessible mountain and refusing in advance ever to move in zigzags, ever to retrace one's steps, or ever to abandon a course once selected, and to try others? And yet people so immature and inexperienced (if youth were the explanation, it would not be so bad; young people are preordained to talk such nonsense for a certain period) have met with support—whether direct or indirect, open or covert, whole or partial, it does not matter—from some members of the Communist Party of Holland.

After the first socialist revolution of the proletariat, and the overthrow of the bourgeoisie in some country, the proletariat of that country remains *for a long time weaker* than the bourgeoisie, simply because of the latter's extensive international links, and also because of the spontaneous and continuous restoration and regeneration of capitalism and the bourgeoisie by the small commodity producers of the country which has overthrown the bourgeoisie. The more powerful enemy can be vanquished only by exerting the utmost effort, and by the most thorough, careful, attentive, skillful, and *obligatory* use of any, even the smallest, rift between the enemies, any conflict of interest among the bourgeoisie of the various countries and among the various groups or types of bourgeoisie within the various countries, and also by taking advantage of any, even the smallest, opportunity of winning a mass ally, even though this ally is temporary, vacillating, unstable, unreliable, and conditional. Those who do not understand this reveal a failure to understand even the smallest grain of Marxism, of modern scientific socialism *in general*. Those who have not proved *in practice*, over a fairly considerable period of time and in fairly varied political situations, their ability to apply this truth in practice have not yet learned to help the revolutionary class in its struggle to emancipate all toiling humanity from the exploiters. And this applies equally to the period *before* and *after* the proletariat has won political power.

Our theory is not a dogma, but a *guide to action*, said Marx and Engels. The greatest blunder, the greatest crime, committed by such "out-and-out" Marxists as Karl Kautsky, Otto Bauer, etc., is that they have not understood this and have been unable to apply it at crucial moments of the proletarian revolution. "Political activity is not like the pavement of Nevsky Prospekt" (the well-kept, broad and level pavement of the perfectly straight principal thoroughfare of St. Petersburg), N. G. Chernyshevsky, the great Russian socialist of the pre-Marxist period, used to say. Since Chernyshevsky's time, disregard or forgetfulness of this truth has cost Russian revolutionaries countless sacrifices. We must strive at all costs to *prevent* the Left Communists and Western European and American revolutionaries that are devoted to the working class from paying *as dearly* as the backward Russians did to learn this truth.

Prior to the downfall of tsarism, the Russian revolutionary Social-Democrats made repeated use of the services of the bourgeois liberals, i.e., they concluded numerous practical compromises with the latter. In 1901–2, even prior to the appearance of Bolshevism, the old editorial board of *Iskra* (consisting of Plekhanov, Axelrod, Zasulich, Martov, Potresov, and myself) concluded (not for long, it is true) a formal political alliance with Struve, the political leader of bourgeois liberalism, while at the same time being able to wage an unremitting and most merciless ideological and political struggle against bourgeois liberalism and against the slightest manifestations of its influence in the working-class movement. The Bolsheviks have always adhered to this policy. Since 1905 they have systematically advocated an alliance between the working class and the peasantry, against the liberal bourgeoisie and tsarism, never, however, refusing to support the bourgeoisie against tsarism (for instance, during second rounds of elections, or during second ballots) and never ceasing their relentless ideological and political struggle against the Socialist-Revolutionaries, the bourgeois-revolutionary peasant party, exposing them as petty-bourgeois democrats who have falsely described themselves as socialists. During the Duma elections of 1907, the Bolsheviks entered briefly into a formal political bloc with the Socialist-Revolutionaries. Between 1903 and 1912, they were periods of several years in which we were formally united with the Mensheviks in a single Social-Democratic Party, but we *never stopped* our ideological and political struggle against them as opportunists and vehicles of bourgeois influence on the proletariat. During the war, we concluded certain compromises with the Kautskyites, with the Left Mensheviks (Martov), and with a section of the Socialist-Revolutionaries (Chernov and Natanson); we were together with them at Zimmerwald and Kienthal, and issued joint manifestos. However, we never ceased and never relaxed our ideological and political struggle against the Kautskyites, Martov and Chernov (when Natanson died in 1919, a "Revolutionary-Communist" Narodnik, he was very close to and almost in agreement with us). At the very moment of the October Revolution, we entered into an informal but very important (and very successful) political bloc with the petty-bourgeois peasantry by adopting the *Socialist-Revolutionary* agrarian program *in its entirety*, without a single alteration—i.e., we effected an undeniable compromise in order to prove to the peasants that we wanted, not to "steam-roller" them but to reach agreement with them. At the same time we proposed (and soon after effected) a formal political bloc, including participation in the government, with the Left Socialist-Revolutionaries, who dissolved this bloc after the conclusion of the Treaty of Brest-Litovsk and then, in July 1918, went to the length of armed rebellion, and subsequently of an armed struggle, against us.

* * *

SEVERAL CONCLUSIONS

* * *

History as a whole, and the history of revolutions in particular, is always richer in content, more varied, more multiform, more lively and ingenious than is imagined by even the best parties, the most class-conscious vanguards of the most advanced classes. This can readily be understood, because even the finest of vanguards express the class-consciousness, will, passion, and imagination of tens of thousands, whereas at moments of great upsurge and the exertion of all human capacities, revolutions are made by the class-consciousness, will, passion, and imagination of tens of millions, spurred on by a most acute struggle of classes. Two very important practical conclusions follow from this: first, that in order to accomplish its task the revolutionary class must be able to master *all* forms or aspects of social activity without exception (completing after the capture of political power—sometimes at great risk and with very great danger—what it did not complete before the capture of power); second, that the revolutionary class must be prepared for the most rapid and brusque replacement of one form by another.

One will readily agree that any army which does not train to use all the weapons, all the means and methods of warfare that the enemy possesses, or may possess, is behaving in an unwise or even criminal manner. This applies to politics even more than it does to the art of war. In politics it is even harder to know in advance which methods of struggle will be applicable and to our advantage in certain future conditions. Unless we learn to apply all the methods of struggle, we may suffer grave and sometimes even decisive defeat, if changes beyond our control in the position of the other classes bring to the forefront a form of activity in which we are especially weak. If, however, we learn to use all the methods of struggle, victory will be certain, because we represent the interests of the really foremost and really revolutionary class, even if circumstances do not permit us to make use of weapons that are most dangerous to the enemy, weapons that deal the swiftest mortal blows. Inexperienced revolutionaries often think that legal methods of struggle are opportunist because, in this field, the bourgeoisie has most frequently deceived and duped the workers (particularly in "peaceful" and non-revolutionary times), while illegal methods of struggle are revolutionary. That, however, is wrong. The truth is that those parties and leaders are opportunists and traitors to the working class that are unable or unwilling (do not say, "I can't"; say, "I shan't") to use illegal methods of struggle in conditions such as those which prevailed, for example, during the imperialist war of 1914–18, when the bourgeoisie of the freest democratic countries most brazenly and brutally deceived the workers, and smothered the truth about the predatory character of the war. But revolutionaries who are incapable of combining illegal forms of struggle with *every* form of legal struggle are poor revolutionaries indeed. It is not difficult to be a revolutionary when revolution has already broken out and is in spate, when all people are joining the revolution just because they are carried away, because it is the vogue, and sometimes even from careerist motives. After its victory, the proletariat has to make most strenuous efforts, even the most painful, so as to "liberate" itself from such pseudo-revolutionaries. It is far more difficult—and far more precious—to be a revolutionary when the conditions for direct, open, really mass and really revolutionary struggle *do not yet exist*, to be able to champion the interests of the revolution (by propaganda, agitation, and organization) in non-revolutionary bodies, and quite often in downright reactionary bodies, in a non-revolutionary situation, among the masses who are incapable of immediately appreciating the need for revolutionary methods of action. To be able to seek, find, and correctly determine the specific path or the particular turn of events that will *lead* the masses to the real, decisive, and final revolutionary struggle—such is the main objective of communism in Western Europe and in America today.

Britain is an example. We cannot tell—no one can tell in advance—how soon a real proletarian revolution will flare up there, and *what immediate cause* will most serve to rouse, kindle, and impel into the struggle the very wide masses, who are still dormant. Hence, it is our duty to carry on all our preparatory work in such a way as to be "well shod on all four feet" (as the late Plekhanov, when he was a Marxist and revolutionary, was fond of saying). It is possible that the breach will be forced, the ice broken, by a parliamentary crisis, or by a crisis arising from colonial and imperialist contradictions, which are hopelessly entangled and are becoming increasingly painful and acute, or perhaps by some third cause, etc. We are not discussing the kind of struggle that will *determine* the fate of the proletarian revolution in Great Britain (no Communist has any doubt on that score; for all of us this is a foregone conclusion): what we are discussing is the *immediate cause* that will bring into motion the now dormant proletarian masses, and lead them right up to revolution. Let us not forget that in the French bourgeois republic, for example, in a situation which, from both the international and the national viewpoints, was a hundred times less revolutionary than it is today, such an "unexpected" and "petty" cause as one of the many thousands of fraudulent machinations of thc reactionary military caste (the Dreyfus case) was enough to bring the people to the brink of civil war!

In Great Britain the Communists should constantly, unremittingly and unswervingly utilize parliamentary elections and all the vicissitudes of the Irish, colonial, and world-imperialist policy of the British Government, and all other fields, spheres and aspects of public life, and work in all of them in a new way, in a communist way, in the spirit of the Third, not the Second, International. I have neither the time nor the space here to describe the "Russian" "Bolshevik" methods of participation in parliamentary elections and in the parliamentary struggle; I can, however, assure foreign Communists that they were quite unlike the usual Western European parliamentary campaigns. From this the conclusion is often drawn: "Well, that was in Russia; in our country parliamentarianism is different." This is a false conclusion. Communists, adherents of the Third International in all countries, exist for the purpose of *changing*—all along the line, in all spheres of life—the old socialist, trade-unionist, syndicalist, and parliamentary type of work into a *new* type of work, the communist. In Russia, too, there was always an abundance of opportunism, purely bourgeois sharp practices and capitalist rigging in the elections. In Western Europe and in America, the communists must learn to create a new, uncustomary, non-opportunist, and non-careerist parliamentarianism; the communist parties must issue their slogans; true proletarians, with the help of the unorganized and downtrodden poor, should distribute leaflets, canvass workers' houses and cottages of the rural proletarians and peasants in the remote villages (fortunately there are many times fewer remote villages in Europe than in Russia, and in Britain the number is very small); they should go into the public houses, penetrate into unions, societies, and chance gatherings of the common people, and speak to the people, not in learned (or very parliamentary) language; they should not at all strive to "get seats" in parliament, but should everywhere try to get people to think, and draw the masses into the struggle, to take the bourgeoisie at its word and utilize the machinery it has set up, the elections it has appointed, and the appeals it has made to the people; they should try to explain to the people what Bolshevism is, in a way that was never possible (under bourgeois rule) outside of election times (exclusive, of course, of times of big strikes, when in Russia a *similar* apparatus for widespread popular agitation worked even more intensively). It is very difficult to do this in Western Europe and extremely difficult in America, but it can and must be done, for the objectives of communism cannot be achieved without effort. We must work to accomplish *practical* tasks, ever more varied and ever more closely connected with all branches of social life, *winning* branch after branch, and sphere after sphere *from the bourgeoisie*.

In Great Britain, further, the work of propaganda, agitation and organization among the armed forces and among the oppressed and underprivileged nationalities in their "*own*" state (Ireland, the colonies) must also be tackled in a new fashion (one that is not socialist, but communist; not reformist, but revolutionary). That is because, in the era of imperialism in general and especially today after a war that was a sore trial to the peoples and has quickly opened their eyes to the truth (i.e., the fact that tens of millions were killed and maimed for the sole purpose of deciding whether the British or the German robbers should plunder the largest number of countries), all these spheres of social life are heavily charged with inflammable material and are creating numerous causes of conflicts, crises, and an intensification of the class struggle. We do not and cannot know which spark —of the innumerable sparks that are flying about in all countries as a result of the world economic and political crisis—will kindle the conflagration, in the sense of raising up the masses; we must, therefore, with our new and communist principles, set to work to stir up all and sundry, even the oldest, mustiest, and seemingly hopeless spheres, for otherwise we shall not be able to cope with our tasks, shall not be comprehensively prepared, shall not be in possession of all the weapons and shall not prepare ourselves either to gain victory over the bourgeoisie (which arranged all aspects of social life—and has now disarranged them—in its bourgeois fashion), or to bring about the impending communist reorganization of every sphere of life, following that victory.

* * *

The Communists must exert every effort to direct the working-class movement and social development in general along the straightest and shortest road to the victory of Soviet power and the dictatorship of the proletariat on a worldwide scale. That is an incontestable truth. But it is enough to take one little step further—a step that might seem to be in the same direction—and truth turns into error. We have only to say, as the German and British Left Communists do, that we recognize only one road, only the direct road, and that we will not permit tacking, conciliatory maneuvers, or compromising—and it will be a mistake which may cause, and in part has already caused and is causing very grave prejudice to communism. Right doctrinarism persisted in recognizing only the old forms, and became utterly bankrupt, for it did not notice the new content. Left doctrinairism persists in the unconditional repudiation of certain old forms, failing to see that the new content is forcing its way through all and sundry forms, that it is our duty as Communists to master all forms, to learn how, with the maximum rapidity, to supplement one form with another, to substitute one for another, and to adapt our tactics to any such change that does not come from our class or from our efforts.

World revolution has been so powerfully stimulated and accelerated by the horrors, vileness, and abominations of the world imperialist war and by the hopelessness of the situation created by it, this revolution is developing in scope and depth with such splendid rapidity, with such a wonderful variety of changing forms, with such an instructive practical refutation of all doctrinairism, that there is every reason to hope for a rapid and complete recovery of the international communist movement from the infantile disorder of "Left-wing" communism.

"TESTAMENT" AND "CODICIL"*

V. I. Lenin

(Written in Moscow, December 1922 to January 1923)

After his second cerebral attack in December 1922, Lenin became convinced that he must act quickly to set Soviet Russia's future in order.

As soon as he was sufficiently recovered to do so, in several sessions between December 23 and 29, he dictated his "Testament," reviewing the credentials of the leading candidates to succeed him, chiefly Trotsky and Stalin. He found fault with both, but, between the two, it would seem he favored Stalin.

But then on January 4, 1923, he dictated a codicil in which he began by stating that Stalin was "too rude," and urged the comrades quickly to find "a way to remove Stalin" and appoint someone else to his position.

What happened between December 29 and January 4 is not, and may never be, known for sure. But it would seem that Lenin became incensed because of Stalin's high-handed and chauvinistic behavior in the Georgian "affair." And then when he learned that Stalin had browbeaten his wife, Krupskaya, and threatened to bring her before the party control commission, Lenin decided that the time for action against Stalin had arrived.

Lenin did not make the "Testament" and the "Codicil" public during his lifetime, nor did the party publish them after his death, choosing to keep Stalin in power. However, in 1926, the New York Times *got a copy of the documents*

* Complete

through its correspondent Max Eastman and published them. For three decades afterward, the West debated whether the "Testament" and the "Codicil" were genuine or two of the many forgeries of Soviet documents manufactured to order in Paris and Stockholm. In 1956, in connection with the "Secret Speech," Khrushchev had them published in the Soviet Union (for the first and last time), thus removing all doubt about their authenticity.

"TESTAMENT"

By the stability of the Central Committee [of the Communist party], of which I spoke before, I mean measures to prevent a split, so far as such measures can be taken. For, of course, the White Guard in Ruskaya Mysl (I think it was S. E. Oldenburg) was right when, in the first place, in his play against Soviet Russia he banked on the hope of a split in our party, and when, in the second place, he banked for that split on serious disagreements in our party.

Our party rests upon two classes, and for that reason its instability is possible, and if there cannot exist agreement between these classes its fall is inevitable. In such an event it would be useless to take any measures or in general to discuss the stability of our Central Committee. In such an event no measures would prove capable of preventing a split. But I trust that is too remote a future, and too improbable an event, to talk about.

I have in mind stability as a guarantee against a split in the near future, and I intend to examine here a series of considerations of a purely personal character.

I think that the fundamental factor in the matter of stability—from this point of view—is such members of the Central Committee as Stalin and Trotsky. The relation between them constitutes, in my opinion, a big half of the danger of that split, which might be avoided, and the avoidance of which might be promoted, in my opinion, by raising the number of members of the Central Committee to fifty or one hundred.

Comrade Stalin, having become General Secretary, has concentrated enormous power in his hands; and I am not sure that he always knows how to use that power with sufficient caution. On the other hand comrade Trotsky, as was proved by his struggle against the Central Committee in connection with the question of the People's Commissariat of Communication, is distinguished not only by his exceptional abilities—personally he is, to be sure, the most able man in the present Central Committee—but also by his too far-reaching self-confidence and a disposition to be too much attracted by the purely administrative side of affairs.

These two qualities of the two most able leaders of the present Central Committee might, quite innocently, lead to a split; if our party does not take measures to prevent it, a split might arise unexpectedly.

I will not further characterize the other members of the Central Committee as to their personal qualities. I will only remind you that the October episode of Zinoviev and Kamenev was not, of course, accidental, but that it ought as little to be used against them personally as the non-Bolshevism of Trotsky.

Of the younger members of the Central Committee I want to say a few words about Bukharin and Piatakov. They are, in my opinion, the most able forces (among the youngest), and in regard to them it is necessary to bear in mind the following: Bukharin is not only the most valuable and most important theoretician of the party, but also may legitimately be considered the favorite of the whole party; but his theoretical views can only with the very greatest doubt be regarded as fully Marxist, for there is something scholastic in them (he never has learned, and I think never has fully understood, the dialectic).

And then Piatakov—a man undoubtedly distinguished in will and ability, but too much given over to administration and the administrative side of things to be relied on in a serious political question.

Of course, both these remarks are made by me merely with a view to the present time, or assuming that these two able and loyal workers may find occasion to increase their knowledge and correct their one-sidedness.

LENIN.

"CODICIL"

Stalin is too rude, and this fault, entirely supportable in relations among us Communists, becomes insupportable in the office of General Secretary. Therefore, I propose to the comrades to find a way to remove Stalin from that position and appoint to it another man who in all respects differs from Stalin in one superiority—namely, that he be more tolerant, more loyal, more polite, and more considerate to comrades, less capricious, etc. This circumstance may seem an insignificant trifle, but I think that from the point of view of preventing a split and from the point of view of the relation between Stalin and Trotsky which I discussed above, it is not a trifle, or it is such a trifle as may acquire decisive significance.

LENIN.

3

THE QUESTION OF THE VICTORY OF SOCIALISM IN ONE COUNTRY*

J. V. Stalin
(From Concerning Questions of Leninism, Published in Moscow, January 1926)

In the aftermath of 1917, the Bolsheviks held that the revolution which had broken out in Russian could not survive unless it spread to the more highly developed capitalist states. However, by the early 1920s it had become clear that although the revolution was not going to spread, it nevertheless had good prospects for survival in Russia. *The question became: What to do next?*

Stalin took the position that attention must now be paid to the internal development of Russia. He indicated that while socialism could not be fully developed in Russia without the spread of the revolution to the West, it was "possible"—later "necessary"—to build "socialism in one country." Because this was not an exceptional position among those now engaged in the struggle to succeed Lenin, little attention was initially paid to it.

In the meantime, the Kamenev–Zinoviev–Stalin trium-

* Complete

virate, attempting to undermine Trotsky, whom all saw as the chief contender for Lenin's power, had attacked Trotsky for the theory of "permanent revolution," which he had formulated in 1905 as a means for speeding the advent of revolution in Russia. At a time when the Russians were exhausted by a decade of war and revolution, "permanent revolution"—even though he disowned it in the contemporary situation—became a millstone around Trotsky's neck, particularly when counterposed to Stalin's advocacy of "socialism in one country," in "our country."

"Socialism in one country" served Stalin in several ways: it indicated his advocacy of stability; it placed him on the side of Russian nationalism; it undermined Trotsky and his "clique" of internationalists, Jews, and intellectuals, who were anathema to the Russian masses and to Stalin personally.

In its implication that what was good for the Soviet Union was, by definition, good for the international movement, "socialism in one country" became a key for determining loyalty to Moscow until World War II—and in some respects beyond.

The pamphlet *The Foundations of Leninism* (May 1924, first edition) contains two formulations on the question of the victory of socialism in one country. The first of these says:

Formerly, the victory of the revolution in one country was considered impossible, on the assumption that it would require the combined action of the proletarians of all or at least of a majority of the advanced countries to achieve victory over the bourgeoisie. Now this point of view no longer fits in with the facts. Now we must proceed from the possibility of such a victory; for the uneven and spasmodic character of the development of the various capitalist countries under the conditions of imperialism, the development within imperialism of catastrophic contradictions leading to inevitable wars, the growth of the revolutionary movement in all countries of the world—all this leads, not only to the possibility, but also to the necessity of the victory of the proletariat in individual countries.

This thesis is quite correct and needs no comment. It is directed against the theory of the Social-Democrats, who regard the seizure of power by the proletariat in one country, without the simultaneous victory of the revolution in other countries, as utopian.

But the pamphlet *The Foundations of Leninism* contains a second formulation, which says:

> But the overthrow of the power of the bourgeoisie and establishment of the power of the proletariat in one country does not yet mean that the complete victory of socialism has been ensured. The principal task of socialism—the organization of socialist production—has still to be fulfilled. Can this task be fulfilled, can the final victory of socialism be achieved in one country, without the joint efforts of the proletarians in several advanced countries? No, it cannot. To overthrow the bourgeoisie the efforts of one country are sufficient; this is proved by the history of our revolution. For the final victory of socialism, for the organization of socialist production, the efforts of one country, particularly of a peasant country like Russia, are insufficient; for that, the efforts of the proletarians of several advanced countries are required.

This second formulation was directed against the assertions of the critics of Leninism, against the Trotskyites, who declared that the dictatorship of the proletariat in one country, in the absence of victory in other countries, could not "hold out in the face of a conservative Europe."

To that extent—but only to that extent—this formulation was then (May 1924) adequate, and undoubtedly it was of some service.

Subsequently, however, when the criticism of Leninism in this sphere had already been overcome in the Party, when a new question had come to the fore—the question of the possibility of building a complete socialist society by the efforts of our country, without help from abroad—the second formulation became obviously inadequate, and therefore incorrect.

What is the defect in this formulation?

Its defect is that it joins two different questions into one:

it joins the question of the *possibility* of building socialism by the efforts of one country—which must be answered in the affirmative—with the question whether a country in which the dictatorship of the proletariat exists can consider itself *fully guaranteed* against intervention, and consequently against the restoration of the old order, without a victorious revolution in a number of other countries—which must be answered in the negative. This is apart from the fact that this formulation may give occasion for thinking that the organization of a socialist society by the efforts of one country is impossible—which, of course, is incorrect.

On this ground I modified and corrected this formulation in my pamphlet *The October Revolution and the Tactics of the Russian Communists* (December 1924); I divided the question into two—into the question of a *full guarantee against the restoration of the bourgeois order*, and the question of the *possibility of building a complete socialist society* in one country. This was effected, in the first place, by treating the "complete victory of socialism" as a "full guarantee against the restoration of the old order," which is possible only through "the joint efforts of the proletarians of several countries"; and, secondly, by proclaiming, on the basis of Lenin's pamphlet *On Cooperation*, the indisputable truth that we have all that is necessary for building a complete socialist society.

It was this new formulation of the question that formed the basis for the well-known resolution of the Fourteenth Party Conference "The Tasks of the Comintern and the RKP(B)," which examines the question of the victory of socialism in one country in connection with the stabilization of capitalism (April 1925), and considers that the building of socialism by the efforts of our country is possible and necessary.

This new formulation also served as the basis for my pamphlet *The Results of the Work of the Fourteenth Conference of the RKP(B)* published in May 1925, immediately after the Fourteenth Party Conference.

With regard to the presentation of the question of the victory of socialism in one country, this pamphlet states:

Our country exhibits two groups of contradictions. One group consists of the internal contradictions that exist between the proletariat and the peasantry (this refers to the building of socialism in one country—*J. St.*). The other group consists of the external contradictions that exist between our country, as the land of socialism, and all the other countries, as lands of capitalism (this refers to the final victory of socialism—*J. St.*). . . . Anyone who confuses the first group of contradictions, which can be overcome entirely by the efforts of one country, with the second group of contradictions, the solution of which requires the efforts of the proletarians of several countries, commits a gross error against Leninism. He is either a muddle-head or an incorrigible opportunist.

On the question of the *victory* of socialism in our country, the pamphlet states:

We can build socialism, and we will build it together with the peasantry under the leadership of the working class. [For] under the dictatorship of the proletariat we possess . . . all that is needed to build a complete socialist society, overcoming all internal difficulties, for we can and must overcome them by our own efforts.

On the question of the *final* victory of socialism, it states:

The final victory of socialism is the full guarantee against attempts at intervention, and hence against restoration; for any serious attempt at restoration can take place only with serious support from outside, only with the support of international capital. Therefore, the support of our revolution by the workers of all countries, and still more the victory of the workers in at least several countries, is a necessary condition for fully guaranteeing the first victorious country against attempts at intervention and restoration, a necessary condition for the final victory of socialism.

Clear, one would think.

It is well known that this question was treated in the same spirit in my pamphlet *Questions and Answers* (June 1925) and in the political report of the Central Committee to Congress XIV of the CPSU(B) (December 1925).

Such are the facts.

These facts, I think, are known to all the comrades, including Zinoviev.

If now, nearly two years after the ideological struggle in the Party and after the resolution that was adopted at the Fourteenth Party Conference (April 1925), Zinoviev finds it possible in his reply to the discussion at Party Congress XIV (December 1925) to dig up the old and quite inadequate formula contained in Stalin's pamphlet written in April 1924, and to make it the basis for deciding the already decided question of the victory of socialism in one country—then this peculiar trick of his only goes to show that he has got completely muddled on this question. To drag the Party back after it has moved forward, to evade the resolution of the Fourteenth Party Conference after it has been confirmed by a plenum of the Central Committee, means to become hopelessly entangled in contradictions, to have no faith in the cause of building socialism, to abandon the path of Lenin, and to acknowledge one's own defeat.

What is meant by the *possibility* of the victory of socialism in one country?

It means the possibility of solving the contradictions between the proletariat and the peasantry by means of the internal forces of our country, the possibility of the proletariat seizing power and using that power to build a complete socialist society in our country, with the sympathy and the support of the proletarians of other countries, but without the preliminary victory of the proletarian revolution in other countries.

Without such a possibility, building socialism is building without prospects, building without being sure that socialism will be completely built. It is no use engaging in building socialism without being sure that we can build it completely, without being sure that the technical backwardness of our country is not an *insuperable* obstacle to the building of a complete socialist society. To deny such a possibility means disbelief in the cause of building socialism, departure from Leninism.

What is meant by the *impossibility* of the complete, final

victory of socialism in one country without the victory of the revolution in other countries?

It means the impossibility of having a full guarantee against intervention, and consequently against the restoration of the bourgeois order, without the victory of the revolution in at least a number of countries. To deny this indisputable thesis means departure from internationalism, departure from Leninism. "We are living," says Lenin,

> not merely in a state, but *in a system of states*, and the existence of the Soviet Republic side by side with imperialist states for a long time is unthinkable. One or the other must triumph in the end. And before that end comes, a series of frightful collisions between the Soviet Republic and the bourgeois states will be inevitable. That means that if the ruling class, the proletariat, wants to, and will hold sway, it must prove this by its military organization also.
>
> We have before us a certain equilibrium, which is in the highest degree unstable, but an unquestionable, an indisputable equilibrium nevertheless. Will it last long? I do not know and, I think, it is impossible to know. And therefore we must exercise very great caution. And the first precept of our policy, the first lesson to be learnt from our governmental activities during the past year, the lesson which all the workers and peasants must learn, is that we must be on the alert, we must remember that we are surrounded by people, classes, and governments who openly express their intense hatred for us. We must remember that we are at all times but a hair's breadth from every manner of invasion.

Clear, one would think.

Where does Zinoviev stand as regards the question of the victory of socialism in one country?

Listen:

> By the final victory of socialism is meant, at least: (1) the abolition of classes, and therefore (2) the abolition of the dictatorship of one class, in this case the dictatorship of the proletariat. . . . In order to get a clearer idea of how the question stands here, in the USSR, in the year 1925, we must distinguish between two things: (1) the assured *possibility* of engaging in building socialism—such a possibility, it stands to reason, is

quite conceivable within the limits of one country; and (2) the final construction and consolidation of socialism, i.e., the achievement of a socialist system, of a socialist society.

What can all this signify?

It signifies that by the final victory of socialism in one country Zinoviev understands, not a guarantee against intervention and restoration, but the possibility of completely building socialist society. And by the victory of socialism in one country Zinoviev understands the kind of building socialism which cannot and should not lead to completely building socialism. Building at haphazard, without prospects, building socialism although completely building a socialist society is impossible—such is Zinoviev's position.

To engage in building socialism *without the possibility* of completely building it, *knowing that it cannot be completely built*—such are the absurdities in which Zinoviev has involved himself.

But this is a mockery of the question, not a solution of it!

Here is another extract from Zinoviev's reply to the discussion at Party Congress XIV:

> Take a look, for instance, at what Comrade Yakovlev went so far as to say at the last Kursk Gubernia Party Conference. He asks: "Is it possible for us, surrounded as we are on all sides by capitalist enemies, to completely build socialism in one country under such conditions?" And he answers: "On the basis of all that has been said, we have the right to say not only that we are building socialism, but that in spite of the fact that for the time being we are alone, that for the time being we are the only Soviet country, the only Soviet state in the world, we shall completely build socialism." (*Kurskaya Pravda*, No. 279, December 8, 1925.) *Is this the Leninist method of presenting the question? Does not this smack of national narrow-mindedness?**

Thus, according to Zinoviev, to recognize the possibility of completely building socialism in one country means adopting the point of view of national narrow-mindedness, while

* My italics.—J. St.

to deny such a possibility means adopting the point of view of internationalism.

But if that is true, it is at all worth while fighting for victory over the capitalist elements in our economy? Does it not follow from this that such a victory is impossible?

Capitulation to the capitalist elements in our economy—that is what the inherent logic of Zinoviev's line of argument leads us to.

And this absurdity, which has nothing in common with Leninism, is presented to us by Zinoviev as "internationalism," as "100 percent Leninism"!

I assert that on this most important question of building socialism, Zinoviev is deserting Leninism and slipping to the standpoint of the Menshevik Sukhanov.

Let us turn to Lenin. Here is what he said about the victory of socialism in one country even before the October Revolution, in August 1915:

> Uneven economic and political development is an absolute law of capitalism. Hence, the victory of socialism is possible first in several or even in one capitalist country taken separately. The victorious proletariat of that country, having expropriated the capitalists and *organized its own socialist production*,* would stand up *against* the rest of the world, the capitalist world, attracting to its cause the oppressed classes of other countries, raising revolts in those countries against the capitalists, and in the event of necessity coming out even with armed force against the exploiting classes and their states.

What is meant by Lenin's phrase "having . . . organized its own socialist production" which I have stressed? It means that the proletariat of the victorious country, having seized power, *can* and *must* organize its own socialist production. And what does "organize socialist production" mean? It means completely building a socialist society. It scarcely needs proof that this clear and definite statement of Lenin's requires no further comment. Otherwise Lenin's call for the seizure of power by the proletariat in October 1917 would be incomprehensible.

You see that this clear thesis of Lenin's, in comparison

* My italics.—J. St.

with Zinoviev's muddled and anti-Leninist "thesis" that we can engage in building socialism "within the limits of one country," although it is *impossible* to build it completely, is as different from the latter as the heavens from the earth.

The statement quoted above was made by Lenin in 1915, before the proletariat had taken power. But perhaps he modified his views after the experience of taking power, after 1917? Let us turn to Lenin's pamphlet *On Cooperation*, written in 1923.

> As a matter of fact, state power over all large-scale means of production, state power in the hands of the proletariat, the alliance of this proletariat with the many millions of small and very small peasants, the assured leadership of the peasantry by the proletariat, etc.— is not this all that is necessary for building a complete socialist society from the cooperatives, from the cooperatives alone, which we formerly looked down upon as huckstering and which from a certain aspect we have the right to look down upon as such now, under NEP? *Is this not all that is necessary for building a complete socialist society?* This is not yet the building of socialist society, but *it is all that is necessary and sufficient for this building.**

In other words, we can and must build a complete socialist society; for we have at our disposal all that is necessary and sufficient for this building.

I think it would be difficult to express oneself more clearly.

Compare this classical thesis of Lenin's with the anti-Leninist rebuke Zinoviev administered to Yakovlev, and you will realize that Yakovlev was only repeating Lenin's words about the possibility of completely building socialism in one country, whereas Zinoviev, by attacking this thesis and castigating Yakovlev, deserted Lenin and adopted the point of view of the Menshevik Sukhanov, the point of view that it is impossible to build socialism completely in our country owing to its technical backwardness.

One can only wonder why we took power in October 1917 if we did not count on completely building socialism.

We should not have taken power in October 1917—this is

* My italics.—J. St.

the conclusion to which the inherent logic of Zinoviev's line of argument leads us.

I assert further that in the highly important question of the victory of socialism, Zinoviev has gone *counter* to the definite decisions of our Party, as registered in the well-known resolution of the Fourteenth Party Conference "The Tasks of the Comintern and the RKP(B) in Connection with the Enlarged Plenum of the ECCI [Executive Committee of the Comintern]."

Let us turn to this resolution. Here is what it says about the victory of socialism in one country:

> The existence of two directly opposite social systems gives rise to the constant menace of capitalist blockade, of other forms of economic pressure, of armed intervention, of restoration. Consequently, the only guarantee of the *final victory of socialism*, i.e., *the guarantee against restoration*, is a victorious socialist revolution in a number of countries. . . . Leninism teaches that the *final* victory of socialism, *in the sense of a full guarantee against the restoration* of bourgeois relationships, is possible only on an international scale. . . . But it *does not follow* from this that it is impossible to build a *complete socialist society** in a backward country like Russia, without the "state aid" (Trotsky) of countries more developed technically and economically.

As you see, the resolution interprets the final victory of socialism as a guarantee against intervention and restoration, *in complete contrast* to Zinoviev's interpretation in his book *Leninism*.

As you see, the resolution recognizes the possibility of building a complete socialist society in a backward country like Russia without the "state aid" of countries more developed technically and economically, *in complete contrast* to what Zinoviev said when he rebuked Yakovlev in his reply to the discussion at Party Congress XIV.

How else can this be described if not as a struggle on Zinoviev's part *against* the resolution of the Fourteenth Party Conference?

Of course, Party resolutions are sometimes not free from

* My italics.—J. St.

error. Sometimes they contain mistakes. Speaking generally, one may assume that the resolution of the Fourteenth Party Conference also contains certain errors. Perhaps Zinoviev thinks that this resolution is erroneous. But then he should say so clearly and openly, as befits a Bolshevik. For some reason or other, however, Zinoviev does not do so. He preferred to choose another path, that of attacking the resolution of the Fourteenth Party Conference from the rear, while keeping silent about this resolution and refraining from any open criticism of the resolution. Zinoviev evidently thinks that this will be the best way of achieving his purpose. And he has but one purpose, namely—to "improve" the resolution, and to amend Lenin "just a little bit." It scarcely needs proof that Zinoviev has made a mistake in his calculations.

What is Zinoviev's mistake due to? What is the root of this mistake?

The root of this mistake, in my opinion, lies in Zinoviev's conviction that the technical backwardness of our country is an *insuperable* obstacle to the building of a complete socialist society; that the proletariat cannot completely build socialism owing to the technical backwardness of our country. Zinoviev and Kamenev once tried to raise this argument at a meeting of the Central Committee of the Party prior to the April Party Conference. But they received a rebuff and were compelled to retreat, and *formally* they submitted to the opposite point of view, the point of view of the majority of the Central Committee. But although he formally submitted to it, Zinoviev has continued to wage a struggle against it all the time. Here is what the Moscow Committee of our Party says about this "incident" in the Central Committee of the RKP(B) in its "Reply" to the letter of the Leningrad Gubernia Party Conference:

> Recently, in the Political Bureau, Kamenev and Zinoviev advocated the point of view that we cannot cope with the internal difficulties due to our technical and economic backwardness unless an international revolution comes to our rescue. We, however, with the majority of the members of the Central Committee, think that we can build socialism, are building it, and will completely build it, notwithstanding our technical back-

wardness and in spite of it. We think that the work of building will proceed far more slowly, of course, than in the conditions of a world victory; nevertheless, we are making progress and will continue to do so. We also believe that the view held by Kamenev and Zinoviev expresses disbelief in the internal forces of our working class and of the peasant masses who follow its lead. We believe that it is a departure from the Leninist position.

This document appeared in the press during the first sittings of Party Congress XIV. Zinoviev, of course, had the opportunity of attacking this document at the congress. It is characteristic that Zinoviev and Kamenev found no arguments against this grave accusation directed against them by the Moscow Committee of our Party. Was this accidental? I think not. The accusation, apparently, hit the mark. Zinoviev and Kamenev "replied" to this accusation by silence, because they had no "card to beat it."

The "New Opposition" is offended because Zinoviev is accused of disbelief in the victory of socialist construction in our country. But if after a whole year of discussion on the question of the victory of socialism in one country; after Zinoviev's viewpoint has been rejected by the Political Bureau of the Central Committee (April 1925); after the Party has arrived at a definite opinion on this question, recorded in the well-known resolution of the Fourteenth Party Conference (April 1925)—if, after all this, Zinoviev ventures to oppose the point of view of the Party in his book *Leninism* (September 1925), if he then repeats this opposition at Party Congress XIV—how can all this, this stubbornness, this persistence in his error, be explained if not by the fact that Zinoviev is infected, hopelessly infected, with disbelief in the victory of socialist construction in our country?

It pleases Zinoviev to regard this disbelief of his as internationalism. But since when have we come to regard departure from Leninism on a cardinal question of Leninism as internationalism?

Will it not be more correct to say that it is not the Party but Zinoviev who is sinning against internationalism and the international revolution? For what is our country, the country "that is building socialism," if not the base of the world revolution? But can it be a real base of the world revolution if it is incapable of completely building a socialist society? Can it remain the mighty center of attraction for the workers of all countries that it undoubtedly is now, if it is incapable of achieving victory at home over the capitalist elements in our economy, the victory of socialist construction? I think not. But does it not follow from this that disbelief in the victory of socialist construction, the dissemination of such disbelief, will lead to our country being discredited as the base of the world revolution? And if our country is discredited, the world revolutionary movement will be weakened. How did Messrs. the Social-Democrats try to scare the workers away from us? By preaching that "the Russians will not get anywhere." What are we beating the Social-Democrats with now, when we are attracting a whole series of workers' delegations to our country and thereby strengthening the position of communism all over the world? By our successes in building socialism. Is it not obvious, then, that whoever disseminates disbelief in our successes in building socialism thereby indirectly helps the Social-Democrats, reduces the sweep of the international revolutionary movement, and inevitably departs from internationalism? . . .

You see that Zinoviev is in no better position in regard to his "internationalism" than in regard to his "100 percent Leninism" on the question of building socialism in one country.

That is why Party Congress XIV rightly defined the views of the "New Opposition" as "disbelief in the cause of socialits construction," as "a distortion of Leninism."

4

STALIN HAS SIGNED THE DEATH CERTIFICATE OF THE THIRD INTERNATIONAL*

L. D. Trotsky
(From The New Militant,
Published in New York, May 1935)

Lenin drew back from the international revolution in 1920 and Stalin moved to "socialism in one country" four years later because it seemed to them that the lack of prospects for the spread of revolution abroad and the continued existence of Soviet Russia required such action. But it is also true that to both Lenin and Stalin—though certainly more to the latter than to the former—the resulting aggrandizement of the role of Russia was not unsatisfactory. Although Lenin had advocated the international revolution and believed before and after 1917 that revolution could be sustained in Russia only if it succeeded abroad, he was interested in the world revolution chiefly because of its necessity for revolution in Russia. As for Stalin, evidence of his Great Russian chauvinism is abundant. His operational principle toward other nations was not that they and Russia should be merged in

* Complete

international brotherhood but that they should be subject to Russian nationhood.

But for other Bolsheviks, the Russianization of the revolution was an apostasy. They had not endured the years in the underground, of imprisonment, exile, and civil war, in order to strengthen Great Russian chauvinism but to free all of mankind. "Socialism in one country" desecrated their aspirations.

Antagonism to "socialism in one country" became a fixture of the opposition. Not even the rise of Hitler—which on the surface increased Stalin's justification for concentrating on specific Russian *interests—deflected Trotsky and his supporters. When, in 1935, Stalin concluded a pact against Hitler with the French government, Trotsky attacked it as an alliance with imperialism against the French proletariat, a further selling out of the international workers' revolution by the Stalin regime.*

Stalin together with the renegade Laval has signed the death certificate of the Third International. Today, there is not a single worker, even the most politically backward, who is unaware that the Soviet bureaucrats have just publicly, decisively, betrayed the international proletariat. For the first time, Stalin has openly said what is—i.e., in full view of the entire world, he has repudiated revolutionary internationalism and passed over to the platform of social patriotism. He has informed his lackeys in France of his open betrayal through the medium of a bourgeois minister, who is himself a traitor to the working class in his own country. The hired bureaucrats of French Stalinism have immediately drawn from it all the necessary conclusions, and Vaillant-Couturier in his article adds ignominy to betrayal.

While the proletarian masses mobilize themselves on the revolutionary road, while the peasant strata are seething and are vigorously intervening in the political struggle, while the petty bourgeoisie, directly hit by the economic crisis that is steadily deepening, is becoming radicalized as a whole, this bureaucrat has the audacity to write that there is no longer any room for the independent activity of the proletariat in its revolutionary struggle against its own bourgeoisie, that all efforts are to no avail, and that to stave off the invasion of the USSR nothing remains except to place faith in French imperialism. Crawling on his belly, he consummates the betrayal of his master.

In the eyes of everyone, the Third International has become the diplomatic agent of Stalinism, loaded down with blunders and crimes, which has just openly taken the decisive step on the road to civil peace.

Let us review the facts.

The Stalin-Laval pact rests on the same plane as the Brest-Litovsk peace. The Soviet government enters into a military alliance with an imperialist government not at its own whim but in order not to be annihilated. In any case, that is its only justification. The Brest-Litovsk peace was a defeat, but the Franco-Russian pact has been proclaimed, for all those who care to listen, a great victory for the USSR. It is unnecessary to attempt a comparison between the relation of forces in 1918 and at the present time. The facts speak for themselves. Whatever the differences in the world situation and in the relationship of forces, the Franco-Soviet treaty from the standpoint of principles and politics rests entirely upon the same plane as the treaty of Brest-Litovsk. *Should, then, the Communists and Socialists vote in parliament for the ratification of the Franco-Soviet agreement*? And this, too, regardless of the question of whether or not Soviet diplomacy was really forced to sign the treaty?

Let us recall the historic example of Brest-Litovsk. The German Social Democrats voted in the Reichstag for ratifying it, claiming that since the Bolsheviks had accepted it, there was no reason whatever for their opposing it. The Bolsheviks replied to them, "You swine. We are objectively compelled to negotiate in order not to be annihilated, but as for you—you are politically free to vote for or against, and your vote implies whether or not you place confidence in your own bourgeoisie."

If we allowed that the Soviet government is really compelled to conclude a military alliance with French imperialism, the proletariat of the latter country does not at all have to do so. By their votes in parliament, the Socialist and Communist deputies are called upon to express themselves not upon the reason and motives for the action of the Soviet government *but solely upon the reasons and motives of the Flandin-Laval government.* If they vote confidence in it, they are the same swine as the German Social Democrats of 1918.

Only yesterday, Thorez and Co. swore that "We love our country, but we cannot countenance national defense under the capitalist regime." If this formula has any meaning, it implies that we cannot confide to the hands of our bourgeoisie the task of defending "our country" (which, besides, is not "ours"). Today we are told, "with throbbing hearts we shall make common cause with our bourgeoisie in the defense of the USSR." We want to know, "how is it that the French bourgeoisie, which is not good enough to defend 'our deeply loved country,' proves itself good enough for the defense of the USSR"? This is the nub of the question. There can be no middle of the road. The very same people will be obliged to proclaim, "with throbbing hearts we shall make common cause with our bourgeoisie to defend our people against the barbarism of Hitler, because the French people has the right to call for the same sacrifices on the part of its heroes as the Russian people."

There is nothing new in the new position of the Communist Party. It is social patriotism.

"But the immediate danger comes from German fascism," it will be said, "so it is necessary to make a bloc against it." Such an argument suffices for this or that diplomatic combination of the Moscow government. But this conception has nothing in common with Marxism. We have always maintained that the danger of war is the inevitable product of world imperialist antagonisms. German fascism as well as the dangers of war are the products of the colossal productive forces of German capitalism that seek for outlets and that must seek for outlets, whatever the political regime of the country. The most progressive capitalist regimes of Europe are stifling within the framework of the national state.

France is marching hand in hand with fascist Italy and with quasi-democratic England against fascist Germany.

Have we forgotten that revolutionary activity during the last war consisted precisely in denouncing the propaganda of the allies who spoke in the name of democracy against the Prussian junkers and the Hohenzollerns? The old catchwords are being refurbished to camouflage imperialist antagonisms by means of sham conflicts between political systems.

On this road one quickly arrives at the idealization of French democracy as such, counterposed to Hitler Germany.

Here again, there is no middle of the road. We repeat: "It is the policy of social patriotism."

The concept of the "aggressor" is very handy for the fiendish work of diplomacy, but it is fatal for the orientation of the proletariat. To checkmate the alleged aggressor, France protects Mussolini, allowing him a free field for action in Abyssinia, and also as regards Austria. And it is precisely the tightening grip of Italy on Austria that may fan to white heat German nationalism and lead to the outbreak of the war. Involved here are the permanent antagonisms that are deepening and sharpening. Their inevitable explosion and the preventive measures of the capitalist states can and must cause the catastrophe.

We will be told in answer, "All this may, perhaps, be true, but isn't it necessary all the same to save ourselves from the most immediate danger, which is the very same Hitler Germany?" Let us observe, first of all, that only yesterday the Comintern advanced in Germany the slogan of "national liberation," which is impossible without a war. Today the Communist International wants to defend the Versailles status quo in order to escape war. He is lost who abandons the position of class struggle and of international revolution and who begins to seek safety outside of the revolutionary struggle against one's own government within one's own country. Today the betrayal will be covered by the plea of the need to "save peace"; tomorrow when war breaks out, nevertheless, the betrayal will be perpetuated in order to save democracy or to save the USSR. But neither peace nor democracy nor the USSR can be saved by the surrender of the French proletariat.

If, after Germany has been annihilated for the second time, France, Italy, and England turn against their temporary ally, does anyone believe that it will be possible on the spur of the moment to sever at a single stroke the proletariat from the bourgeoisie that, with the aid of the working-class parties, will have succeeded in raising itself as the master of the nation and that has gagged and demoralized the working class through civil peace?

To fritter away the only capital we possess, the revolutionary independence of the proletariat, in return for precarious, equivocal, and unstable diplomatic combinations would be tantamount to walling up the avenue to the revolutionary future. The basic crime of reformism lies precisely in the fact that, chasing after the shadows of reforms, it castrated the proletariat by class collaboration. This policy is ten times, one hundred times, a thousand times more criminal at a time when it is a question not of a peaceful period of parliamentary combinations but of a war that concentrates all the instruments of oppression and destruction in the hands of the bourgeoisie and leaves the proletariat its one and only weapon: its political independence, its hatred of the bourgeoisie, its revolutionary will.

Moreover, who has the right to declare that the docile submissiveness of the French proletariat to its own bourgeoisie must inevitably frighten German fascism and force it to retreat? This indeed would be a gratuitous assertion; just the opposite result would occur in the long run.

Hitler has not yet morally crushed the German proletariat. In order to succeed in this, his propaganda revolves around the weighty argument, "we are encircled, we are hated, they seek our destruction." It is a question of the race struggle. Already the fact that the workers' state was compelled to fraternize with the French bourgeoisie against Germany has strengthened the position of the Nazis against the German working class. Should the French proletariat deliberately participate in this alliance by surrendering its class independence, the theory of the race struggle will make great headway in Germany to the detriment of the theory of the class struggle. Driven by the irresistible national spirit that he has himself incited, Hitler may be compelled to unleash the war.

On the other hand, the open, irresistible, thunderous opposition of the French proletariat to its own imperialism will be a disavowal of racism and will give a powerful impetus to the German revolution.

The USSR participated actively at Geneva in the elaboration of measures against terrorism and terrorists. The assassination of the king of Yugoslavia was the reason for this incident. We Marxists have always been the opponents of individual terrorism, but we have also assumed the defense of national terrorists against imperialist oppression. This elementary tradition has now been abandoned; the USSR has taken its place in the sphere of national struggles as the pillar of the established order and of the status quo.

In the light of the Stalin-Laval communiqué, the international working class is beginning to gain a better understanding of why Stalin undertook a new persecution of the Bolshevik-Leninists and of the Zinoviev group. Before finally delivering the Kremlin to the bourgeoisie, he found it necessary to overwhelm and exterminate all those who might raise their voices in protest.

The enemy is Stalinism! But the point in question is not to forget or overlook reformism. The treacherous policy of the Stalinists provides them with tremendous support. From now on, Blum and Paul Faure openly spread the idea of the defense of the "national soil" because these philistines themselves, likewise, do not approve of "unconditional" defense. This stupidity of wishing to "condition" the defense of the national bourgeoisie or of the proletarian state is clear to everyone. If our country, as it is, is worthy of being defended, it must be defended no matter what the origin of the war may be: it would be absurd to punish "our country" for the idiocy of Laval and his colleagues. *To us, it is the class character that is decisive* and not the policy of the government. We are committed to oppose the war budgets of the most democratic governments of the bourgeois states, and we are pledged to defend the USSR despite and against Stalin and his infamy.

But the absurdity of the "conditional" defense of the bourgeois state bears, nevertheless, a grave political meaning. Were Blum to render to the bourgeoisie all that the latter demands, he would be unable to differentiate himself from Herriot or even from Louis Marin. He would lose the confidence of the working class and become a cipher. By resorting to pacifism right up to the outbreak of the war, he retains the possibility of rendering a double service to the bourgeoisie during the war; a large section of the working class will say to itself: "If this tried-and-true pacifist now joins the ranks of 'civil peace,' it is because the war has been foisted upon us, it is because the defense is just." In order to be able to achieve this mission, Blum must reject as invalid the orders of Stalin. This perfidious game is enormously facilitated by the social-patriotic turn of the Stalinists.

Leon Blum and Co. lament that the communiqué does not sufficiently conform to the statutes of the League. Yet the CAP [National Council of the SFIO] as early as January elaborated its famous program that proclaims the necessity of destroying the bourgeois state and of opposing to it the interests of the working people, including the interests of the country. What is the League of Nations? It is also the mechanism of the bourgeois state or of several bourgeois states acting jointly and, at the same time, antagonistic to one another. If the mechanism of the bourgeois state deserves only to be destroyed, how can anyone stake the hopes for a better future upon the League of Nations, which is the by-product of this very same mechanism?

It is the doctrine of Jaurèsism that democracy or the democratic state ("the bourgois mechanism") envisages constant improvement of its fate and advances slowly but surely toward socialism. Viewed in this perspective, the League of Nations must naturally have its place to regulate the international relations of the democrats.

Today not only Pivert and Zyromsky but also Blum and Paul Faure are obliged to recognize the necessity of overthrowing and destroying the mechanism of the bourgeois state. *Under these conditions, how can they maintain their faith in the League of Nations?*

The same question presents itself on the subject of disarmament. Zyromsky expresses his regrets at the sight of his newly acquired friend Litvinov abandoning the slogans of disarmament in favor of collective security. The very same Zyromsky refuted, in his previous article, "social pacifism" in domestic policies, i.e., the hope of settling the social question amicably. Zyromsky is unable to understand that external social pacifism is the reverse side of the coin of internal social pacifism. If the bourgeoisie allows itself to be disarmed in order to secure peace, it will be, at the same time, disarmed in the struggle against the proletariat. We find here the same contradiction as in the question concerning the League of Nations. We have at least the verbal recognition of the need for the proletariat to arm itself and to gain powerful strongholds in the bourgeois army in order to lead to the victory of the internal class struggle. At the same time, one busies oneself with securing peace under the capitalist regime through general disarmament. Why then make a revolution against a humanitarian bourgeoisie that will be disarmed through a covenant of the League of Nations?

The solution of this enigma is quite simple. These people haven't the slightest confidence either in a revolution or in the destruction of the mechanism of the bourgeois army. Moreover, they demonstrate this by reiterating the slogan, "disarm the fascist leagues." Zyromsky is unaware that this famous revolutionary demand is the most stupid incarnation of social pacifism.

In refutation it will be said, "Yet you Bolshevik-Leninists yourselves recognize the right of the Soviet government to conclude alliances with imperialist states for its immediate safety. Is it, then, not our duty as French workers to support these alliances insofar as they are useful to the workers' government?"

No, never! We have already pointed out why the German Socialists were duty bound to fight against the Brest-Litovsk peace, although it was absolutely necessary for the continued existence of the Soviets at the given moment.

Let us take this very same question more concretely and more practically. Revolutionary defeatism doesn't at all imply the sabotage of the sham national defense by an active minority. It would be absurd to attribute to revolutionary workers the idea of blowing up bridges and railroads, etc., etc. . . . in case of war. The revolutionary workers, *insofar as they are the minority*, participate in the war as the slaves of imperialism who are conscious of their enslavement. At the same time, they prepare through agitation the transformation of the imperialist war into a civil war.

Should the USSR succeed in securing the military assistance of the French bourgeoisie in the event of aggression on the part of German imperialism (which is, by the way, by no means certain), this assistance supplied by the bourgeoisie in power will in no way be hindered by the fact that the revolutionary minority will continue to fulfill its duty in incessantly preparing for the overthrow of the bourgeoisie, whatever may be the military assistance of the imperialist general staff (and it will always be precarious, equivocal, and perfidious).

The revolutionary repercussions that will be engendered in Germany by the revolutionary movement in France will provide another sort of effective assistance for the salvation of the USSR, as well as for the development of the world revolution.

Should the revolutionary movement in France, in the event of war, gain such force as to directly threaten the military machine of the bourgeoisie and imperil its alliance with the USSR, it would imply that the French proletariat is capable of seizing power at the height of the struggle. Should they perhaps be restrained in such a situation? Let them say it. Will we run the risk of defeat? Obviously. Revolution, like war, carries risk with it since danger is the essential element in it. But only wretched philistines would wish to emerge from an international situation that is brimful of mortal dangers without incurring any risks whatever.

Thus revolutionary defeatism does not prevent the Soviet government on its own responsibility from profiting by such-and-such a pact or this-and-that imperialist military assistance. But these fleeting transactions cannot and must not in any way commit the French and the world proletariat whose task is, above all during the time of war, to prepare for the liquidation of imperialism through the victorious revolution.

The pact indicates weakness and not strength on the part of the USSR. This new treaty is the product of the defeats in China, in Germany, in Austria, and in Spain.

Since the world revolutionary factor has been weakened, the government of the USSR has found itself forced to adapt to the imperialist factor. That is the only correct formula for the Franco-Soviet treaty.

The Kremlin bureaucrats, who see only the strengthening of the USSR, thereby posit the independence of the workers' state from the world working-class movement; the more defeats the latter suffers, the stronger becomes the international position of the USSR. These are the statements of charlatans—they must be nailed to the pillory.

But if, because of annihilation of the proletariat in a number of countries, the Soviet government is compelled to fraternize temporarily with the oppressors of the French working class, this cannot be the ground for further weakening the latter by demoralizing it and thus still further worsening the international situation, forcing the revolution to retreat and consequently placing the USSR directly in danger.

When events of worldwide importance are at stake, the revolutionary party has no right to permit itself to be motivated by secondary, episodic, conjunctural, and always problematic considerations. It is necessary to be farsighted, preserving and accumulating the revolutionary strength of the class; it is in this manner that one can also best exert influence on all secondary questions; revolutionary policy is always the most practical. *The enemy is Stalinism!* It weakened the USSR because it delivered the Chinese workers and peasants to the bureaucracy of the Kuomintang, the English workers to the bureaucracy of the trade unions, etc. . . . Frightened by the consequences, it sought to play the card of adventurism, "third period." The results proved themselves even more fatal. Today Stalin and Co. have lost all confidence in the revolutionary forces. They resort to pure diplomacy—that is to say, to the filthiest sort. They refuse to see anything except combinations with this or that imperialism against some other. They are, above all, afraid lest the French workers compromise their combinations. Thorez and Co. subscribe to this disgraceful attitude. They also deem the revolutionary movement to be an obstacle to the safety of the USSR. They accept the order to penalize and hamstring the revolution.

They openly become the Stalinist police over the French proletariat, and, what is more, the Stalinist police become, at the same time, the police of French imperialism.

When we, the Bolshevik-Leninists, began our struggle against the theory of socialism in one country, it may have seemed that only an academic question was under discussion. Today the historical function of this formula may be clearly seen: its task is the severing of the fate of the USSR from the fate of the world proletariat. It has created a national base for the Soviet bureaucracy that allowed it to concentrate all the power in its own hands. The new law that extends capital punishment to children twelve years old reveals with fearful eloquence not only that the USSR is still a considerable distance from socialism but also that under the domination of the omnipotent bureaucracy the social decomposition of wide strata of workers and peasants has attained formidable proportions despite all the technological conquests bought so dearly by the workers and peasants. And it is precisely at the moment when the war danger threatens the state founded by the October Revolution that the government of the USSR draws the final conclusions from the theory of socialism in one country, prostituting the ABC of Marxism and degrading the Comintern to the role played by Scheidemann, Noske, Renaudel, Vandervelde and Co.

When, after the capitulation of the Communist International before Hitler, we proclaimed: it is the "August 4" of the Third International, we met with not a few protests. "August 4," we were told, was a conscious betrayal, while the capitulation before Hitler was the inevitable consequence of false policy. Today we see how superficial are such purely psychological evaluations. The capitulation was the expression of the internal degeneration, a consequence of accumulated blunders and crimes. This degeneration implied in its turn the capitulation to imperialist war and a prelude to the capitulation before the imperialist bourgeoisie, which is preparing for war. That is why the "August 4" of the Third International was already lodged in the capitulation to Hitler. It is the great merit of the Bolshevik-Leninists that they stated this in time.

Leninism is betrayed and vilified by Stalinism.

The urgent task of the hour is to reconstitute the ranks of the vanguard of the international proletariat. For this a banner and a program are necessary, and they can only be the banner and the program of the Fourth International.

The Third International is dead. Long live the Fourth International!

5

RESOLUTION CONCERNING THE SITUATION IN THE COMMUNIST PARTY OF YUGOSLAVIA*

Cominform
(Published 28 June 1948)

"Socialism in one country" in practice meant that the interest of the Russian party and the Soviet Union came before the interest of all other countries and parties. So long as there was only one country where a communist party had taken over (putting aside sparsely populated Outer Mongolia where the Soviets had installed a puppet regime in the 1920s), the Russian party could successfully enforce the "socialism in one country" doctrine on the international movement—though not entirely without dissent. However, by the end of World War II there were socialist regimes in half a dozen countries.

The new countries of the socialist camp, both more highly populated and more highly developed than Outer Mongolia, grew restive under the harsh yoke of Stalin's insistence that the USSR come first. However, in most of these countries, the communist leadership had been placed in power by the Red Army, and lacked authority among the people over

* Complete

whom it ruled. Only in Yugoslavia, where Tito's partisan forces had been instrumental in liberating the country and Tito had set up a popular regime with minimal Soviet help, was there a serious questioning of the emphasis on Soviet interests—and Soviet control.

Stalin, infuriated by the Yugoslav temerity in questioning Soviet primacy, tried a variety of means to bring Tito to toe the line. Failing these, and still not prepared to resort to military intervention, he summoned a meeting of the Cominform (the post–World War II successor to the Comintern) to meet in Bucharest. There, in late June, at the behest of Stalin, who was trying to shock the Yugoslavs into compliance—for they would be frightened at the prospect of being alone in a hostile world—the Cominform issued a resolution declaring that "the Central Committee of the Communist Party of Yugoslavia has placed itself and the Yugoslav party outside the family of the fraternal communist parties."

The Information Bureau, composed of the representatives of the Bulgarian Workers' Party (Communists), Rumanian Workers' Party, Hungarian Workers' Party, Polish Workers' Party, The Communist Party of the Soviet Union (Bolsheviks), Communist Party of France, Communist Party of Czechoslovakia and the Communist Party of Italy, upon discussing the situation in the Communist Party of Yugoslavia and announcing that the representatives of the Communist Party of Yugoslavia had refused to attend the meeting of the Information Bureau, unanimously reached the following conclusions:

1. The Information Bureau notes that recently the leadership of the Communist Party of Yugoslavia has pursued an incorrect line on the main questions of home and foreign policy, a line which represents a departure from Marxism-Leninism. In this connection, the Information Bureau approves the action of the Central Committee of the CPSU(B), which took the initiative in exposing this incorrect policy of the Central Committee of the Communist Party of

Yugoslavia, particularly the incorrect policy of Comrades Tito, Kardelj, Djilas, and Rankovic.

2. The Information Bureau declares that the leadership of the Yugoslav Communist Party is pursuing an unfriendly policy toward the Soviet Union and the CPSU(B). An undignified policy of defaming Soviet military experts and discrediting the Soviet Union has been carried out in Yugoslavia. A special regime was instituted for Soviet civilian experts in Yugoslavia, whereby they were under surveillance of Yugoslav state security organs and were continually followed. The representative of the CPSU(B) in the Information Bureau, Comrade Yudin, and a number of official representatives of the Soviet Union in Yugoslavia, were followed and kept under observation by Yugoslav state security organs.

All these and similar facts show that the leaders of the Communist Party of Yugoslavia have taken a stand unworthy of Communists, and have begun to identify the foreign policy of the Soviet Union with the foreign policy of the imperialist powers, behaving toward the Soviet Union in the same manner as they behave to the bourgeois states. Precisely because of this anti-Soviet stand, slanderous propaganda about the "degeneration" of the CPSU(B), about the "degeneration" of the USSR, and so on, borrowed from the arsenal of counter-revolutionary Trotskyism, is current within the Central Committee of the Communist Party of Yugoslavia.

The Information Bureau denounces this anti-Soviet attitude of the leaders of the Communist Party of Yugoslavia, as being incompatible with Marxism-Leninism and only appropriate to nationalists.

3. In home policy, the leaders of the Communist Party of Yugoslavia are departing from the positions of the working class and are breaking with the Marxist theory of classes and class struggle. They deny that there is a growth of capitalist elements in their country, and consequently, a sharpening of the class struggle in the countryside. This denial is the direct result of the opportunist tenet that the class struggle does not become sharper during the period of transition from

capitalism to socialism, as Marxism-Leninism teaches, but dies down, as was affirmed by opportunists of the Bukharin type, who propagated the theory of the peaceful growing over of capitalism into socialism.

The Yugoslav leaders are pursuing an incorrect policy in the countryside by ignoring the class differentiation in the countryside and by regarding the individual peasantry as a single entity, contrary to the Marxist-Leninist doctrine of classes and class struggle, contrary to the well-known Lenin thesis that small individual farming gives birth to capitalism and the bourgeoisie continually, daily, hourly, spontaneously, and on a mass scale. Moreover, the political situation in the Yugoslav countryside gives no grounds for smugness and complacency. In the conditions obtaining in Yugoslavia, where individual peasant farming predominates, where the land is not nationalized, where there is private property in land, and where land can be bought and sold, where much of the land is concentrated in the hands of kulaks, and where hired labor is employed—in such conditions there can be no question of educating the Party in the spirit of glossing over the class struggle and of reconciling class contradictions without by so doing disarming the Party itself in face of the difficulties connected with the construction of socialism.

Concerning the leading role of the working class, the leaders of the Yugoslav Communist Party, by affirming that the peasantry is the "most stable foundation of the Yugoslav state" are departing from the Marxist-Leninist path and are taking the path of a populist, kulak party. Lenin taught that the proletariat as the "only class in contemporary society which is revolutionary to the end . . . must be the leader in the struggle of the entire people for a thorough democratic transformation, in the struggle of all working people and the exploited against the oppressors and exploiters."

The Yugoslav leaders are violating this thesis of Marxism-Leninism.

As far as the peasantry is concerned, it may be that the majority—that is, the poor and medium peasants—are already in alliance with the working class, with the working class having the leading role in this alliance.

The attitude of the Yugoslav leaders disregards these theses of Marxism-Leninism.

As can be seen, this attitude also reflects views appropriate to petty-bourgeois nationalism, but not to Marxists-Leninists.

4. The Information Bureau considers that the leadership of the Communist Party of Yugoslavia is revising the Marxist-Leninist teachings about the Party. According to the theory of Marxism-Leninism, the Party is the main guiding and leading force in the country, which has its own, specific program, and does not dissolve itself among the non-Party masses. The Party is the highest form of organization and the most important weapon of the working class.

In Yugoslavia, however, the People's Front, and not the Communist Party, is considered to be the main leading force in the country. The Yugoslav leaders belittle the role of the Communist Party and actually dissolve the Party in the non-party People's Front, which is composed of the most varied class elements (workers, peasants engaged in individual farming, kulaks, traders, small manufacturers, bourgeois intelligentsia, etc.) as well as mixed political groups which include certain bourgeois parties. The Yugoslav leaders stubbornly refuse to recognize the falseness of their tenet that the Communist Party of Yugoslavia allegedly cannot and should not have its own specific program and that it should be satisfied with the program of the People's Front.

The fact that in Yugoslavia it is only the People's Front which figures in the political arena, while the Party and its organizations do not appear openly before the people in its own name, not only belittles the role of the Party in the political life of the country, but also undermines the Party as an independent political force, which has the task of winning the growing confidence of the people and of influencing ever broader masses of the working people by open political activity and open propaganda of its views and program. The leaders of the Yugoslav Communist Party are repeating the mistakes of the Russian Mensheviks regarding the dissolution of the Marxist party into a non-party, mass organization.

All this reveals the existence of liquidation tendencies in the Communist Party of Yugoslavia.

The Information Bureau believes that this policy of the Central Committee of the Communist Party of Yugoslavia threatens the very existence of the Communist Party, and ultimately carries with it the danger of the degeneration of the People's Republic of Yugoslavia.

5. The Information Bureau considers that the bureaucratic regime created inside the Party by its leaders is disastrous for the life and development of the Yugoslav Communist Party. There is no inner Party democracy, no elections, and no criticism and self-criticism in the Party. Despite the unfounded assurances of Comrades Tito and Kardelj, the majority of the Central Committee of the Communist Party of Yugoslavia is composed of co-opted, and not of elected members. The Communist Party is actually in a position of semi-legality. Party meetings are either not held at all, or meet in secret—a fact which can only undermine the influence of the Party among the masses. This type of organization of the Yugoslav Communist Party cannot be described as anything but a sectarian-bureaucratic organization. It leads to the liquidation of the Party as an active, self-acting organism, it cultivates military methods of leadership in the Party similar to the methods advocated in his day by Trotsky.

It is a completely intolerable state of affairs when the most elementary rights of members in the Yugoslav Communist Party are suppressed, when the slightest criticism of incorrect measures in the Party is brutally repressed.

The Information Bureau regards as disgraceful such actions as the expulsion from the Party and the arrest of the Central Committee members, Comrades Djuiovic and Hebrang, because they dared to criticize the anti-Soviet attitude of the leaders of the Yugoslav Communist Party, and called for friendship between Yugoslavia and the Soviet Union.

The Information Bureau considers that such a disgraceful, purely Turkish, terrorist regime cannot be tolerated in the Communist Party. The interests of the very existence and development of the Yugoslav Communist Party demand that an end be put to this regime.

6. The Information Bureau considers that the criticism made by the Central Committee of the CPSU(B) and Central Committees of the other Communist parties of the mistakes of the Central Committee of the Communist Party of Yugoslavia, and who in this way rendered fraternal assistance to the Yugoslav Communist Party, provides the Communist Party of Yugoslavia with all the conditions necessary to speedily correct the mistakes committed.

However, instead of honestly accepting this criticism and taking the Bolshevik path of correcting these mistakes, the leaders of the Communist Party of Yugoslavia, suffering from boundless ambition, arrogance, and conceit, met this criticism with belligerence and hostility. They took the anti-Party path of indiscriminately denying all their mistakes, violated the doctrine of Marxism-Leninism regarding the attitude of a political party to its mistakes and thus aggravated their anti-Party mistakes.

Unable to face the criticism of the Central Committee of the CPSU(B) and the Central Committees of the other fraternal Parties, the Yugoslav leaders took the path of outrightly deceiving their Party and people by concealing from the Yugoslav Communist Party the criticism of the Central Committee's incorrect policy and also by concealing from the Party and the people the real reasons for the brutal measures against Comrades Djuiovic and Hebrang.

Recently, even after the Central Committee of the CPSU(B) and fraternal parties had criticized the mistakes of the Yugoslav leaders, the latter tried to bring in a number of new leftist laws. They hastily decreed the nationalization of medium industry and trade, though the basis for this is completely unprepared. In view of such haste the new decision only hampers the supply of goods to the population. In a similar hurried manner they brought in a new grain tax for which the way is also not prepared and which can, therefore, only dislocate grain supplies to the urban population. Finally, only recently the Yugoslav leaders in loud declarations declared their love for and devotion to the Soviet

Union, although it is known that in practice they are pursuing an unfriendly policy toward the Soviet Union.

Nor is this all. Of late the leaders of the Communist Party of Yugoslavia have, with perfect aplomb, been declaiming a policy of liquidating the capitalist elements in Yugoslavia. In a letter to the Central Committee of the CPSU(B), dated 13 April, Tito and Kardelj wrote that "the plenum of the Central Committee approved the measures proposed by the Political Bureau of the Central Committee to liquidate the remnants of capitalism in the country."

In accordance with this line Kardelj, speaking in the Skupschina on 25 April, declared: "In our country the days of the last remnants of the exploitation of man by man are numbered."

In the conditions prevailing in Yugoslavia this position of the leaders of the Communist Party in regard to the liquidation of the capitalist elements, and hence, the kulaks as a class, cannot be qualified as other than adventurous, and non-Marxist. For it is impossible to solve this task as long as individual peasant economy predominates in the country, which inevitably gives birth to capitalism; as long as conditions have not been created for the large-scale collectivization of agriculture; and as long as the majority of the working peasantry is not convinced of the advantages of collective methods of farming. The experience of the CPSU(B) shows that the elimination of the last and biggest exploiting class—the kulak class—is possible only on the basis of the mass collectivization of agriculture, that the elimination of the kulaks as a class is an organic and integral part of the collectivization of agriculture.

In order to eliminate the kulaks as a class, and hence, to eliminate the capitalist elements in the countryside, it is necessary for the Party to engage in detailed preparatory work to restrict the capitalist elements in the countryside, to strengthen the alliance of the working class and the peasantry under the leadership of the working class, to make socialist industry capable of producing machinery for the collective administration of agriculture. Haste in this matter can only lead to irreparable harm.

Only on the basis of these measures, carefully prepared and consistently carried out, is it possible to go over from restriction of the capitalist elements in the countryside to their liquidation.

All attempts by the Yugoslav leaders to solve this problem hastily and by means of decrees signify either that the venture is foredoomed to failure or that it is a boastful and empty demagogic declaration.

The Information Bureau considers that by means of these false and demagogic tactics, the Yugoslav leaders are endeavoring to demonstrate that they are not only for class struggle, but that they go even further, beyond those demands which—taking into account the real possibilities—could be advanced by the Communist Party of Yugoslavia in the matter of restricting the capitalist elements.

The Information Bureau considers that since these leftist decrees and declarations of the Yugoslav leadership are demagogic and impracticable in the present conditions, they can but compromise the banner of socialist construction in Yugoslavia.

That is why the Information Bureau considers such adventurist tactics as an undignified maneuver and an impermissible political gamble.

As we see, these leftist demagogic measures and declarations on the part of the Yugoslav leaders are designed to cover up their refusal to recognize mistakes and honestly correct them.

7. Taking into account the situation in the Communist Party of Yugoslavia, and seeking to show the leaders of the Party the way out of this situation, the Central Committee of the CPSU(B) and the Central Committees of other fraternal parties suggested that the matter of the Yugoslav Communist Party should be discussed at a meeting of the Information Bureau, on the same normal party footing as that on which the activities of other Communist Parties were discussed at the first meeting of the Information Bureau.

However, the Yugoslav leaders rejected the repeated suggestions of the fraternal Communist Parties to discuss the situation in the Yugoslav Party at a meeting of the Information Bureau.

Attempting to avoid the just criticism of the fraternal parties in the Information Bureau, the Yugoslav leaders invented the fable of their allegedly "unequal position." There is not a grain of truth in this story. It is generally known that when the Information Bureau was set up, the Communist Parties based their work on the indisputable principle that any party could report to the Information Bureau in the same way that any party had the right to criticize other parties.

At the first meeting of the Nine Communist Parties, the Yugoslav Communist Party took full advantage of this right.

The refusal of the Yugoslav Party to report to the Information Bureau on its actions and to listen to criticism by other Communist Parties means, in practice, a violation of the equality of the Communist Parties and is, in fact, tantamount to a demand for a privileged position for the Communist Party of Yugoslavia in the Information Bureau.

8. In view of this, the Information Bureau expresses complete agreement with the estimation of the situation in the Yugoslav Communist Party, with the criticism of the mistakes of the Central Committee of the Party, and with the political analysis of these mistakes contained in letters from the Central Committee of the CPSU(B) to the Central Committee of the Communist Party of Yugoslavia between March and May 1948.

The Information Bureau unanimously concludes that by their anti-Party and anti-Soviet views, incompatible with Marxism-Leninism, by their whole attitude and their refusal to attend the meeting of the Information Bureau, the leaders of the Communist Party of Yugoslavia have placed themselves in opposition to the Communist Parties affiliated to the Information Bureau, have taken the path of seceding from the united socialist front against imperialism, have taken the path of betraying the cause of international solidarity of the working people, and have taken up a position of nationalism.

The Information Bureau condemns this anti-Party policy

and attitude of the Central Committee of the Communist Party of Yugoslavia.

The Information Bureau considers that, in view of all this, the Central Committee of the Communist Party of Yugoslavia has placed itself and the Yugoslav Party outside the family of the fraternal Communist Parties, outside the united Communist front and consequently outside the ranks of the Information Bureau.

The Information Bureau considers that the basis of these mistakes made by the leadership of the Communist Party of Yugoslavia lies in the undoubted fact that nationalist elements, which previously existed in a disguised form, managed in the course of the past five or six months to reach a dominant position in the leadership of the Communist Party of Yugoslavia, and that consequently the leadership of the Yugoslav Communist Party has broken with the international traditions of the Communist Party of Yugoslavia and has taken the road of nationalism.

Considerably overestimating the internal, national forces of Yugoslavia and their influence, the Yugoslav leaders think that they can maintain Yugoslavia's independence and build socialism without the support of the Communist Parties of other countries, without the support of the people's democracies, without the support of the Soviet Union. They think that the new Yugoslavia can do without the help of these revolutionary forces.

Showing their poor understanding of the international situation and their intimidation by the blackmailing threats of the imperialists, the Yugoslav leaders think that by making concessions they can curry favor with the Imperialist states. They think they will be able to bargain with them for Yugoslavia's independence and, gradually, get the people of Yugoslavia oriented on these states, that is, on capitalism. In this they proceed tacitly from the well-known bourgeois-nationalist thesis that "capitalist states are a lesser danger to the independence of Yugoslavia than the Soviet Union."

The Yugoslav leaders evidently do not understand or, probably, pretend they do not understand, that such a nationalist line can only lead to Yugoslavia's degeneration into an ordinary bourgeois republic, to the loss of its independence and to its transformation into a colony of the imperialist countries.

The Information Bureau does not doubt that inside the Communist Party of Yugoslavia there are sufficient healthy elements, loyal to Marxism-Leninism, to the international traditions of the Yugoslav Communist Party, and to the united socialist front.

Their task is to compel their present leaders to recognize their mistakes openly and honestly and to rectify them; to break with nationalism, return to internationalism; and in every way to consolidate the united socialist front against imperialism.

Should the present leaders of the Yugoslav Communist Party prove incapable of doing this, their job is to replace them and to advance a new internationalist leadership of the Party.

The Information Bureau does not doubt that the Communist Party of Yugoslavia will be able to fulfil this honorable task.

6

REPORT OF AN INVESTIGATION INTO THE PEASANT MOVEMENT IN HUNAN*

To the Central Committee of the Chinese Communist Party

Mao Tse-tung
(February 1927)

The Yugoslav challenge to the implications of "socialism in one country" was viewed by Stalin as a major threat to Soviet primacy, but it palled before still another threat of just a year or two later: the victory of the Mao forces in China and the establishment of the People's Republic of China.

China was no backwater satellite, such as Bulgaria, Rumania, or Poland, but the most populous nation on earth, with an ancient, highly developed culture and a strong will to dominate. And it was led by a man of whom Stalin had been suspicious for decades. Mao Tse-tung was not Moscow-trained, not even Moscow-oriented. He was, first of all, a fiercely independent Chinese nationalist—and Moscow had had more than an inkling of that since 1927 when Mao wrote his "Report" from Hunan.

* Complete

It is a basic tenet of Marxism that the material of the revolution is the urban proletariat. The Chinese communists in the 1920s accepted this orthodoxy and worked among the proletarians of Canton, Wuhan, and Shanghai. But as the forces of the revolution spread northward out of Kwangtung province in 1926, they inspired fierce peasant uprisings in their wake. Millions of peasants turned against their landlords and took over local governments.

In January 1927, Mao was sent by the Central Committee to his native Hunan to observe and evaluate the jacqueries. He was forever impressed by what he saw. In four months time, he wrote, the peasant world has changed, "the broad peasant masses have risen to fulfill their historical mission." Mao now asserted that the poor peasantry, not the proletariat, was the basis of revolution, the "vanguard."

Not many among the top echelon of Chinese communists agreed with Mao in 1927, and the "Report" did not create much of a stir among the Russian comrades. But, in time, it became a fundamental part of Mao's basic doctrine—and its significance and that of its writer were not lost on Moscow.

THE IMPORTANCE OF THE PEASANT PROBLEM

During my recent visit to Hunan I conducted an investigation on the spot into the conditions in the five counties of Hsiangtan, Hsianghsiang, Hengshan, Liling, and Changsha. In the 32 days from January 4 to February 5, in villages and in county towns, I called together for fact-finding conferences experienced peasants and comrades working for the peasant movement, and listened attentively to their reports and collected a lot of material. Many of the hows and whys of the peasant movement were quite the reverse of what I had heard from the gentry in Hankow and Changsha. And many strange things there were that I had never seen or heard before. I think these conditions exist in many other places. All kinds of arguments against the peasant movement must be speedily set right. The erroneous measures taken by the revolutionary authorities concerning the peasant movement must be speedily changed. Only thus can any good be done for the future of the revolution. For the rise of the present peasant movement is a colossal event. In a very short time, in China's central, southern, and northern provinces several hundred million peasants will rise like a tornado or tempest, a force so extraordinarily swift and violent that no power, however great, will be able to suppress it. They will break through all shackles that now bind them and dash forward along the road to liberation. They will send all imperialists, warlords, corrupt officials, local bullies, and bad gentry to their graves. All revolutionary parties and all revolutionary comrades will stand before them to be tested, and to be accepted or rejected as they decide. To march at their head and lead them? Or to follow at their rear, gesticulating at them and criticizing them? Or to face them as opponents? Every Chinese is free to choose among the three, but circumstances demand that a quick choice be made.

GET ORGANIZED!

The peasant movement in Hunan, so far as it concerns the counties in central and southern sections of the province, where the movement is already developed, can be roughly divided into two periods. The first period was the period of organization, extending from January to September of last year [1926]. In this period, there were the stage from January to June—a stage of underground activities, and the stage from July to September when the revolutionary army expelled Chao Heng-ti[1]—a stage of open activities. In this period, the membership of the peasant association totaled only 300,000 to 400,000, and the masses it could directly lead numbered only little more than a million; as there was hardly any struggle in the rural areas, so very little criticism was made on the association. Since its members served as guides, scouts, and carriers, officers in the Northern Expedition Army even had a good word or two for the peasant association. The second period was the period of revolution-

1. The ruler of Hunan and agent of the warlords of the Northern clique.

ary action, extending from last October to this January. The membership of the peasant association jumped to two million and the masses over whom it could exercise direct leadership increased to ten million people. As the peasants mostly entered only one name for each family when joining the association, a membership of two million therefore means a mass following of about ten million. Of all the peasants in Hunan, almost half are organized. In counties like Hsiangtan, Hsianghsiang, Liuyang, Changsha, Liling, Ninghsiang, Pingchiang, Hsiangyin, Hengshan, Hengyang, Leiyang, Chenhsien, and Anhua, nearly all the peasants have rallied organizationally in the association and followed its leadership. The peasants, with their extensive organization, went right into action and within four months brought about a great and unprecedented revolution in the countryside.

DOWN WITH THE LOCAL BULLIES AND BAD GENTRY! ALL POWER TO THE PEASANT ASSOCIATION!

The peasants attack as their main targets the local bullies and bad gentry and the lawless landlords, hitting in passing against patriarchal ideologies and institutions, corrupt officials in the cities, and evil customs in the rural areas. In force and momentum, the attack is just like a tempest or hurricane; those who submit to it survive and those who resist it perish. As a result, the privileges which the feudal landlords have enjoyed for thousands of years are shattered to pieces. The dignity and prestige of the landlords are dashed to the ground. With the fall of the authority of the landlords, the peasant association becomes the sole organ of authority, and what people call "All power to the peasant association" has come to pass. Even such a trifle as a quarrel between man and wife has to be settled at the peasant association. Nothing can be settled in the absence of people from the association. The association is actually dictating in all matters in the countryside, and it is literally true that "whatever it says, goes." The public can only praise the association and must not condemn it. The local bullies and bad gentry and the lawless landlords have been totally deprived of the right to have their say, and no one dare mutter the word "No." To be safe from the power and pressure of the peasant association, the first-rank local bullies and bad gentry fled to Shanghai; the second-rank ones, to Hankow; the third-rank ones, to Changsha; and the fourth-rank ones, to the county towns; the fifth-rank ones and even lesser fry can only remain in the countryside and surrender to the peasant association.

"I'll donate ten dollars, please admit me to the peasant association," one of the smaller gentry would say.

"Pshaw! Who wants your filthy money!" the peasants would reply.

Many middle and small landlords, rich peasants, and middle peasants, formerly opposed to the peasant association, now seek admission in vain. Visiting various places, I often came across such people, who solicited my help; "I beg the committeeman from the provincial capital to be my guarantor!" they would say.

The census book compiled by the local authorities under the Manchu regime consisted of a regular register and a special register; in the former, honest people were entered, and in the latter, burglars, bandits, and other undesirables. The peasants in some places now use the same method to threaten people formerly opposed to the association: "Enter them in the special register!"

Such people, afraid of being entered in the special register, try various means to seek admission to the association and do not feel at ease until, as they eagerly desire, their names are entered in its register. But they are as a rule sternly turned down, and so spend their days in a constant state of suspense; barred from the doors of the association, they are like homeless people. In short, what was generally sneered at four months ago as the "peasants' gang" has now become something most honorable. Those who prostrated themselves before the power of the gentry now prostrate themselves before the power of the peasants. Everyone admits that the world has changed since last October.

"AN AWFUL MESS!" AND "VERY GOOD INDEED!"

The revolt of the peasants in the countryside disturbed the sweet dreams of the gentry. When news about the countryside reached the cities, the gentry there immediately burst into an uproar. When I first arrived in Changsha, I met people from various circles and picked up a good deal of street gossip. From the middle strata upwards to the right-wingers of the Kuomintang, there was not a single person who did not summarize the whole thing in one phrase: "An awful mess!" Even quite revolutionary people, carried away by the opinion of the "awful mess" school which prevailed like a storm over the whole city, became downhearted at the very thought of the conditions in the countryside, and could not deny the word "mess." The very progressive people could only remark, "Indeed a mess but inevitable in the course of the revolution." In a word, nobody could categorically deny the word "mess." But the fact is, as stated above, that the broad peasant masses have risen to fulfill their historical mission, that the democratic forces in the rural areas have risen to overthrow the rural feudal power. The patriarchal-feudalistic class of local bullies, bad gentry, and lawless landlords has formed the basis of autocratic government for thousands of years, the cornerstone of imperialism, warlordism, and corrupt officialdom. To overthrow this feudal power is the real objective of the national revolution. What Dr. Sun Yat-sen wanted to do in the forty years he devoted to the national revolution but failed to accomplish, the peasants have accomplished in a few months. This is a marvelous feat which has never been achieved in the last forty or even thousands of years. It is very good indeed. It is not "a mess" at all. It is anything but "an awful mess." To give credit where it is due, if we allot ten points to the accomplishments of the democratic revolution, then the achievements of the urban dwellers and the military units rate only three points, while the remaining seven points should go to the peasants in their rural revolution.[2] "An awful mess"—that is obviously a theory which in line with the interests of the landlords aims at combating the rise of the peasants, a theory of the landlord class for preserving the old order of feudalism and obstructing the establishment of a new order of democracy, and a counterrevolutionary theory. No revolutionary comrade should blindly repeat it. If you have firmly established the revolutionary viewpoint and have furthermore gone the round of the villages for a look, you will feel overjoyed as never before. There, great throngs of tens of thousands of slaves, i.e., the peasants, are overthrowing their cannibal enemies. Their actions are absolutely correct; their actions are very good indeed! "Very good indeed!" is the theory of the peasants and all other revolutionaries. Every revolutionary comrade should know that the national revolution requires a profound change in the countryside. The Revolution of 1911 did not bring about this change, hence its failure. Now the change takes place, which is an important factor necessary for completing the revolution. Every revolutionary comrade must support this change, or he will be taking the counterrevolutionary stand.

THE QUESTION OF "GOING TOO FAR"

There is another section of people who say, "Although the peasant association ought to be formed, it has gone rather too far in its present actions." This is the opinion of the middle-of-the-roaders. But how do matters stand in reality? True, the peasants do in some ways "act unreasonably" in the countryside. The peasant association, supreme in authority, does not allow the landlords to have their say and makes a clean sweep of all their prestige. This is tantamount to trampling the landlords underfoot after knocking them down. The peasants threaten: "Put you in the special register"; they impose fines on the local bullies and bad gentry and demand contributions; they smash their sedan chairs.

2. This sentence was omitted from some post-1949 editions, presumably so as not to offend Moscow's proletarian orthodoxy (Ed. note).

Crowds of people swarm into the homes of the local bullies and bad gentry who oppose the peasant association, slaughtering their pigs and consuming their grain. They may even loll for a minute or two on the ivory beds of the young mesdames and mesdemoiselles in the families of the bullies and gentry. At the slightest provocation they make arrests, crown the arrested with tall paper hats, and parade them through the villages: "You bad gents, now you know who we are!" Doing whatever they like and turning everything upside down, they have even created a kind of terrorism in the countryside. This is what some people call "going too far," or "going beyond the proper limit to right a wrong," or "really too outrageous." The opinion of this group, reasonable on the surface, is erroneous at bottom. First, the things described above have all been the inevitable results of the doings of the local bullies and bad gentry and lawless landlords themselves. For ages these people, with power in their hands, tyrannized over the peasants and trampled them underfoot; that is why the peasants have now risen in such a great revolt. The most formidable revolts and the most serious troubles invariably occur at places where the local bullies and bad gentry and the lawless landlords are the most ruthless in their evil deeds. The peasants' eyes are perfectly discerning. As to who is bad and who is not, who is the most ruthless and who is less so, and who is to be severely punished and who is to be dealt with lightly, the peasants keep perfectly clear accounts and very seldom has there been any discrepancy between the punishment and the crime. So even Mr. Tang Meng-hsiao once said: "When the peasants attacked the bullies and bad gentry in the villages, in nine cases out of ten they were correct."[3] Secondly, a revolution is not the same as inviting people to dinner or writing an essay, or painting a picture, or doing fancy needlework; it cannot be anything so refined, so calm and gentle, or so mild, kind, courteous, restrained, and magnanimous.[4] A revolution is an uprising, an act of violence

3. This sentence was also omitted from some post-1949 editions (Ed. note).
4. These were the virtues of Confucius, as described by one of his disciples.

whereby one class overthrows another. A rural revolution is a revolution by which the peasantry overthrows the authority of the feudal landlord class. If the peasants do not use the maximum of their strength, they can never overthrow the authority of the landlords which has been deeply rooted for thousands of years. In the rural areas, there must be a great, fervent revolutionary upsurge, which alone can arouse hundreds and thousands of the people to form a great force. All the actions mentioned above, labeled as "going too far," are caused by the power of the peasants, generated by a great, fervent revolutionary upsurge in the countryside. Such actions were quite necessary in the second period of the peasant movement (the period of revolutionary action). In this period, it was necessary to establish the absolute authority of the peasants. It was necessary to prevent mailcious criticisms against the peasant association. It was necessary to overthrow all the authority of the gentry, to knock them down, and even stamp them underfoot. All actions labeled as "going too far" had a revolutionary significance in the second period. To put it bluntly, it was necessary to bring about a brief reign of terror in every rural area; otherwise one can never suppress the activities of the counterrevolutionaries in the countryside or overthrow the authority of the gentry. To right a wrong it is necessary to exceed the proper limit, and the wrong cannot be righted without the proper limit being exceeded. The opinion of this school that the peasants are "going too far" is on the surface different from the opinion of the other school mentioned earlier that the peasant movement is "an awful mess," but in essence it adheres to the same viewpoint, and is likewise a theory of the landlords which supports the interests of the privileged classes. Since this theory hinders the rise of the peasant movement and consequently disrupts the revolution, we must oppose it resolutely.

THE SO-CALLED "MOVEMENT OF THE RIFFRAFF"

The right wing of the Kuomintang says, "The peasant movement is a movement of the riffraff, a movement of the lazy peasants." This opinion has gained much currency in Changsha. I went to the countryside and heard the gentry say, "It is all right to set up the peasant association, but the people now running it are incompetent; better put others on the job!" This opinion and the dictum of the right wing come to the same thing; both admit that the peasant movement may be carried on (as the peasant movement has already risen, no one dare say that it shouldn't), but regard people leading the movement as incompetent and hate particularly those in charge of the associations at the lower levels, labeling them "riffraff." In short, all those who were formerly despised or kicked into the gutter by the gentry, who had no social standing, and who were denied the right to have a say, have now, to one's surprise, raised their heads. They have not only raised their heads, but have also taken power into their hands. They are now running the *hsiang* peasant association (peasant association at the lowest level), which has been turned into a formidable force in their hands. They raise their rough, blackened hands and lay them on the heads of the gentry. They bind the bad gentry with ropes, put tall paper hats on them, and lead them in a parade through the villages. (This is called "parading through the *hsiang*" in Hsiangtan and Hsianghsiang, and "parading through the fields" in Liling.) Every day the coarse, harsh sound of their denunciation more or less pierces the ears of the gentry. They are giving orders and directions in all matters. They rank above everybody else, they who used to rank below everyone else—that is what people mean by upside down."

VANGUARD OF THE REVOLUTION

When there are two opposite approaches to a thing or a kind of people, there will be two opposite opinions. "An awful mess" and "very good indeed," "riffraff" and "vanguard of the revolution," are both suitable examples.

We have seen the peasants' accomplishment of a revolutionary task for many years left unaccomplished and their important contributions to the national revolution. But have all the peasants taken part in accomplishing such a great revolutionary task and making important contributions? No. The peasantry consists of three sections—the rich peasants, the middle peasants, and the poor peasants. The circumstances of the three sections differ, and so do their reactions to the revolution. In the first period, what reached the ears of the rich peasants was that the Northern Expedition Army met with a crushing defeat in Kiangsi, that Chiang Kai-shek had been wounded in the leg and had flown back to Kwangtung, and that Wu Pei-fu had recaptured Yochou. So they thought that the peasant association certainly could not last long and the Three People's Principles[5] could never succeed, because such things were never heard of before. The officials of a *hsiang* peasant association (generally of the so-called "riffraff" type), bringing the membership register and entering the house of a rich peasant, said to him, "Please join the peasant association." How would the rich peasant answer? "Peasant association? For decades I have lived here and tilled the fields here; I have not seen anything like the peasant association but I get along all the same. You had better give it up!"—this from a moderate rich peasant. "What peasant association? Association for having one's head chopped off—don't get people into trouble!"—this from a violent rich peasant. Strangely enough, the peasant association has been established for several months, and has even dared to oppose the gentry. Some gentry in the neighborhood were arrested by the association and paraded through the villages because they refused to surrender their opium-smoking kits. In the county towns, moreover, prominent members of the gentry were put to death, such as Yen Yung-chiu of Hsiangtan and Yang Chih-tse of Ninghsiang. At the meeting celebrating the anniversary of the October Revolution, the anti-British rallies, and the grand celebration of the victory of the Northern Expedition, at least ten thousand peasants in every county, carrying big and small banners, with poles and hoes thrown in, marched in demonstrations

5. The Three People's Principles—Nationalism, Democracy, and the People's Welfare—were proposed by Sun Yat-sen as guiding principles for China.

in great columns like rolling waves. When all this happened, the rich peasants began to feel perplexed. In the grand celebration of the victory of the Northern Expedition, they learnt that Kiukiang had been taken, that Chiang Kai-shek had not been wounded in the leg, and that Wu Pei-fu had been finally defeated. Furthermore, "Long live the Three People's Principles!" "Long live the peasant association!" and "Long live the peasants!" were clearly written on the "decrees on red and green paper" (posters). " 'Long live the peasants!' Are these people to be regarded as emperors?" The rich peasants were greatly puzzled. So the peasant association put on grand airs. People from the association said to the rich peasants, "We'll enter you in the special register," or, "In another month, the admission fee will be ten dollars!" It was only in these circumstances that the rich peasants tardily joined the peasant association, some paying fifty cents or a dollar (the regular fee being only ten cents), others securing admission only after people have put in for them a good word or two at their request. There are also quite a number of diehards who, even up to the present, have not joined the association. When the rich peasants join the association they generally enter the name of some old man of 60 or 70 of their family, for they are always afraid of "the drafting of the adult males." After joining the association they never work for it enthusiastically. They remain inactive throughout.

How about the middle peasants? Their attitude is vacillating. They think that the revolution will not do them much good. They have rice in their pot and are not afraid of creditors knocking at their doors at midnight. They too, judging a thing by whether it ever was there before, knit their brows and think hard: "Can the peasant association really stand on its own legs?" "Can the Three People's Principles succeed?" Their conclusion is, "Afraid not." They think that all these things depend entirely on the will of Heaven: "To run a peasant association? Who knows if Heaven wills it or not?" In the first period, people from the peasant association, registers in hand, entered the house of a middle peasant and said to him, "Please join the peasant association!" "No hurry!" replied the middle peasant. It was not until the second period, when the peasant association enjoyed great power, that the middle peasants joined up. In the association they behave better than the rich peasants, but are as yet not very active, and still want to wait and see. It is entirely necessary for the peasant association to explain a good deal more to the middle peasants in order to get them to join.

The main force in the countryside which has always put up the bitterest fight is the poor peasants. Throughout both the period of underground organization and that of open organization the poor peasants have fought militantly all along. They accept most willingly the leadership of the Communist Party. They are the deadliest enemies of the local bullies and bad gentry and attack their strongholds without the slightest hesitation. They alone are prepared to do the destructive work.[6] They say to the rich peasants: "We joined the peasant association long ago. Why do you still hesitate?" The rich peasants answer in a mocking tone, "You people have neither a tile over your head nor a pinpoint of land beneath your feet. What should have kept you from joining!" Indeed, the poor peasants are not afraid of losing anything. Many of them really have "neither a tile over their head nor a pinpoint of land beneath their feet"—what should have kept them from joining the association? According to a survey of Changsha County, the poor peasants comprise 70 percent of the rural population; the middle peasants, 20 percent; and the rich peasants and landlords, 10 percent. The poor peasants who comprise 70 percent can be subdivided into two groups, the utterly impoverished and the less impoverished. The completely dispossessed, i.e., those who have neither land nor money, and who, without any means of livelihood, are forced to leave home and become mercenary soldiers, or hired laborers, or tramp about as beggars—all belong to the "utterly impoverished" and comprise 20 percent. The partly dispossessed, i.e., those who have a little land or a little money but consume more than they receive and live in the midst of toil and worry all the

6. This sentence also omitted from some post-1949 editions (Ed. note).

year round, e.g., the handicraftsmen, tenant-peasants (except the rich tenant-peasants), and semitenant peasants—all belong to the "less impoverished" and comprise 50 percent. This enormous mass of poor peasants, altogether comprising 70 percent of the rural population, are the backbone of the peasant association, the vanguard in overthrowing the feudal forces, and the foremost heroes who have accomplished the great revolutionary undertaking left unaccomplished for many years. Without the poor peasants (the "riff-raff" as the gentry call them), it would never have been possible to bring about in the countryside the present state of revolution, to overthrow the local bullies and bad gentry, or to complete the democratic revolution. Being the most revolutionary, the poor peasants have won the leadership in the peasant association. Almost all the posts of chairmen and committee members in the peasant associations at the lowest level were held by poor peasants in both the first and second periods (of the officials in the *hsiang* associations in Hengshan the utterly impoverished comprise 50 percent, the less impoverished comprise 40 percent, and the impoverished intellectuals comprise 10 percent). This leadership of the poor peasants is absolutely necessary. Without the poor peasants there can be no revolution. To reject them is to reject the revolution. To attack them is to attack the revolution. Their general direction of the revolution has never been wrong. They have hurt the dignity of the local bullies and bad gentry. They have knocked the big and small local bullies and bad gentry to the ground and trampled them underfoot. Many of their deeds in the period of revolutionary action, described as "gone too far," were in fact the very needs of the revolution. Some of the county governments, county headquarters of the party,[7] and county peasant associations in Hunan have committed a number of mistakes; there are even some which at the request of the landlords sent soldiers to arrest the lower officials of the peasant associations. Many chairmen and committeemen of the *hsiang* associations are imprisoned in the jails in Hengshen and

7. The Kuomintang, not the Chinese Communist Party.

Hsianghsiang. This is a serious mistake which greatly encourages the arrogance of the reactionaries. To judge whether or not it is a mistake, one need only see how, as soon as the chairmen and committeemen of the peasant associations are arrested, the local lawless landlords are elated and reactionary sentiments mount. We must oppose such counterrevolutionary calumnies as "riffraff movement" and "movement of the lazy peasants" and must be especially careful not to commit the mistake of helping the local bullies and bad gentry to attack the poor peasants. As a matter of fact, although some of the poor-peasant leaders certainly had shortcomings in the past, most of them have reformed themselves by now. They are themselves energetically prohibiting gambling and exterminating banditry. Where the peasant association is powerful, gambling and banditry have vanished. In some places it is literally true that people do not pocket articles dropped on the road and that doors are not bolted at night. According to a survey of Hengshan, 85 percent of the poor-peasant leaders have now turned out to be quite reformed, capable, and energetic. Only 15 percent of them retain some bad habits. They can only be regarded as "the few undesirables," and we must not echo the local bullies and bad gentry in condemning indiscriminately everybody as "riffraff." To tackle this problem of "the few undesirables," we can only, on the basis of the association's slogan of strengthening discipline, carry on propaganda among the masses and educate the undesirables themselves so that the discipline of the association may be strengthened, but we must not wantonly send soldiers to make arrests, lest we should undermine the prestige of the poor peasantry and fan up the arrogance of the local bullies and bad gentry. This is a point we must particularly attend to.

7

"SECRET SPEECH" TO PARTY CONGRESS XX*

N. S. Khrushchev
(Moscow, 24 February 1956)

Few events have so rocked the communist world as Khrushchev's "Secret Speech." Without it, it is unlikely that the Polish developments and the Hungarian uprising would have occurred, or that the crises in communist unity and identity would have developed, at least in the manner and to the extent that they did. Ripping the mask from the Stalin persona created shockwaves that undermined the authority of communism and communist leadership everywhere and did great violence to the myth of the communist monolith.

Khrushchev did not foresee the extremes of the consequences he was setting in motion by his "Secret Speech." But, he was certainly aware of the seriousness of what he was about to do; and he had to be pushed into action. As Party Congress XX progressed, it became apparent that if Khrushchev did not lead the onslaught against Stalin's ghost, others, high in the ranks of the party, would. The information would come out—unless it was to be suppressed in ruthless Stalin fashion. But Khrushchev realized that even if the

* Complete

latter option was open, it would only result in strengthening the claims to power of others like Molotov and Kaganovich, who had been closer to Stalin longer than he had been. If he went in the opposite direction, he could use the crimes of Stalin to destroy those who continued to identify with Stalin and who stood in the way of his own rise to power.

He decided to attack Stalin.

Even so, he sought to bring balance to his portrayal of the former generalissimo. And Khrushchev tried to keep the speech within the party. He did not want to broadcast the party's disgrace—and his, for he, like all of those in the top ranks of the party, had played Stalin's game. Nevertheless, one or more copies found their way into the hands of the U.S. Department of State, which released the document in early June 1956.

THE CULT OF THE INDIVIDUAL

Comrades! In the report of the Central Committee of the party at the Twentieth Congress, in a number of speeches by delegates to the Congress, as also formerly during the plenary CC/CPSU [Central Committee of the Communist Party of the Soviet Union] sessions, quite a lot has been said about the cult of the individual and about its harmful consequences.

After Stalin's death, the Central Committee of the party began to implement a policy of explaining concisely and consistently that it is impermissible and foreign to the spirit of Marxism-Leninism to elevate one person, to transform him into a superman possessing supernatural characteristics akin to those of a god. Such a man supposedly knows everything, sees everything, thinks for everyone, can do anything, is infallible in his behavior.

Such a belief about a man, and specifically about Stalin, was cultivated among us for many years.

The objective of the present report is not a thorough evaluation of Stalin's life and activity. Concerning Stalin's merits an entirely sufficient number of books, pamphlets and studies had already been written in his lifetime. The role of Stalin in the preparation and execution of the Socialist Revolution, in the Civil War, and in the fight for the construction of Socialism in our country is universally known. Everyone knows this well. At present we are concerned with a question which has immense importance for the party now and for the future—with how the cult of the person of Stalin has been gradually growing, the cult which became at a certain specific stage the source of a whole series of exceedingly serious and grave perversions of party principles, of party democracy, of revolutionary legality.

Because of the fact that not all as yet realize fully the practical consequences resulting from the cult of the individual, the great harm caused by the violation of the principle of collective leadership of the party and because of the accumulation of immense and limitless power in the hands of one person—the Central Committee of the party considers it absolutely necessary to make the material pertaining to this matter available to the Twentieth Congress of the Communist Party of the Soviet Union.

Allow me first of all to remind you how severely the classics of Marxism-Leninism denounced every manifestation of the cult of the individual. In a letter to the German political worker, Wilhelm Bloss, Marx stated: "From my antipathy to any cult of the individual, I never made public during the existence of the International the numerous addresses from various countries which recognized my merits and which annoyed me. I did not even reply to them, except sometimes to rebuke their authors. Engels and I first joined the secret society of Communists on the condition that everything making for superstitious worship of authority would be deleted from its statute. Lassalle subsequently did quite the opposite."

Some time later Engels wrote: "Both Marx and I have always been against any public manifestation with regard to individuals, with the exception of cases when it had an important purpose; and we most strongly opposed such manifestations which during our lifetime concerned us personally."

The great modesty of the genius of the Revolution, Vladimir Ilyich Lenin, is known. Lenin had always stressed the role of the people as the creator of history, the directing and organizational role of the party as a living and creative organism, and also the role of the Central Committee.

Marxism does not negate the role of the leaders of the working class in directing the revolutionary liberation movement.

While ascribing great importance to the role of the leaders and organizers of the masses, Lenin at the same time mercilessly condemned every manifestation of the cult of the individual, inexorably combated the views, alien to Marxism, about the "hero" and the "crowd" and countered all efforts to oppose a "hero" to the masses and to the people.

Lenin taught that the party's strength depends on its indissoluble unity with the masses, on the fact that behind the party follow the people—workers, peasants, and intelligentsia. "Only he will win and retain the power," said Lenin, "who believes in the people, who submerges himself in the fountain of the living creativeness of the people."

Lenin spoke with pride about the Bolshevik Communist Party as the leader and teacher of the people; he called for the presentation of all the most important questions before the opinion of the conscious workers, before the opinion of their party. He said, "We believe in it, we see in it the wisdom, the honor, and the conscience of our epoch."

Lenin resolutely stood against every attempt aimed at belittling or weakening the directing role of the party in the structure of the Soviet state. He worked out Bolshevik principles of party leadership and norms of party life, stressing that the guiding principle of party leadership is its collegiality [leadership by a group]. Already during the prerevolutionary years Lenin called the Central Committee of the party a collective of leaders and the guardian and interpreter of party principles. "During the period between congresses," pointed out Lenin, "the Central Committee guards and interprets the principles of the party."

Underlining the role of the Central Committee of the party and its authority, Vladimir Ilyich pointed out: "Our

Central Committee constituted itself as a closely centralized and highly authoritative group . . ."

During Lenin's life the Central Committee of the party was a real expression of collective leadership of the party and of the nation. Being a militant Marxist-revolutionist, always unyielding in matters of principle, Lenin never imposed by force his views on his co-workers. He tried to convince; he patiently explained his opinions to others. Lenin always diligently observed that the norms of party life were realized, that the party statute was enforced, that the party congresses and the plenary sessions of the Central Committee took place at the proper intervals.

LENIN ON STALIN

In addition to the great accomplishments of V. I. Lenin for the victory of the working class and of the working peasants, for the victory of our party and for the application of the ideas of scientific Communism to life, his acute mind expressed itself also in this—that he detected in Stalin in time those negative characteristics which resulted later in grave consequences. Fearing the future fate of the party and of the Soviet nation, V. I. Lenin made a completely correct characterization of Stalin, pointing out that it was necessary to consider the question of transferring Stalin from the position of the Secretary General because of the fact that Stalin was excessively rude, that he did not have a proper attitude toward his comrades, that he was capricious and abused his power.

In December 1922, in a letter to the Party Congress, Vladimir Ilyich wrote: "After taking over the position of Secretary General, Comrade Stalin accumulated in his hands immeasurable power and I am not certain whether he will be always able to use this power with the required care."

This letter—a political document of tremendous importance, known in the party history as Lenin's "Testament"—was distributed among the delegates to the Twentieth Party Congress. You have read it and will undoubtedly read it again more than once. You might reflect on Lenin's plain words, in which expression is given to Vladimir Ilyich's anxiety concerning the party, the people, the state, and the future direction of party policy.

Vladimir Ilyich said: "Stalin is excessively rude, and this defect, which can be freely tolerated in our midst and in contacts among us Communists, becomes a defect which cannot be tolerated in one holding the position of the Secretary General. Because of this, I propose that the comrades consider the method by which Stalin would be removed from this position and by which another man would be selected for it, a man who, above all, would differ from Stalin in only one quality—namely, greater tolerance, greater loyalty, greater kindness and a more considerate attitude toward the comrades, a less capricious temper, etc."

This document of Lenin's was made known to the delegates at the Thirteenth Party Congress, who discussed the question of transferring Stalin from the position of Secretary General. The delegates declared themselves in favor of retaining Stalin in this post, hoping that he would heed the critical remarks of Vladimir Ilyich and would be able to overcome the defects which caused Lenin serious anxiety.

Comrades! The Party Congress should become acquainted with two new documents, which confirm Stalin's character as already outlined by Vladimir Ilyich Lenin in his "testament." These documents are a letter from Nadezhda Konstantinovna Krupskaya to Kamenev, who was at that time head of the Political Bureau, and a personal letter from Vladimir Ilyich Lenin to Stalin.

I will now read these documents:

LEV BORISOVICH!

Because of a short letter which I had written in words dictated to me by Vladimir Ilyich by permission of the doctors, Stalin allowed himself yesterday an unusually rude outburst directed at me. This is not my first day in the party. During all these thirty years I have never heard from any comrade one word of rudeness. The business of the party and of Ilyich are not less dear to me than to Stalin. I need at present the maximum of self-control. What one can and what one cannot discuss with Ilyich—I know better than any doctor, because I know what makes him nervous and what does not, in any case I know better than Stalin. I am turning to you and to Grigory [Zinoviev], as much closer comrades of V. I., and I beg you to protect me from rude interference with my private life and from vile invectives and threats. I have no doubt as to what will be the unanimous decision of the control commission, with which Stalin sees fit to threaten me; however, I have neither the strength nor the time to waste on this foolish quarrel. And I am a living person and my nerves are strained to the utmost.

N. KRUPSKAYA

Nadezhda Konstantinovna wrote this letter on 23 December 1922. After two and a half months, in March 1923, Vladimir Ilyich Lenin sent Stalin the following letter:

TO COMRADE STALIN:
COPIES FOR: KAMENEV AND ZINOVIEV.
Dear Comrade Stalin!
You permitted yourself a rude summons of my wife to the telephone and a rude reprimand of her. Despite the fact that she told you that she agreed to forget what was said, nevertheless Zinoviev and Kamenev heard about it from her. I have no intention to forget so easily that which is being done against me, and I need not stress here that I consider as directed against me that which is being done against my wife. I ask you, therefore, that you weigh carefully whether you are agreeable to retracting your words and apologizing or whether you prefer the severance of relations between us.

SINCERELY: LENIN

MARCH 1923

(*Commotion in the hall.*)

THE ORIGINS OF REPRESSION

Comrades! I will not comment on these documents. They speak eloquently for themselves. Since Stalin could behave in this manner during Lenin's life, could behave thus toward Nadezhda Konstantinovna Krupskaya—whom the party knows well and values highly as a loyal friend of Lenin and as an active fighter for the cause of the party since its creation—we can easily imagine how Stalin treated other people. These negative characteristics of his developed steadily and during the last years acquired an absolutely insufferable character.

As later events have proven, Lenin's anxiety was justified: In the first period after Lenin's death Stalin still paid attention to his advice, but later he began to disregard the serious admonitions of Vladimir Ilyich.

When we analyze the practice of Stalin in regard to the direction of the party and of the country, when we pause to consider everything which Stalin perpetrated, we must be convinced that Lenin's fears were justified. The negative characteristics of Stalin, which, in Lenin's time, were only incipient, transformed themselves during the last years into a grave abuse of power by Stalin, which caused untold harm to our party.

We have to consider seriously and analyze correctly this matter in order that we may preclude any possibility of a repetition in any form whatever of what took place during the life of Stalin, who absolutely did not tolerate collegiality in leadership and in work, and who practiced brutal violence, not only toward everything which opposed him, but also toward that which seemed, to his capricious and despotic character, contrary to his concepts.

Stalin acted not through persuasion, explanation, and patient cooperation with people, but by imposing his concepts and demanding absolute submission to his opinion. Whoever opposed this concept or tried to prove his viewpoint and the correctness of his position was doomed to removal from the leading collective and to subsequent moral and physical annihilation. This was especially true during the period following the Seventeenth Party Congress, when many prominent party leaders and rank-and-file party workers, honest and dedicated to the cause of Communism, fell victim to Stalin's despotism.

We must affirm that the party fought a serious fight against the Trotskyites, the Rightists, and Bourgeois Nationalists, and that it disarmed ideologically all the enemies of Leninism. This ideological fight was carried on successfully, as a result of which the party became strengthened and tempered. Here Stalin played a positive role.

The party led a great political-ideological struggle against those in its own ranks who proposed anti-Leninist theses, who represented a political line hostile to the party and to the cause of socialism. This was a stubborn and a difficult fight but a necessary one, because the political line of both the Trotskyite-Zinovievite bloc and of the Bukharinites led actually toward the restoration of capitalism and capitulation to the world bourgeoisie. Let us consider for a moment what would have happened if in 1928–29 the political line of right deviation had prevailed among us, or orientation toward "cotton-dress industrialization," or toward the kulak, etc. We would not now have a powerful heavy industry, we would not have the *kolkhozes*, we would find ourselves disarmed and weak in a capitalist encirclement.

It was for this reason that the party led an inexorable ideological fight and explained to all party members and to the non-party masses the harm and the danger of the anti-Leninist proposals of the Trotskyite opposition and the rightist opportunists. And this great work of explaining the party line bore fruit; both the Trotskyites and the rightist opportunists were politically isolated; the overwhelming party majority supported the Leninist line and the party was able to awaken and organize the working masses to apply the Leninist party line and to build socialism.

Worth noting is the fact that, even during the progress of the furious ideological fight against the Trotskyites, the Zinovievites, the Bukharinites and others, extreme repressive measures were not used against them. The fight was on ideological grounds. But some years later, when socialism in our country was fundamentally constructed, when the exploiting classes were generally liquidated, when the Soviet social structure had radically changed, when the social basis for political movements and groups hostile to the party had violently contracted, when the ideological opponents of the party had long since been defeated politically—then the repression directed against them began.

It was precisely during this period (1935 to 1937–38) that the practice of mass repression through the Government apparatus was born, first against the enemies of Leninism—

Trotskyites, Zinovievites, Bukharinites, long since politically defeated by the party—and subsequently also against many honest Communists, against those party cadres who had borne the heavy load of the Civil War and the first and most difficult years of industrialization and collectivization, who actively fought against the Trotskyites and the rightists, for the Leninist party line.

Stalin originated the concept "enemy of the people." This term automatically rendered it unnecessary that the ideological errors of a man or men engaged in a controversy be proved; this term made possible the usage of the most cruel repression, violating all norms of revolutionary legality, against anyone who in any way disagreed with Stalin, against those who were only suspected of hostile intent, against those who had bad reputations. This concept "enemy of the people" actually eliminated the possibility of any kind of ideological fight or the making of one's views known on this or that issue, even those of a practical character. In the main, and in actuality, the only proof of guilt used, against all norms of current legal science, was the "confession" of the accused himself; and, as subsequent investigation proved, "confessions" were secured through physical pressures against the accused. This led to glaring violations of revolutionary legality and to the fact that many entirely innocent persons, who in the past had defended the party line, became victims.

We must assert that, in regard to those persons who in their time had opposed the party line, there were often no sufficiently serious reasons for their physical annihilation. The formula "enemy of the people" was specifically introduced for the purpose of physically annihilating such individuals.

LENIN AND ENEMIES

It is a sad fact that many persons who were later annihilated as enemies of the party and people had worked with Lenin during his life. Some of these persons had made errors during Lenin's life, but despite this, Lenin benefited by their work; he corrected them and he did everything possible to retain them in the ranks of the party; he induced them to follow him.

In this connection the delegates to the Party Congress should familiarize themselves with an unpublished note by V. I. Lenin directed to the Central Committee's Political Bureau in October 1920. Outlining the duties of the Control Commission, Lenin wrote that the commission should be transformed into a real "organ of party and proletarian conscience."

> As a special duty of the Control Commission there is recommended a deep individualized relationship with, and sometimes even a type of therapy for, the representatives of the so-called opposition—those who have experienced a psychological crisis because of failure in their Soviet or party career. An effort should be made to quiet them, to explain the matter to them in a way used among comrades, to find for them (avoiding the method of issuing orders) a task for which they are psychologically fitted. Advice and rules relating to this matter are to be formulated by the Central Committee's Organizational Bureau, etc.

Everyone knows how irreconcilable Lenin was with the ideological enemies of Marxism, with those who deviated from the correct party line. At the same time, however, Lenin, as is evident from the given document, in his practice in leading the party demanded the most intimate party contact with people who had shown indecision or temporary non-conformity with the party line, but whom it was possible to return to the party path. Lenin advised that such people should be patiently educated without the application of extreme methods.

Lenin's wisdom in dealing with people was evident in his work with cadres.

An entirely different relationship with people characterized Stalin. Lenin's traits—patient work with people, stubborn and painstaking education of them, the ability to induce people to follow him without using compulsion, but rather through the ideological influence on them of the whole collective—were entirely foreign to Stalin. He discarded the Leninist method of convincing and educating, he abandoned the method of ideological struggle for that of administrative violence, mass repressions, and terror. He acted on an increasingly larger scale and more stubbornly through punitive organs, at the same time often violating all existing norms of morality and of Soviet laws.

Arbitrary behavior by one person encouraged and permitted arbitrariness in others. Mass arrests and deportations of many thousands of people, execution without trial and without normal investigation created conditions of insecurity, fear and even despair.

This, of course, did not contribute toward unity of the party ranks and of all strata of working people, but, on the contrary, brought about annihilation and the expulsion from the party of workers who were loyal but inconvenient to Stalin.

Our party fought for the implementation of Lenin's plans for the construction of socialism. This was an ideological fight. Had Leninist principles been observed during the course of this fight, had the party's devotion to principles been skillfully combined with a keen and solicitous concern for people, had they not been repelled and wasted but rather drawn to our side, we certainly would not have had such a brutal violation of revolutionary legality and many thousands of people would not have fallen victim to the method of terror. Extraordinary methods would then have been resorted to only against those people who had in fact committed criminal acts against the Soviet system.

Let us recall some historical facts.

In the days before the October Revolution, two members of the Central Committee of the Bolshevik party—Kamenev and Zinoviev—declared themselves against Lenin's plan for an armed uprising.

In addition, on October 18 they published in the Menshevik newspaper, *Novaya Zhizn*, a statement declaring that the Bolsheviks were making preparations for an uprising and that they considered it adventuristic. Kamenev and Zinoviev thus disclosed to the enemy the decision of the Central Committee to stage the uprising, and that the uprising had been organized to take place within the very near future.

This was treason against the party and against the Revolution. In this connection, V. I. Lenin wrote: "Kamenev and Zinoviev revealed the decision of the Central Committee of their party on the armed uprising to Rodzyanko and Kerensky . . ." He put before the Central Committee the question of Zinoviev's and Kamenev's expulsion from the party.

However, after the Great Socialist October Revolution, as is known, Zinoviev and Kamenev were given leading positions. Lenin put them in positions in which they carried out most responsible party tasks and participated actively in the work of the leading party and Soviet organs. It is known that Zinoviev and Kamenev committed a number of other serious errors during Lenin's life. In his "Testament" Lenin warned that "Zinoviev's and Kamenev's October episode was of course not an accident." But Lenin did not pose the question of their arrest and certainly not their shooting.

Or, let us take the example of the Trotskyites. At present, after a sufficiently long historical period, we can speak about the fight with the Trotskyites with complete calm and can analyze this matter with sufficient objectivity. After all, around Trotsky were people whose origin cannot by any means be traced to bourgeois society. Part of them belonged to the party intelligentsia and a certain part were recruited from among the workers. We can name many individuals who, in their time, joined the Trotskyites; however, these same individuals took an active part in the workers' movement before the Revolution, during the Socialist October Revolution itself, and also in the consolidation of the victory of this greatest of revolutions. Many of them broke with Trotskyism and returned to Leninist positions. Was it necessary to annihilate such people? We are deeply convinced that, had Lenin lived, such an extreme method would not have been used against any of them.

Such are only a few historical facts. But can it be said that Lenin did not decide to use even the most severe means against enemies of the Revolution when this was actually necessary? No, no one can say this. Vladimir Ilyich demanded uncompromising dealings with the enemies of the Revolution and of the working class and when necessary resorted ruthlessly to such methods. You will recall only V. I. Lenin's fight with the Socialist-Revolutionary organizers of the anti-Soviet uprising, with the counterrevolutionary kulaks in 1918 and with others, when Lenin without hesitation used the most extreme methods against the enemies. Lenin used such methods, however, only against actual class enemies and not against those who blunder, who err, and whom it was possible to lead through ideological influence and even retain in the leadership. Lenin used severe methods only in the most necessary cases, when the exploiting classes were still in existence and were vigorously opposing the Revolution, when the struggle for survival was decidedly assuming the sharpest forms, even including a civil war.

STALIN'S ATTITUDE TOWARD THE ROLE OF THE PARTY

Stalin, on the other hand, used extreme methods and mass repressions at a time when the Revolution was already victorious, when the Soviet state was strengthened, when the exploiting classes were already liquidated and socialist relations were rooted solidly in all phases of national economy, when our party was politically consolidated and had strengthened itself both numerically and ideologically.

It is clear that here Stalin showed in a whole series of cases his intolerance, his brutality, and his abuse of power. Instead of proving his political correctness and mobilizing the masses, he often chose the path of repression and physical annihilation, not only against actual enemies, but also against individuals who had not committed any crimes against the party and the Soviet Government. Here we see no wisdom but only a demonstration of the brutal force which had once so alarmed V. I. Lenin.

Lately, especially after the unmasking of the Beria gang, the Central Committee looked into a series of matters fabricated by this gang. This revealed a very ugly picture of brutal willfulness connected with the incorrect behavior of Stalin. As facts prove, Stalin, using his unlimited power, allowed himself many abuses, acting in the name of the Central Committee, not asking for the opinion of the Committee members nor even of the members of the Central Committee's Political Bureau; often he did not inform them about his personal decisions concerning very important party and government matters.

Considering the question of the cult of the individual, we must first of all show everyone what harm this caused to the interests of our party.

Vladimir Ilyich Lenin had always stressed the party's role and significance in the direction of the socialist government of workers and peasants; he saw in this the chief precondition for a successful building of socialism in our country. Pointing to the great responsibility of the Bolshevik party, as the ruling party of the Soviet state, Lenin called for the most meticulous observance of all norms of party life; he called for the realization of the principles of collegiality in the direction of the party and the state.

Collegiality of leadership flows from the very nature of our party, a party built on the principles of democratic centralism. "This means," said Lenin, "that all party matters are accomplished by all party members—directly or through representatives—who, without any exceptions, are subject to the same rules; in addition, all administrative members, all directing collegia, all holders of party positions are elective, they must account for their activities and are recallable."

It is known that Lenin himself offered an example of the most careful observance of these principles. There was no matter so important that Lenin himself decided it without asking for advice and approval of the majority of the Central Committee members or of the members of the Central Committee's Political Bureau. In the most difficult period for our party and our country, Lenin considered it necessary regularly to convoke congresses, party conferences and plenary sessions of the Central Committee at which all the most important questions were discussed and where resolutions, carefully worked out by the collective of leaders, were approved.

We can recall, for an example, the year 1918 when the country was threatened by the attack of the imperalistic interventionists. In this situation the Seventh Party Congress was convened in order to discuss a vitally important matter which could not be postponed—the matter of peace. In 1919, while the civil war was raging, the Eighth Party Congress convened, which adopted a new party program, decided such important matters as the relationship with the peasant masses, the organization of the Red Army, the leading role of the party in the work of the soviets, the correction of the social composition of the party, and other matters. In 1920 the Ninth Party Congress was convened, which laid down guiding principles pertaining to the party's work in the sphere of economic construction. In 1921 the Tenth Party Congress accepted Lenin's New Economic Policy and the historical resolution called "About Party Unity."

During Lenin's life, party congresses were convened regularly; always when a radical turn in the development of the party and the country took place, Lenin considered it absolutely necessary that the party discuss at length all the basic matters pertaining to internal and foreign policy and to questions bearing on the development of party and government.

It is very characteristic that Lenin addressed to the Party Congress as the highest party organ his last articles, letters and remarks. During the period between congresses, the Central Committee of the party, acting as the most authoritative leading collective, meticulously observed the principles of the party and carried out its policy.

So it was during Lenin's life. Were our party's holy Leninist principles observed after the death of Vladimir Ilyich?

Whereas, during the first few years after Lenin's death, party congresses and Central Committee plenums took place more or less regularly, later, when Stalin began increasingly to abuse his power, these principles were brutally violated. This was especially evident during the last fifteen years of his life. Was it a normal situation when over thirteen years elapsed between the Eighteenth and Nineteenth Party Congresses, years during which our party and our country had experienced so many important events? These events demanded categorically that the party should have passed resolutions pertaining to the country's defense during the

Patriotic War [World War II] and to peacetime construction after the war. Even after the end of the war a Congress was not convened for over seven years. Central Committee plenums were hardly ever called. It should be sufficient to mention that during all the years of the Patriotic War not a single Central Committee plenum took place. It is true that there was an attempt to call a Central Committee plenum in October 1941, when Central Committee members from the whole country were called to Moscow. They waited two days for the opening of the plenum, but in vain. Stalin did not even want to meet and talk to the Central Committee members. This fact shows how demoralized Stalin was in the first months of the war and how haughtily and disdainfully he treated the Central Committee members.

In practice, Stalin ignored the norms of party life and trampled on the Leninist principle of collective party leadership.

SEVENTEENTH PARTY CONGRESS

Stalin's willfulness *vis-à-vis* the party and its Central Committee became fully evident after the Seventeenth Party Congress which took place in 1934.

Having at its disposal numerous data showing brutal arbitrariness toward party cadres, the Central Committee has created a party commission under the control of the Central Committee Presidium; it was charged with investigating what made possible the mass repressions against the majority of the Central Committee members and candidates elected at the Seventeenth Congress of the All-Union Communist Party (Bolsheviks).

The commission has become acquainted with a large quantity of materials in the NKVD archives and with other documents and has established many facts pertaining to the fabrication of cases against Communists, to false accusations, to glaring abuses of socialist legality, which resulted in the death of innocent people. It became apparent that many party, Soviet, and economic activists, who were branded in 1937–38 as "enemies," were actually never enemies, spies, wreckers, etc., but were always honest Communists; they were only so stigmatized and, often, no longer able to bear barbaric tortures, they charged themselves (at the order of the investigative judges—falsifiers) with all kinds of grave and unlikely crimes.

The commission has presented to the Central Committee Presidium lengthy and documented materials pertaining to mass repressions against the delegates to the Seventeenth Party Congress and against members of the Central Committee elected at that Congress. These materials have been studied by the Presidium of the Central Committee.

It was determined that of the 139 members and candidates of the party's Central Committee who were elected at the Seventeenth Congress, 98 persons, i.e., 70 percent, were arrested and shot (mostly in 1937–38). *(Indignation in the hall.)* What was the composition of the delegates to the Seventeenth Congress? It is known that 80 percent of the voting participants of the Seventeenth Congress joined the party during the years of conspiracy before the Revolution and during the civil war; this means before 1921. By social origin the basic mass of the delegates to the Congress were workers (60 percent of the voting members).

For this reason, it was inconceivable that a congress so composed would have elected a Central Committee a majority of whom would prove to be enemies of the party. The only reason why 70 percent of Central Committee members and candidates elected at the Seventeenth Congress were branded as enemies of the party and of the people was that honest Communists were slandered, accusations against them were fabricated, and revolutionary legality was gravely undermined.

The same fate met not only the Central Committee members but also the majority of the delegates to the Seventeenth Party Congress. Of 1,966 delegates with either voting or advisory rights, 1,108 persons were arrested on charges of revolutionary crimes, i.e., decidedly more than a majority. This very fact shows how absurd, wild and contrary to common sense were the charges of counterrevolutionary crimes made out, as we now see, against a majority of participants at the Seventeenth Party Congress. (*Indignation in the hall.*)

We should recall that the Seventeenth Party Congress is historically known as the Congress of Victors. Delegates to the Congress were active participants in the building of our socialist state; many of them suffered and fought for party interests during the pre-Revolutionary years in the conspiracy and at the civil-war fronts; they fought their enemies valiantly and often nervelessly looked into the face of death.

How, then, can we believe that such people could prove to be "two-faced" and had joined the camps of the enemies of socialism during the era after the political liquidation of Zinovievites, Trotskyites, and Rightists and after the great accomplishments of socialist construction? This was the result of the abuse of power by Stalin, who began to use mass terror against the party cadres.

What is the reason that mass repressions against activists increased more and more after the Seventeenth Party Congress? It was because at that time Stalin had so elevated himself above the party and above the nation that he ceased to consider either the Central Committee or the party.

While he still reckoned with the opinion of the collective before the Seventeenth Congress, after the complete political liquidation of the Trotskyites, Zinovievites, and Bukharinites, when as a result of that fight and socialist victories the party achieved unity, Stalin ceased to an ever greater degree to consider the members of the party's Central Committee and even the members of the Political Bureau. Stalin thought that now he could decide all things alone and all he needed were people to fill the stage; he treated all others in such a way that they could only listen to and praise him.

THE CASE OF S. M. KIROV

After the criminal murder of S. M. Kirov, mass repressions and brutal acts of violation of socialist legality began. On the evening of 1 December 1934 on Stalin's initiative (without the approval of the Political Bureau—which approved it two days later, casually) the secretary of the Presidium of the Central Executive Committee, Yenukidze, signed the following directive:

1. Investigative agencies are directed to speed up the cases of those accused of the preparation or execution of acts of terror.
2. Judicial organs are directed not to hold up the execution of death sentences pertaining to crimes of this category in order to consider the possibility of pardon, because the Presidium of the Central Executive Committee of the USSR does not consider as possible the receiving of petitions of this sort.
3. The organs of the Commissariat of Internal Affairs are directed to execute the death sentences against criminals of the above-mentioned category immediately after the passage of sentences.

This directive became the basis for mass acts of abuse against socialist legality. During many of the fabricated court cases the accused were charged with "the preparation" of terroristic acts; this deprived them of any possibility that their cases might be reexamined, even when they stated before the court that their "confessions" were secured by force, and when, in a convincing manner, they disproved the accusations against them.

It must be asserted that to this day the circumstances surrounding Kirov's murder hide many things which are inexplicable and mysterious and demand a most careful examination. There are reasons for the suspicion that the killer of Kirov, Nikolayev, was assisted by someone from among the people whose duty it was to protect the person of Kirov.

A month and a half before the killing, Nikolayev was arrested on the grounds of suspicious behavior but he was released and not even searched. It is an unusually suspicious circumstance that when the Chekist assigned to protect Kirov was being brought for an interrogation, on 2 December 1934, he was killed in a car "accident" in which no other occupants of the car were harmed.

After the murder of Kirov, top functionaries of the Leningrad NKVD were given very light sentences, but in 1937 they were shot. We can assume that they were shot in order to cover the traces of the organizers of Kirov's killing.

Mass repressions grew tremendously from the end of 1936 after a telegram from Stalin and Zhdanov, dated from Sochi on 25 September 1936, was addressed to Kaganovich, Molotov, and other members of the Political Bureau. The content of the telegram was as follows:

We deem it absolutely necessary and urgent that Comrade Yezhov be nominated to the post of People's Commissar for Internal Affairs. Yagoda has definitely proved himself to be incapable of unmasking the Trotskyite-Zinovievite bloc. The OGPU is four years behind in this matter. This is noted by all party workers and by the majority of the representatives of the NKVD.

Strictly speaking, we should stress that Stalin did not meet with and, therefore, could not know the opinion of party workers.

This Stalinist formulation that the "NKVD is four years behind" in applying mass repression and that there is need of "catching up" with the neglected work, directly pushed the NKVD workers on the path of mass arrests and executions.

We should state that this formulation was also forced on the February–March plenary session of the Central Committee of the All-Union Communist Party (Bolsheviks) in 1937. The plenary resolution approved it on the basis of Yezhov's report, "Lessons Flowing from the Harmful Activity, Diversion, and Espionage of the Japanese-German-Trotskyite agents," stating:

The plenum of the Central Committee of the All-Union Communist Party (Bolsheviks) considers that all facts revealed during the investigation into the matter of an anti-Soviet Trotskyite center and of its followers in the provinces show that the People's Commissariat of Internal Affairs has fallen behind at least four years in the attempt to unmask these most inexorable enemies of the people.

The mass repressions at this time were made under the slogan of a fight against the Trotskyites. Did the Trotskyites at this time actually constitute such a danger to our party and to the Soviet state? We should recall that in 1927, on the eve of the Fifteenth Party Congress, only some 4,000 votes were cast for the Trotskyite-Zinovievite opposition while there were 724,000 for the party line. During the 10 years which passed between the Fifteenth Party Congress and the February-March Central Committee plenum, Trotskyism was completely disarmed; many former Trotskyites had changed their former views and worked in the various sectors building socialism. It is clear that in the situation of socialist victory there was no basis for mass terror in the country.

Stalin's report at the February–March Central Committee plenum in 1937, "Deficiencies of Party Work and Methods for the Liquidation of the Trotskyites and of Other Two-facers," contained an attempt at theoretical justification of the mass terror policy under the pretext that as we march forward toward Socialism, class war must allegedly sharpen. Stalin asserted that both history and Lenin taught him this.

Actually Lenin taught that the application of revolutionary violence is necessitated by the resistance of the exploiting classes, and this referred to the era when the exploiting classes existed and were powerful. As soon as the nation's political situation had improved, when in January 1920, the Red Army took Rostov and thus won a most important victory over Denikin, Lenin instructed Dzerzhinsky to stop mass terror and to abolish the death penalty. Lenin justified this important political move of the Soviet state in the following manner in his report at the session of the All-Union Central Executive Committee on 2 February 1920:

> We were forced to use terror because of the terror practiced by the Entente, when strong world powers threw their hordes against us, not avoiding any type of conduct. We would not have lasted two days had we not answered these attempts of officers and White Guardists in a merciless fashion; this meant the use of terror, but this was forced upon us by the terrorist methods of the Entente.
>
> But as soon as we attained a decisive victory, even before the end of the war, immediately after taking Rostov, we gave up the use of the death penalty and thus proved that we intend to execute our own program in the manner that we promised. We say

that the application of violence flows out of the decision to crush the exploiters, the large landowners and the capitalists; as soon as this was accomplished we gave up the use of all extraordinary methods. We have proved this in practice.

Stalin deviated from these clear and plain precepts of Lenin. Stalin put the party and the NKVD up to the use of mass terror when the exploiting classes had been liquidated in our country and when there were no serious reasons for the use of extraordinary mass terror.

This terror was actually directed not at the remnants of the defeated exploiting classes but against the honest workers of the party and of the Soviet state; against them were made lying, slanderous and absurd accusations concerning "two-facedness," "espionage," "sabotage," preparation of fictitious "plots," etc.

At the February–March Central Committee plenum in 1937 many members actually questioned the rightness of the established course regarding mass repressions under the pretext of combating "two-facedness."

Comrade Postyshev most ably expressed these doubts. He said:

I have philosophized that the severe years of fighting have passed. Party members who have lost their backbones have broken down or have joined the camp of the enemy; healthy elements have fought for the party. These were the years of industrialization and collectivization. I never thought it possible that after this severe era had passed Karpov and people like him would find themselves in the camp of the enemy. [Karpov was a worker in the Ukrainian Central Committee whom Postyshev knew well.] And now, according to the testimony, it appears that Karpov was recruited in 1934 by the Trotskyites. I personally do not believe that in 1934 an honest party member who had trod the long road of unrelenting fight against enemies for the party and for socialism, would now be in the camp of the enemies. I do not believe it. . . . I cannot imagine how it would be possible to travel with the party during the difficult years and then, in 1934, join the Trotskyites. It is an odd thing. . . .(*Movement in the hall.*)

Using Stalin's formulation, namely, that the closer we are to Socialism the more enemies we will have, and using the resolution of the February–March Central Committee plenum passed on the basis of Yezhov's report—the *provocateurs* who had infiltrated the organs of state security, together with conscienceless careerists began to cover with the party name the mass terror against party cadres, cadres of the Soviet state and ordinary Soviet citizens. It should suffice to say that the number of arrests based on charges of counterrevolutionary crimes grew ten times between 1936 and 1937.

"CONFESSIONS"

It is known that brutal willfulness was practiced against leading party workers. The Party Statutes, approved at the Seventeenth Party Congress, were based on Leninist principles expressed at the Tenth Party Congress. They stated that, in order to apply an extreme method such as exclusion from the party against a Central Committee member, against a Central Committee candidate, and against a member of the Party Control Commission, "it is necessary to call a Central Committee plenum and to invite to the plenum all Central Committee candidate members and all members of the Party Control Commission"; only if two thirds of the members of such a general assembly of responsible party leaders find it necessary, only then can a Central Committee member or candidate be expelled.

The majority of the Central Committee members and candidates elected at the Seventeenth Congress and arrested in 1937–38 were expelled from the party illegally through the brutal abuse of the Party Statutes, because the question of their expulsion was never studied at the Central Committee plenum.

Now, when the cases of some of these so-called spies and saboteurs were examined, it was found that all their cases were fabricated. Confessions of guilt of many arrested and charged with enemy activity were gained with the help of cruel and inhuman tortures.

At the same time, Stalin, as we have been informed by members of the Political Bureau of that time, did not show them the statements of many accused political activists when they retracted their confessions before the military tribunal and asked for an objective examination of their cases. There were many such declarations, and Stalin without doubt knew of them.

The Central Committee considers it absolutely necessary to inform the Congress of many such fabricated "cases" against the members of the party's Central Committee elected at the Seventeenth Party Congress.

An example of vile provocation, of odious falsification and of criminal violation of revolutionary legality is the case of the former candidate member of the Central Committee Political Bureau, one of the most eminent workers of the party and of the Soviet Government, Comrade Eikhe, who was a party member since 1905. *(Commotion in the hall.)*

Comrade Eikhe was arrested on 29 April 1938 on the basis of slanderous materials, without the sanction of the Prosecutor of the USSR, which was finally received fifteen months after the arrest.

Investigation of Eikhe's case was made in a manner which most brutally violated Soviet legality and was accompanied by willfulness and falsification.

Eikhe was forced under torture to sign ahead of time a protocol of his confession prepared by the investigative judges, in which he and several other eminent party workers were accused of anti-Soviet activity.

On 1 October 1939 Eikhe sent his declaration to Stalin in which he categorically denied his guilt and asked for an examination of his case. In his declaration he wrote, "There is no more bitter misery than to sit in the jail of a government for which I have always fought."

A second declaration of Eikhe has been preserved which he sent to Stalin on 27 October 1939; in it he cited facts very convincingly and countered the slanderous accusations made against him, arguing that this provocatory accusation was on the one hand the work of real Trotskyites whose arrests he had sanctioned as First Secretary of the West Siberian Krai [Territory] Party Committee and who conspired in order to take revenge on him, and, on the other hand, the result of the base falsification of materials by the investigative judges.

Eikhe wrote in his declaration:

On 25 October of this year I was informed that the investigation in my case has been concluded and I was given access to the materials of this investigation. Had I been guilty of only one hundredth of the crimes with which I am charged, I would not have dared to send you this pre-execution declaration; however, I have not been guilty of even one of the things with which I am charged and my heart is clean of even the shadow of baseness. I have never in my life told you a word of falsehood and now, finding my two feet in the grave, I am also not lying. My whole case is a typical example of provocation, slander, and violation of the elementary basis of revolutionary legality. . . .

. . . The confessions which were made part of my file are not only absurd but contain some slander of the Central Committee of the All-Union Communist Party (Bolsheviks) and the Council of People's Commissars because correct resolutions of the Central Committee of the All-Union Communist Party (Bolsheviks) and of the Council of People's Commissars which were made not on my initiative and without my participation are presented as hostile acts of counterrevolutionary organizations made at my suggestion. . . .

I am now alluding to the most disgraceful part of my life and to my really grave guilt against the party and against you. This is my confession of counterrevolutionary activity. . . . The case is as follows: Not being able to suffer the tortures to which I was submitted by Ushakov and Nikolayev—and especially by the first one—who utilized the knowledge that my broken ribs have not properly mended and have caused me great pain, I have been forced to accuse myself and others.

The majority of my confession has been suggested or dictated by Ushakov, and the remainder is my reconstruction of NKVD materials from Western Siberia for which I assumed all responsibility. If some part of the story which Ushakov fabricated and which I signed did not properly hang together, I was forced to sign another variation. The same thing was done to Rukhimovich, who was at first designated as a member of the reserve net and whose name later was removed without telling me anything about it; the same was also done with the leader of the reserve net, supposedly created by Bukharin in 1935. At first I wrote my name in, and then I was instructed to insert Mezhlauk. There were other similar incidents.

. . . I am asking and begging you that you again examine my case, and this not for the purpose of sparing me but in order to

> unmask the vile provocation which, like a snake, wound itself around many persons in a great degree due to my meanness and criminal slander. I have never betrayed you or the party. I know that I perish because of vile and mean work of the enemies of the party and of the people, who fabricated the provocation against me.

It would appear that such an important declaration was worth an examination by the Central Committee. This, however, was not done, and the declaration was transmitted to Beria while the terrible maltreatment of the Political Bureau candidate, Comrade Eikhe, continued.

On 2 February 1940 Eikhe was brought before the court. Here he did not confess any guilt but said the following:

> In all the so-called confessions of mine there is not one letter written by me with the exception of my signatures under the protocols which were forced from me. I have made my confession under pressure from the investigative judge who from the time of my arrest tormented me. After that I began to write all this nonsense. . . . The most important thing for me is to tell the court, the party, and Stalin that I am not guilty. I have never been guilty of any conspiracy. I will die believing in the truth of party policy as I have believed in it during my whole life.

On 4 February Eikhe was shot. *(Indignation in the hall.)*

It has been definitely established now that Eikhe's case was fabricated; he has been posthumously rehabilitated.

Comrade Rudzutak, candidate-member of the Political Bureau, member of the party since 1905, who spent 10 years in a tsarist hard-labor camp, completely retracted in court the confession which was forced from him. The protocol of the session of the Collegium of the Supreme Military Court contains the following statement by Rudzutak:

> The only plea which he places before the court is that the Central Committee of the All-Union Communist Party (Bolsheviks) be informed that there is in the NKVD an as yet not liquidated center which is craftily manufacturing cases, which forces innocent persons to confess; there is no opportunity to prove one's nonparticipation in crimes to which the confessions of various persons testify. The investigative methods are such that they force people to lie and to slander entirely innocent persons in

addition to those who already stand accused. He asks the Court that he be allowed to inform the Central Committee of the All-Union Communist Party (Bolsheviks) about all this in writing. He assures the Court that he personally never had any evil designs in regard to the policy of our party because he had always agreed with the party policy pertaining to all spheres of economic and cultural activity.

This declaration of Rudzutak was ignored, despite the fact that Rudzutak was in his time the chief of the Central Control Commission which was called into being in accordance with Lenin's concept for the purpose of fighting for party unity. . . . In this manner fell the chief of this highly authoritative party organ, a victim of brutal willfulness; he was not even called before the Central Committee's Political Bureau because Stalin did not want to talk to him. Sentence was pronounced on him in twenty minutes and he was shot. *(Indignation in the hall.)*

After careful examination of the case in 1955, it was established that the accusation against Rudzutak was false and that it was based on slanderous materials. Rudzutak has been rehabilitated posthumously.

FABRICATING PLOTS

The way in which the former NKVD workers manufactured various fictitious "anti-Soviet centers" and "blocs" with the help of provocatory methods is seen from the confession of Comrade Rozenblum, party member since 1906, who was arrested in 1937 by the Leningrad NKVD.

During the examination in 1955 of the Komarov case, Rozenblum revealed the following fact: When Rozenblum was arrested in 1937, he was subjected to terrible torture during which he was ordered to confess false information concerning himself and other persons. He was then brought to the office of Zakovsky, who offered him freedom on condition that he make before the court a false confession fabricated in 1937 by the NKVD concerning "sabotage, espionage, and diversion in a terroristic center in Leningrad." *(Movement in the hall.)*

With unbelievable cynicism, Zakovsky told about the vile "mechanism" for the crafty creation of fabricated "anti-Soviet plots."

"In order to illustrate it to me," stated Rozenblum,

> Zakovsky gave me several possible variants of the organization of this center and its branches. After he detailed the organization to me, Zakovsky told me that the NKVD would prepare the case of this center, remarking that the trial would be public. Before the court were to be brought four or five members of this center: Chudov, Ugarov, Smorodin, Pozern, Shaposhnikova (Chudov's wife), and others together with two or three members from the branches of this center. . . .
>
> . . . The case of the Leningrad center has to be built solidly, and for this reason witnesses are needed. Social origin (of course, in the past) and the party standing of the witness will play more than a small role.
>
> "You, yourself," said Zakovsky, "will not need to invent anything. The NKVD will prepare for you a ready outline for every branch of the center; you will have to study it carefully and to remember well all questions and answers which the Court might ask. This case will be ready in four or five months, or perhaps a half year. During all this time you will be preparing yourself so that you will not compromise the investigation and yourself. Your future will depend on how the trial goes and on its results. If you begin to lie and testify falsely, blame yourself. If you manage to endure it, you will save your head and we will feed and clothe you at the Government's cost until your death."

These are the kind of vile things which were then practiced. *(Movement in the hall.)*

Even more widely was the falsification of cases practiced in the provinces. The NKVD headquarters of the Sverdlov Oblast "discovered" the so-called Ural Uprising Staff—an organ of the bloc of rightists, Trotskyites, Socialist-Revolutionaries, church leaders—whose chief supposedly was the Secretary of the Sverdlov Oblast Party Committee and a member of the Central Committee, All-Union Communist Party (Bolsheviks), Kabakov, who had been a party member since 1914. The investigative materials of that time show that in almost all *krais*, *oblasts*, and republics there supposedly existed "rightist Trotskyite, espionage-terror, and diversionary-sabotage organizations and centers" and that the heads of such organizations as a rule—for no known reasons—were first secretaries of *oblast* or republic Communist Party committees or central committees. *(Movement in the hall.)*

Many thousands of honest and innocent Communists have died as a result of this monstrous falsification of such "cases," as a result of the fact that all kinds of slanderous "confessions" were accepted, and as a result of the practice of forcing accusations against oneself and others. In the same manner were fabricated the "cases" against eminent party and state workers—Kossior, Chubar, Postyshev, Kosaryev, and others.

In those years repressions on a mass scale were applied which were based on nothing tangible and which resulted in heavy cadre losses to the party.

The vicious practice was condoned of having the NKVD prepare lists of persons whose cases were under the jurisdiction of the Military Collegium and whose sentences were prepared in advance. Yezhov would send these lists to Stalin personally for his approval of the proposed punishment. In 1937–38, 383 such lists containing the names of many thousands of party, Soviet, Komsomol, Army, and economic workers were sent to Stalin. He approved these lists.

A large part of these cases are being reviewed now and a great part of them are being voided because they were baseless and falsified. Suffice it to say that from 1954 to the present time the Military Collegium of the Supreme Court has rehabilitated 7,679 persons, many of whom were rehabilitated posthumously.

Mass arrests of party, Soviet, economic, and military workers caused tremendous harm to our country and to the cause of socialist advancement.

Mass repressions had a negative influence on the moral-political condition of the party, created a situation of uncertainty, contributed to the spreading of unhealthy suspicion, and sowed distrust among Communists. All sorts of slanderers and careerists were active.

Resolutions of the January plenum of the Central Committee, All-Union Communist Party (Bolsheviks), in 1938 brought some measure of improvement to the party organizations. However, widespread repression also existed in 1938.

Only because our party has at its disposal such great moral-political strength was it possible for it to survive the difficult events in 1937–38 and to educate new cadres. There is, however, no doubt that our march forward toward Socialism and toward the preparation for the country's defense would have been much more successful were it not for the tremendous loss in the cadres suffered as a result of the baseless and false mass repressions in 1937–38.

STALIN'S RESPONSIBILITY

We are justly accusing Yezhov for the degenerate practices of 1937. But we have to answer these questions:

Could Yezhov have arrested Kossior, for instance, without the knowledge of Stalin? Was there an exchange of opinions or a Political Bureau decision concerning this?

No, there was not, as there was none regarding other cases of this type.

Could Yezhov have decided such important matters as the fate of such eminent party figures?

No, it would be a display of naïveté to consider this the work of Yezhov alone. It is clear that these matters were decided by Stalin, and that without his orders and his sanction Yezhov could not have done this.

We have examined the cases and have rehabilitated Kossior, Rudzutak, Postyshev, Kosaryev and others. For what causes were they arrested and sentenced? The review of evidence shows that there was no reason for this. They, like many others, were arrested without the prosecutor's knowledge.

In such a situation, there is no need for any approval, for what sort of an approval could there be when Stalin decided everything? He was the chief prosecutor in these cases. Stalin not only agreed to, but on his own initiative issued, arrest orders. We must say this so that the delegates to the

Congress can clearly undertake and themselves assess this and draw the proper conclusions.

Facts prove that many abuses were made on Stalin's orders without reckoning with any norms of party and Soviet legality. Stalin was a very distrustful man, morbidly suspicious; we knew this from our work with him. He could look at a man and say: "Why are your eyes so shifty today?" or "Why are you turning so much today and why do you avoid looking directly into my eyes?"

This sickly suspicion created in him a general distrust even toward eminent party workers whom he had known for years. Everywhere and in everything he saw "enemies," "two-facers," and "spies."

Possessing unlimited power, he indulged in great willfulness and choked a person morally and physically. A situation was created where one could not express one's own will.

When Stalin said that one or another should be arrested, it was necessary to accept on faith that he was an "enemy of the people." Meanwhile, Beria's gang, which ran the organs of state security, outdid itself in proving the guilt of the arrested and the truth of materials which it falsified. And what proofs were offered? The confessions of the arrested. And the investigative judges accepted these "confessions."

And how is it possible that a person confesses to crimes which he has not committed? Only in one way—because of application of physical methods of pressuring him, tortures, bringing him to a state of unconsciousness, deprivation of his judgment, taking away of his human dignity. In this manner were "confessions" secured.

When the wave of mass arrests began to recede in 1939, and the leaders of territorial party organizations began to accuse the NKVD workers of using methods of physical pressure on the arrested, Stalin dispatched a coded telegram on 20 January 1939 to the committee secretaries of *oblasts* and *krais*, to the Central Committees of republic communist parties, to the People's Commissars of Internal Affairs and to the heads of NKVD organizations. The telegram stated:

The Central Committee of the All-Union Communist Party (Bolsheviks) explains that the application of methods of physical pressure in NKVD practice is permissible from 1937 on, in accordance with permission of the Central Committee of the All-Union Communist Party (Bolsheviks). . . . It is known that all bourgeois intelligence services use methods of physical influence against representatives of the socialist proletariat and that they use them in their most scandalous forms.

The question arises as to why the socialist intelligence service should be more humanitarian against the mad agents of the bourgeosie, against the deadly enemies of the working class and of the *kolkhoz* workers. The Central Committee of the All-Union Communist Party (Bolsheviks) considers that physical pressure should still be used obligatorily, as an exception applicable to known and obstinate enemies of the people, as a method both justifiable and appropriate.

Thus, Stalin sanctioned in the name of the Central Committee of the All-Union Communist Party (Bolsheviks) the most brutal violation of socialist legality—torture and oppression—which led as we have seen to the slandering and self-accusation of innocent people.

Not long ago—only several days before the present Congress—we called to the Central Committee Presidium session and interrogated the investigative judge Rodos, who in his time investigated and interrogated Kossior, Chubar, and Kosaryev. He is a vile person, with the brain of a bird, and morally completely degenerate. And it was this man who was deciding the fate of prominent party workers; he was making judgments also concerning the politics in these matters, because, having established their "crime," he provided therewith materials from which important political implications could be drawn.

The question arises whether a man with such an intellect could alone make the investigation in a manner to prove the guilt of people such as Kossior and others. No, he could not have done it without proper directives. At the Central Committee Presidium session he told us: "I was told that Kossior and Chubar were people's enemies and for this reason, I, as an investigative judge, had to make them confess that they are enemies." (*Indignation in the hall.*)

He could do this only through long tortures, which he did, receiving detailed instructions from Beria. We must say that at the Central Committee Presidium session he cynically declared, "I thought that I was executing the orders of the party."

In this manner, Stalin's orders concerning the use of methods of physical pressure against the arrested were in practice executed.

These and many other facts show that all norms of correct party solution of problems were invalidated and everything was dependent upon the willfulness of one man.

STALIN IN THE PATRIOTIC WAR

The power accumulated in the hands of one person, Stalin, led to serious consequences during the Great Patriotic War.

When we look at many of our novels, films, and historical "scientific studies," the role of Stalin in the Patriotic War appears to be entirely improbable. Stalin has foreseen everything. The Soviet Army, on the basis of a strategic plan prepared by Stalin long before, used the tactics of so-called active defense, i.e., tactics which, as we know, allowed the Germans to come up to Moscow and Stalingrad. Using such tactics, the Soviet Army, supposedly, thanks only to Stalin's genius, turned the offensive and subdued the enemy. The epic victory gained through the armed might of the land of the Soviets, through our heroic people, is ascribed in this type of novel, film, and "scientific study" as being completely due to the strategic genius of Stalin.

We have to analyze this matter carefully because it has a tremendous significance not only from the historical, but especially from the political, educational, and practical point of view.

What are the facts of this matter?

Before the war, our press and all our political-educational work was characterized by its bragging tone: When an enemy violates the holy Soviet soil, then for every blow of the enemy we will answer three blows, and we will battle the enemy on his soil and we will win without much harm to ourselves. But these positive statements were not based in all areas on concrete facts, which would actually guarantee the immunity of our borders.

During the war and after the war, Stalin put forward the thesis that the tragedy which our nation experienced in the first part of the war was the result of the "unexpected" attack of the Germans against the Soviet Union. But, comrades, this is completely untrue. As soon as Hitler came to power in Germany he assigned to himself the task of liquidating communism. The fascists were saying this openly; they did not hide their plans.

In order to attain this aggressive end, all sorts of pacts and blocs were created, such as the famous Berlin-Rome-Tokyo Axis. Many facts from the prewar period clearly showed that Hitler was going all out to begin a war against the Soviet state, and that he had concentrated large armed forces, including armored units, near the Soviet borders.

Documents which have now been published show that by 3 April 1941, Churchill, through his ambassador to the USSR, Cripps, personally warned Stalin that the Germans had begun regrouping their armed units with the intent of attacking the Soviet Union.

It is self-evident that Churchill did not do this at all because of his friendly feeling toward the Soviet nation. He had in this his own imperialistic goals—to bring Germany and the USSR into a bloody war and thereby to strengthen the position of the British Empire.

Just the same, Churchill affirmed in his writings that he sought to "warn Stalin and call his attention to the danger which threatened him." Churchill stressed this repeatedly in his dispatches of 18 April and in the following days.

However, Stalin took no heed of these warnings. What is more, Stalin ordered that no credence be given to information of this sort, in order not to provoke the initiation of military operations.

We must assert that information of this sort concerning the threat of German armed invasion of Soviet territory was coming in also from our own military and diplomatic sources; however, because the leadership was conditioned against such information, such data were dispatched with fear and assessed with reservation.

Thus, for instance, information sent from Berlin on 6 May 1941 by the Soviet military attaché, Captain Vorontsov, stated: "Soviet citizen . . . Bozer communicated to the deputy naval attaché that according to a statement of a certain German officer from Hitler's headquarters, Germany is preparing to invade the USSR on 14 May through Finland, the Baltic countries, and Latvia. At the same time Moscow and Leningrad will be heavily raided and paratroopers landed in border cities."

In his report of 22 May 1941, the deputy military attaché in Berlin, Khlopov, communicated that "the attack of the German Army is reportedly scheduled for 15 June, but it is possible that it may begin in the first days of June."

A cable from our London Embassy dated 18 June 1941 stated:

> As of now Cripps is deeply convinced of the inevitability of armed conflict between Germany and the USSR which will begin not later than the middle of June. According to Cripps, the Germans have presently concentrated 147 divisions (including air force and service units) along the Soviet borders.

Despite these particularly grave warnings, the necessary steps were not taken to prepare the country properly for defense and to prevent it from being caught unawares.

Did we have time and the capabilities for such preparations? Yes, we had the time and capabilities. Our industry was already so developed that it was capable of supplying fully the Soviet Army with everything that it needed. This is proven by the fact that although during the war we lost almost half of our industry and important industrial and food-production areas as the result of enemy occupation of the Ukraine, Northern Caucasus, and other western parts of the country, the Soviet nation was still able to organize the production of military equipment in the eastern parts of the country, install there equipment taken from the western industrial areas, and supply our armed forces with everything which was necessary to destroy the enemy.

Had our industry been mobilized properly and in time to supply the Army with the necessary matériel, our wartime losses would have been decidedly smaller. Such mobilization had not been, however, started in time. And already in the first days of the war it became evident that our Army was badly armed, that we did not have enough artillery, tanks and planes to throw the enemy back.

Soviet science and technology produced excellent models of tanks and artillery pieces before the war. But mass production of all this was not organized, and, as a matter of fact, we started to modernize our military equipment only on the eve of the war.

As a result, at the time of the enemy's invasion of the Soviet land, we did not have sufficient quantities either of old machinery which was no longer used for armament production or of new machinery which we had planned to introduce into armament production.

The situation with antiaircraft artillery was especially bad; we did not organize the production of antitank ammunition. Many fortified regions proved to be indefensible as soon as they were attacked, because the old arms had been withdrawn and new ones were not yet available there.

This pertained, alas, not only to tanks, artillery, and planes. At the outbreak of the war we did not even have sufficient numbers of rifles to arm the mobilized manpower. I recall that in those days I telephoned to Comrade Malenkov from Kiev and told him, "People have volunteered for the new Army and demand arms. You must send us arms."

Malenkov answered me, "We cannot send you arms. We are sending all our rifles to Leningrad and you have to arm yourselves." *(Movement in the hall.)*

Such was the armament situation.

In this connection we cannot forget, for instance, the following fact: Shortly before the invasion of the Soviet Union by the Hitlerite Army, Kirponos, who was chief of the Kiev Special Military District (he was later killed at the front) wrote to Stalin that the German armies were at the Bug River, were preparing for an attack and in the very near future would probably start an offensive. In this connection, Kirponos proposed that a strong defense be organized, that 300,000 people be evacuated from the border areas and that several strong points be organized there: antitank ditches, trenches for the soldiers, etc.

Moscow answered this proposition with the assertion that this would be a provocation, that no preparatory defense work should be undertaken at the borders, that the Germans were not to be given any pretext for the initiation of military action against us. Thus, our borders were insufficiently prepared to repel the enemy.

STALIN AND THE FIRST DAYS OF THE WAR

When the fascist armies had actually invaded Soviet territory and military operation had begun, Moscow issued the order that the German fire was not to be returned. Why? It was because Stalin, despite evident facts, thought that the war had not yet started, that this was only a provocative action on the part of several undisciplined sections of the German Army, and that our reaction might serve as a reason for the Germans to begin the war.

The following fact is also known: On the eve of the invasion of the territory of the Soviet Union by the Hitlerite Army, a certain German citizen crossed our border and stated that the German armies had received orders to start the offensive against the Soviet Union on the night of 22 June at three o'clock. Stalin was informed about this immediately, but even this warning was ignored.

As you see everything was ignored: warnings of certain Army commanders, declarations of deserters from the enemy army, and even the open hostility of the enemy. Is this an example of the alertness of the chief of the party and of the state at this particularly significant historical moment?

And what were the results of this carefree attitude, this disregard of clear facts? The result was that in the first hours and days the enemy destroyed in our border regions a large part of our Air Force, artillery and other military equipment; he annihilated large numbers of our military cadres and disorganized our military leadership; consequently we could not prevent the enemy from marching deep into the country.

Very grievous consequences, especially in reference to the beginning of the war, followed Stalin's annihilation of many military commanders and political workers during 1937–41 because of his suspiciousness and through slanderous accusations. During these years repressions were instituted against certain parts of military cadres beginning literally at the company and battalion commander level and extending to the higher military centers; during this time the cadre of leaders who had gained military experience in Spain and in the Far East was almost completely liquidated.

The policy of large-scale repression against the military cadres led also to undermined military discipline, because for several years officers of all ranks and even soldiers in the party and Komsomol cells were taught to "unmask" their superiors as hidden enemies. *(Movement in the hall.)*

It is natural that this caused a negative influence on the state of military discipline in the early war period.

And, as you know, we had before the war excellent military cadres which were unquestionably loyal to the party and to the Fatherland. Suffice it to say that those of them who managed to survive despite severe tortures to which they were subjected in the prisons, have from the first war days shown themselves real patriots and heroically fought for the glory of the Fatherland; I have here in mind such comrades as Rokossovsky (who, as you know, had been jailed), Gorbatov, Maretskov (who is a delegate at the present Congress), Podlas (he was an excellent commander who perished at the front), and many, many others. However, many such commanders perished in camps and jails and the Army saw them no more.

All this brought about the situation which existed at the beginning of the war and which was the great threat to our Fatherland.

It would be incorrect to forget that, after the first severe disaster and defeats at the front, Stalin thought that this was the end. In one of his speeches in those days he said: "All that which Lenin created we have lost forever."

After this Stalin for a long time actually did not direct the military operations and ceased to do anything whatever. He returned to active leadership only when some members of the Political Bureau visited him and told him that it was necessary to take certain steps immediately in order to improve the situation at the front.

Therefore, the threatening danger which hung over our Fatherland in the first period of the war was largely due to the faulty methods of directing the nation and the party by Stalin himself.

However, we speak not only about the moment when the war began, which led to serious disorganization of our Army and brought us severe losses. Even after the war began, the nervousness and hysteria which Stalin demonstrated, interfering with actual military operation, caused our Army serious damage.

Stalin was very far from an understanding of the real situation which was developing at the front. This was natural because, during the whole Patriotic War, he never visited any section of the front or any liberated city except for one short ride on the Mozhaisk highway during a stabilized situation at the front. To this incident were dedicated many literary works full of fantasies of all sorts and so many paintings. Simultaneously, Stalin was interfering with the operations and issuing orders which did not take into consideration the real situation at a given section of the front and which could not help but result in huge personnel losses.

I will allow myself in this connection to bring out one characteristic fact which illustrates how Stalin directed operations at the fronts. There is present at this Congress Marshal Bagramyan who was once the Chief of Operations in the headquarters of the southwestern front and who can corroborate what I will tell you.

When there developed an exceptionally serious situation for our Army in 1942 in the Kharkov region, we had correctly decided to drop an operation whose objective was to encircle Kharkov, because the real situation at that time would have threatened our Army with fatal consequences if this operation were continued.

We communicated this to Stalin, stating that the situation demanded changes in operational plans so that the enemy would be prevented from liquidating a sizable concentration of our Army.

Contrary to common sense, Stalin rejected our suggestion and issued the order to continue the operation aimed at the encirclement of Kharkov, despite the fact that at this time many Army concentrations were themselves actually threatened with encirclement and liquidation.

I telephoned to Vasilevsky and begged him:

"Alexander Mikhailovich, take a map"—Vasilevsky is present here—"and show Comrade Stalin the situation which has developed." We should note that Stalin planned operations on a globe. *(Animation in the hall.)*

Yes, comrades, he used to take the globe and trace the front line on it. I said to Comrade Vasilevsky: "Show him the situation on a map; in the present situation we cannot continue the operation which was planned. The old decision must be changed for the good of the cause."

Vasilevsky replied, saying that Stalin had already studied this problem and that he, Vasilevsky, would not see Stalin further concerning this matter, because the latter didn't want to hear any arguments on the subject of this operation.

After my talk with Vasilevsky, I telephoned to Stalin at his villa. But Stalin did not answer the telephone and Malenkov was at the receiver. I told Comrade Malenkov that I was calling from the front and that I wanted to speak personally to Stalin. Stalin informed me through Malenkov that I should speak with Malenkov. I stated for the second time that I wished to inform Stalin personally about the grave situation which had arisen for us at the front. But Stalin did not consider it convenient to raise the phone and again stated that I should speak to him through Malenkov, although he was only a few steps from the telephone.

After "listening" in this manner to our plea, Stalin said: "Let everything remain as it is!"

And what was the result of this? The worst that we had expected. The Germans surrounded our Army concentrations and consequently we lost hundreds of thousands of our soldiers. This is Stalin's military "genius"; this is what it cost us. *(Movement in the hall.)*

On one occasion after the war, during a meeting of Stalin with members of the Political Bureau, Anastas Ivanovich Mikoyan mentioned that Khrushchev must have been right when he telephoned concerning the Kharkov operation and that it was unfortunate that his suggestion had not been accepted.

You should have seen Stalin's fury! How could it be admitted that he, Stalin, had not been right! He is after all a "genius," and a genius cannot help but be right! Everyone can err, but Stalin considered that he never erred, that he was always right. He never acknowledged to anyone that he had made any mistake, large or small, despite the fact that he made not a few mistakes in the matter of theory and in his practical activity. After the Party Congress we shall probably have to reevaluate many wartime military operations and to present them in their true light.

The tactics on which Stalin insisted without knowing the essence of the conduct of battle operations cost us much blood until we succeeded in stopping the opponent and going over to the offensive.

The military know that already by the end of 1941, instead of great operational maneuvers flanking the opponent and penetrating behind his back, Stalin demanded incessant frontal attacks and the capture of one village after another. Because of this we paid with great losses until our generals, on whose shoulders rested the whole weight of conducting the war, succeeded in changing the situation and shifting to flexible-maneuver operations, which immediately brought serious changes at the front favorable to us.

STALIN AND HIS GENERALS

All the more shameful was the fact that after our great victory over the enemy which cost us so much, Stalin began to downgrade many of the commanders who contributed so much to the victory over the enemy, because Stalin excluded every possibility that services rendered at the front should be credited to anyone but himself.

Stalin was very much interested in the assessment of Comrade Zhukov as a military leader. He asked me often for my opinion of Zhukov. I told him then, "I have known Zhukov for a long time; he is a good general and a good military leader."

After the war Stalin began to tell all kinds of nonsense about Zhukov, among other things the following, "You praised Zhukov, but he does not deserve it. It is said that before each operation at the front Zhukov used to behave as follows: He used to take a handful of earth, smell it, and say, 'We can begin the attack,' or the opposite, 'The planned operation cannot be carried out.' " I stated at that time, "Comrade Stalin, I do not know who invented this, but it is not true."

It is possible that Stalin himself invented these things for the purpose of minimizing the role and military talents of Marshal Zhukov.

In this connection, Stalin very energetically popularized himself as a great leader; in various ways he tried to inculcate in the people the version that all victories gained by the Soviet nation during the Great Patriotic War were due to the courage, daring, and genius of Stalin and of no one else. Exactly like Kuzma Kryuchkov [a famous Cossack who performed heroic feats against the Germans], he put one dress on seven people at the same time. *(Animation in the hall.)*

In the same vein, let us take, for instance, our historical and military films and some literary creations; they make us feel sick. Their true objective is the propagation of the theme of praising Stalin as a military genius. Let us recall the film, *The Fall of Berlin*. Here only Stalin acts; he issues orders in the hall in which there are many empty chairs and only one man approaches him and reports something to him—that is Poskrebyshev, his loyal shield-bearer. *(Laughter in the hall.)*

And where is the military command? Where is the Political Bureau? Where is the Government? What are they doing and with what are they engaged? There is nothing about them in the film. Stalin acts for everybody; he does not reckon with anyone; he asks no one for advice. Everything is shown to the nation in his false light. Why? In order to surround Stalin with glory, contrary to the facts and contrary to historical truth.

The question arises: And where are the military, on whose shoulders rested the burden of the war? They are not in the film; with Stalin in, no room was left for them.

Not Stalin, but the party as a whole, the Soviet Government, our heroic Army, its talented leaders and brave soldiers, the whole Soviet nation—these are the ones who assured the victory in the Great Patriotic War. *(Tempestuous and prolonged applause.)*

The Central Committee members, ministers, our economic leaders, leaders of Soviet culture, directors of territorial party and Soviet organizations, engineers, and technicians—every one of them in his own place of work generously gave of his strength and knowledge toward ensuring victory over the enemy.

Exceptional heroism was shown by our hard core—surrounded by glory is our whole working class, our *kolkhoz* peasantry, the Soviet intelligentsia, who under the leadership of party organizations overcame untold hardships and, bearing the hardships of war, devoted all their strength to the cause of the defense of the Fatherland.

Great and brave deeds during the war were accomplished by our Soviet women who bore on their backs the heavy load of production work in the factories, on the *kolkhozes*, and in various economic and cultural sectors; many women participated directly in the Great Patriotic War at the fronts; our brave youth contributed immeasurably at the front and at home to the defense of the Soviet Fatherland and to the annihilation of the enemy.

Immortal are the services of the Soviet soldiers, of our commanders and political workers of all ranks; after the loss of a considerable part of the Army in the first war months they did not lose their heads and were able to reorganize during the progress of combat; they created and toughened during the progress of the war a strong and heroic Army and not only stood off pressures of the strong and cunning enemy but also smashed him.

The magnificent and heroic deeds of hundreds of millions of people of the East and of the West during the fight against the threat of fascist subjugation which loomed before us will live centuries and millennia in the memory of thankful humanity. *(Thunderous applause.)*

The main role and the main credit for the victorious ending of the war belongs to our Communist Party, to the armed forces of the Soviet Union, and to the tens of millions of Soviet people raised by the party. *(Thunderous and prolonged applause.)*

STALIN COMMITS GENOCIDE AND OTHER CRIMES

Comrades, let us reach for some other facts. The Soviet Union is justly considered as a model of a multinational state because we have in practice assured the equality and friendship of all nations which live in our great Fatherland.

All the more monstrous are the acts whose initiator was Stalin and which are rude violations of the basic Leninist principles of the nationality policy of the Soviet state. We refer to the mass deportations from their native places of whole nations, together with all Communists and Komsomols without any exception; this deportation action was not dictated by any military considerations.

Thus, already at the end of 1943, when there occurred a permanent breakthrough at the fronts of the Great Patriotic War benefiting the Soviet Union, a decision was taken and executed concerning the deportation of all the Karachai from the lands on which they lived.

In the same period, at the end of December, 1943, the same lot befell the whole population of the Autonomous Kalmyk Republic. In March, 1944, all the Chechen and Ingush peoples were deported and the Chechen-Ingush Autonomous Republic was liquidated. In April, 1944, all

Balkars were deported to faraway places from the territory of the Kabardino-Balkar Autonomous Republic and the Republic itself was renamed the Autonomous Kabardian Republic. The Ukrainians avoided meeting this fate only because there were too many of them and there was no place to which to deport them. Otherwise, he would have deported them also. *(Laughter and animation in the hall.)*

Not only a Marxist-Leninist but also no man of common sense can grasp how it is possible to make whole nations responsible for inimical activity, including women, children, old people, Communists, and Komsomols, to use mass repression against them, and to expose them to misery and suffering for the hostile acts of individual persons or groups of persons.

After the conclusion of the Patriotic War, the Soviet nation stressed with pride the magnificent victories gained through great sacrifices and tremendous efforts. The country experienced a period of political enthusiasm. The party came out of the war even more united; in the fire of the war, party cadres were tempered and hardened. Under such conditions nobody could have even thought of the possibility of some plot in the party.

And it was precisely at this time that the so-called Leningrad affair was born. As we have now proven, this case was fabricated. Those who innocently lost their lives included Comrades Voznesensky, Kuznetsov, Rodionov, Popkov, and others.

As is known, Voznesensky and Kuznetsov were talented and eminent leaders. Once they stood very close to Stalin. It is sufficient to mention that Stalin made Voznesensky first deputy to the chairman of the Council of Ministers and Kuznetsov was elected secretary of the Central Committee. The very fact that Stalin entrusted Kuznetsov with the supervision of the state-security organs shows the trust which he enjoyed.

How did it happen that these persons were branded as enemies of the people and liquidated?

Facts prove that the "Leningrad affair" is also the result of willfullness which Stalin exercised against party cadres.

Had a normal situation existed in the party's Central Committee and in the Central Committee Political Bureau, affairs of this nature would have been examined there in accordance with party practice, and all pertinent facts assessed; as a result, such an affair, as well as others, would not have happened.

We must state that, after the war, the situation became even more complicated. Stalin became even more capricious, irritable, and brutal; in particular his suspicion grew. His persecution mania reached unbelievable dimensions. Many workers were becoming enemies before his very eyes. After the war, Stalin separated himself from the collective even more. Everything was decided by him alone without any consideration for anyone or anything.

This unbelievable suspicion was cleverly taken advantage of by the abject *provocateur* and vile enemy, Beria, who had murdered thousands of Communists and loyal Soviet people. The elevation of Voznesensky and Kuznetsov alarmed Beria. As we have now proven, it had been precisely Beria who had "suggested" to Stalin the fabrication by him and by his confidante of materials in the form of declarations and anonymous letters, and in the form of various rumors and talks.

The party's Central Committee has examined this so-called Leningrad affair; persons who innocently suffered are now rehabilitated and honor has been restored to the glorious Leningrad party organization. Abakumov and others who fabricated this affair were brought before a court; their trial took place in Leningrad and they received what they deserved.

The question arises: Why is it that we see the truth of this affair only now, and why did we not do something earlier, during Stalin's life, in order to prevent the loss of innocent lives? It was because Stalin personally supervised the "Leningrad affair," and the majority of the Political Bureau members did not, at that time, know all of the circumstances in these matters, and could not therefore intervene.

When Stalin received certain material from Beria and Abakumov, without examining these slanderous materials, he ordered an investigation of the "affair" of Voznesensky and Kuznetsov. With this, their fate was sealed.

Instructive in the same way is the case of the Mingrelian nationalist organization which supposedly existed in Georgia. As is known, resolutions by the Central Committee of the Communist Party of the Soviet Union were adopted concerning this case in November 1951 and in March 1952. These resolutions were adopted without prior discussion with the Political Bureau. Stalin had personally dictated them. They made serious accusations against many loyal Communists. On the basis of falsified documents, it was proved that there existed in Georgia a supposedly nationalistic organization whose objective was the liquidation of the Soviet power in that republic with the help of imperialistic powers.

In this connection, a number of responsible party and Soviet workers were arrested in Georgia. As was later proved, this was a slander directed against the Georgian party organization.

We know that there have been at times manifestations of local bourgeois nationalism in Georgia as in several other republics. The question arises: Could it be possible that in the period during which the resolutions referred to above were adopted, nationalist tendencies grew so much that there was a danger of Georgia's leaving the Soviet Union and joining Turkey? *(Animation in the hall, laughter.)*

This is, of course, nonsense. It is impossible to imagine how such assumptions could enter anyone's mind. Everyone knows how Georgia has developed economically and culturally under Soviet rule.

Industrial production of the Georgian Republic is 27 times greater than it was before the Revolution. Many new industries have arisen in Georgia which did not exist there before the Revolution: iron smelting, an oil industry, a machine-construction industry, etc. Illiteracy has long since been liquidated, which, in pre-Revolutionary Georgia, included 78 percent of the population.

Could the Georgians, comparing the situation in their republic with the hard situation of the working masses in

Turkey, be aspiring to join Turkey? In 1955, Georgia produced 18 times as much steel per person as Turkey. Georgia produces 9 times as much electrical energy per person as Turkey. According to the available 1950 census, 65 per cent of Turkey's total population are illiterate, and, of the women, 80 per cent are illiterate. Georgia has 19 institutions of higher learning which have about 39,000 students; this is 8 times more than in Turkey (for each 1,000 inhabitants). This prosperity of the working people has grown tremendously in Georgia under Soviet rule.

It is clear that, as the economy and culture develop, and as the socialist consciousness of the working masses in Georgia grows, the source from which bourgeois nationalism draws its strength evaporates.

As it developed, there was no nationalistic organization in Georgia. Thousands of innocent people fell victim to willfulness and lawlessness. All of this happened under the "genial" leadership of Stalin, "the great son of the Georgian nation," as Georgians like to refer to Stalin. *(Animation in the hall.)*

STALIN AS DIPLOMAT

The willfulness of Stalin showed itself not only in decisions concerning the internal life of the country but also in the international relations of the Soviet Union.

The July plenum of the Central Committee studied in detail the reasons for the development of conflict with Yugoslavia. It was a shameful role which Stalin played here. The "Yugoslavia affair" contained no problems which could not have been solved through party discussions among comrades. There was no significant basis for the development of the "affair"; it was completely possible to have prevented the rupture of relations with that country. This does not mean, however, that the Yugoslav leaders did not make mistakes or did not have shortcomings. But these mistakes and shortcomings were magnified in a monstrous manner by Stalin, which resulted in a break of relations with a friendly country.

I recall the first days when the conflict between the Soviet Union and Yugoslavia began artificially to be blown up. Once, when I came from Kiev to Moscow, I was invited to visit Stalin who, pointing to the copy of a letter lately sent to Tito, asked me, "Have you read this?"

Not waiting for my reply, he answered, "I will shake my little finger—and there will be no more Tito. He will fall."

We have dearly paid for this "shaking of the little finger." This statement reflected Stalin's delusions of grandeur, but he acted just that way: "I will shake my little finger—and there will be no Kossior"; "I will shake my little finger once more and Postyshev and Chubar will be no more"; "I will shake my little finger again—and Voznesensky, Kuznetsov, and many others will disappear."

But this did not happen to Tito. No matter how much or how little Stalin shook, not only his little finger but everything else that he could shake, Tito did not fall. Why? The reason was that, in this case of disagreement with the Yugoslav comrades, Tito had behind him a state and a people who had gone through a severe school of fighting for liberty and independence, a people which gave support to its leaders.

You see to what Stalin's delusions of grandeur led. He had completely lost consciousness of reality; he demonstrated his suspicion and haughtiness not only in relation to individuals in the USSR, but in relation to whole parties and nations.

We have carefully examined the case of Yugoslavia and have found a proper solution which is approved by the peoples of the Soviet Union and of Yugoslavia as well as by the working masses of all the people's democracies and by all progressive humanity. The liquidation of the abnormal relationship with Yugoslavia was done in the interest of the whole camp of Socialism, in the interest of strengthening peace in the whole world.

Let us also recall the "affair of the doctor-plotters." *(Animation in the hall.)*

Actually there was no "affair" outside of the declaration of the woman doctor Timashuk, who was probably influenced or ordered by someone (after all, she was an unofficial collaborator of the organs of state security) to write Stalin a letter in which she declared that doctors were applying supposedly improper methods of medical treatment.

Such a letter was sufficient for Stalin to reach an immediate conclusion that there are doctor-plotters in the Soviet Union. He issued orders to arrest a group of eminent Soviet medical specialists. He personally issued advice on the conduct of the investigation and the method of interrogation of the arrested persons. He said that the academician Vinogradov should be put in chains, another one should be beaten. Present at this Congress as a delegate is the former Minister of State Security, Comrade Ignatiev. Stalin told him curtly, "If you do not obtain confessions from the doctors, we will shorten you by a head." *(Tumult in the hall.)*

Stalin personally called the investigative judge, gave him instructions, advised him on which investigative methods should be used; these methods were simple—beat, beat and, once again, beat.

Shortly after the doctors were arrested, we members of the Political Bureau received protocols containing the doctors' confessions of guilt. After distributing these protocols, Stalin told us, "You are blind like young kittens; what will happen without me? The country will perish because you do not know how to recognize enemies."

The case was so presented that no one could verify the facts on which the investigation was based. There was no possibility of trying to verify facts by contacting those who had made the confessions of guilt.

We felt, however, that the case of the arrested doctors was questionable. We knew some of these people personally because they had once treated us. When we examined this "case" after Stalin's death, we found it to be fabricated from beginning to end.

This ignominious "case" was set up by Stalin; he did not, however, have the time in which to bring it to an end (as he conceived that end), and for this reason the doctors are still alive. Now all have been rehabilitated; they are working in the same places they were working before; they treat top individuals, not excluding members of the Government; they have our full confidence; and they execute their duties honestly, as they did before.

THE CRIMES OF BERIA

In organizing the various dirty and shameful cases, a very base role was played by the rabid enemy of our party, an agent of a foreign intelligence service—Beria, who had stolen into Stalin's confidence. In what way could this *provocateur* gain such a position in the party and in the state, so as to become the first deputy chairman of the Council of Ministers of the Soviet Union and a member of the Central Committee Political Bureau? It has now been established that this villain had climbed up the Government ladder over an untold number of corpses.

Were there any signs that Beria was an enemy of the party? Yes, there were. Already in 1937, at a Central Committee plenum, former People's Commissar of Health Protection Kaminsky said that Beria had worked for the Mussavat intelligence service. But the Central Committee plenum had barely concluded when Kaminsky was arrested and then shot. Had Stalin examined Kaminsky's statement? No, because Stalin believed in Beria, and that was enough for him. And when Stalin believed in anyone or anything, then no one could say anything which was contrary to his opinion; anyone who would dare to express opposition would have met the same fate as Kaminsky.

There were other signs, also. The declaration which Comrade Snegov made at the party's Central Committee is interesting. (Parenthetically speaking, he was also rehabilitated not long ago, after seventeen years in prison camps.) In this declaration, Snegov writes:

> In connection with the proposed rehabilitation of the former Central Committee member, Kartvelishvili-Lavryentiev, I have entrusted to the hands of the representative of the Committee of State Security a detailed deposition concerning Beria's role in the disposition of the Kartvelishvili case and concerning the criminal motives by which Beria was guided.

In my opinion, it is indispensable to recall an important fact pertaining to this case and to communicate it to the Central Committee, because I did not consider it as proper to include in the investigation documents.

On 30 October 1931, at the session of the Organizational Bureau of the Central Committee, All-Union Communist Party (Bolsheviks), Kartvelishvili, secretary of the Trans-Caucasian Krai Committee, made a report. All members of the executive of the Krai Committee were present; of them I alone am alive.

During this session, J. V. Stalin made a motion at the end of his speech concerning the organization of the secretariat of the Trans-Caucasian Krai Committee composed of the following: first secretary, Kartvelishvili; second secretary, Beria (it was then, for the first time in the party's history, that Beria's name was mentioned as a candidate for a party position). Kartvelishvili answered that he knew Beria well and for that reason refused categorically to work together with him. Stalin proposed then that this matter be left open and that it be solved in the process of the work itself. Two days later a decision was arrived at that Beria would receive the party post and that Kartvelishvili would be deported from the Trans-Caucasus.

This fact can be confirmed by Comrades Mikoyan and Kaganovich, who were present at that session.

The long, unfriendly relations between Kartvelishvili and Beria were widely known; they date back to the time when Comrade Sergo [Ordzhonikidze] was active in the Trans-Caucasus; Kartvelishvili was the closest assistant of Sergo. The unfriendly relationship impelled Beria to fabricate a "case" against Kartvelishvili.

It is a characteristic thing that in this "case" Kartvelishvili was charged with a terroristic act against Beria.

The indictment in the Beria case contains a discussion of his crimes. Some things should, however, be recalled, especially since it is possible that not all delegates to the Congress have read this document. I wish to recall Beria's bestial disposition of the cases of Kedrov, Golubiev, and Golubiev's adopted mother, Baturina—persons who wished to inform the Central Committee concerning Beria's treacherous activity. They were shot without any trial and the sentence was passed ex post facto, after the execution.

Here is what the old Communist, Comrade Kedrov, wrote to the Central Committee through Comrade Andreyev (Comrade Andreyev was then a Central Committee secretary):

I am calling to you for help from a gloomy cell of the Lefortorsky prison. Let my cry of horror reach your ears; do not remain deaf; take me under your protection; please, help remove the nightmare of interrogations and show that this is all a mistake.

I suffer innocently. Please believe me. Time will testify to the truth. I am not an *agent provocateur* of the tsarist Okhrana [secret police]; I am not a spy; I am not a member of an anti-Soviet organization of which I am being accused on the basis of denunciations. I am also not guilty of any other crimes against the party and the Government. I am an old Bolshevik, free of any stain; I have honestly fought for almost forty years in the ranks of the party for the good and the prosperity of the nation. . . .

. . . Today I, a 62-year-old man, am being threatened by the investigative judges with more severe, cruel, and degrading methods of physical pressure. They (the judges) are no longer capable of becoming aware of their error and of recognizing that their handling of my case is illegal and impermissible. They try to justify their actions by picturing me as a hardened and raving enemy and are demanding increased repressions. But let the party know that I am innocent and that there is nothing which can turn a loyal son of the party into an enemy, even right up to his last dying breath.

But I have no way out. I cannot divert from myself the hastily approaching new and powerful blows.

Everything, however, has its limits. My torture has reached the extreme. My health is broken, my strength and my energy are waning, the end is drawing near. To die in a Soviet prison, branded as a vile traitor to the Fatherland—what can be more monstrous for an honest man? And how monstrous all this is! Unsurpassed bitterness and pain grips my heart. No! No! This will not happen; this cannot be, I cry. Neither the party, nor the Soviet government, nor the people's commissar, L. P. Beria, will permit this cruel, irreparable injustice. I am firmly certain that, given a quiet, objective examination, without any foul rantings, without any anger and without the fearful tortures, it would be easy to prove the baselessness of the charges. I believe deeply that truth and justice will triumph. I believe. I believe.

The old Bolshevik, Comrade Kedrov, was found innocent by the Military Collegium. But, despite this, he was shot at Beria's order. *(Indignation in the hall.)*

Beria also handled cruelly the family of Comrade Ordzhonikidze. Why? Because Ordzhonikidze had tried to prevent Beria from realizing his shameful plans. Beria had cleared from his way all persons who could possibly interfere with him. Ordzhonikidze was always an opponent of Beria, which he told to Stalin. Instead of examining this affair and taking appropriate steps, Stalin allowed the liquidation of Ordzhonikidze's brother and brought Ordzhonikidze himself to such a state that he was forced to shoot himself. *(Indignation in the hall.)*

Such was Beria.

Beria was unmasked by the party's Central Committee shortly after Stalin's death. As a result of the particularly detailed legal proceedings, it was established that Beria had committed monstrous crimes and Beria was shot.

The question arises why Beria, who had liquidated tens of thousands of party and Soviet workers, was not unmasked during Stalin's life. He was not unmasked earlier because he had utilized very skillfully Stalin's weaknesses; feeding him with suspicions, he assisted Stalin in everything and acted with his support.

BUILDING UP THE CULT OF THE INDIVIDUAL

Comrades:

The cult of the individual acquired such monstrous size chiefly because Stalin himself, using all conceivable methods, supported the glorification of his own person. This is supported by numerous facts. One of the most characteristic examples of Stalin's self-glorification and of his lack of even elementary modesty is the edition of his *Short Biography*, which was published in 1948.

This book is an expression of the most dissolute flattery, an example of making a man into a godhead, of transforming him into an infallible sage, "the greatest leader, sublime strategist of all times and nations." Finally, no other words could be found with which to lift Stalin up to the heavens.

We need not give here examples of the loathsome adulation filling this book. All we need to add is that they all were approved and edited by Stalin personally and some of them were added in his own handwriting to the draft text of the book.

What did Stalin consider essential to write into this book? Did he want to cool the ardor of his flatterers who were composing his *Short Biography*? No! He marked the very places where he thought that the praise of his services was insufficient. Here are some examples characterizing Stalin's activity, added in Stalin's own hand:

> In this fight against the skeptics and capitulators, the Trotskyites, Zinovievites, Bukharinites, and Kamenevites, there was definitely welded together, after Lenin's death, that leading core of the party . . . that upheld the great banner of Lenin, rallied the party behind Lenin's behests, and brought the Soviet people into the broad road of industrializing the country and collectivizing the rural economy. The leader of this core and the guiding force of the party and the state was Comrade Stalin.

Thus writes Stalin himself! Then he adds:

> Although he performed his task of leader of the party and the people with consummate skill and enjoyed the unreserved support of the entire Soviet people, Stalin never allowed his work to be marred by the slightest hint of vanity, conceit or self-adulation.

Where and when could a leader so praise himself? Is this worthy of a leader of the Marxist-Leninist type? No. Precisely against this did Marx and Engels take such a strong position. This also was always sharply condemned by Vladimir Ilich Lenin.

In the draft text of his book appeared the following sentence: "Stalin is the Lenin of today." This sentence appeared to Stalin to be too weak, so, in his own handwriting, he changed it to read: "Stalin is the worthy continuer of Lenin's work, or, as it is said in our party, Stalin is the Lenin of today." You see how well it is said, not by the people but by Stalin himself.

It is possible to give many such self-praising appraisals written into the draft text of that book in Stalin's hand. Especially generously does he endow himself with praises pertaining to his military genius, to his talent for strategy.

I will cite one more insertion made by Stalin concerning the theme of the Stalinist military genius.

"The advanced Soviet science of war received further development," he writes,

> at Comrade Stalin's hands. Comrade Stalin elaborated the theory of the permanently operating factors that decide the issue of wars, of active defense and the laws of counteroffensive and offensive, of the cooperation of all services and arms in modern warfare, of the role of big tank masses and air forces in modern war, and of the artillery as the most formidable of the armed services. At the various stages of the war Stalin's genius found the correct solutions that took account of all the circumstances of the situation. (*Movement in the hall.*)

And, further, writes Stalin:

> Stalin's military mastership was displayed both in defense and offense. Comrade Stalin's genius enabled him to divine the enemy's plans and defeat them. The battles in which Comrade Stalin directed the Soviet armies are brilliant examples of operational military skill.

In this manner was Stalin praised as a strategist. Who did this? Stalin himself, not in his role as a strategist but in the role of an author-editor, one of the main creators of his self-adulatory biography. Such, comrades, are the facts. We should rather say shameful facts.

And one additional fact from the same *Short Biography* of Stalin. As is known, *The Short Course of the History of the All-Union Communist Party (Bolsheviks)* was written by a commission of the party Central Committee.

This book, parenthetically, was also permeated with the

cult of the individual and was written by a designated group of authors. This fact was reflected in the following formulation on the proof copy of the *Short Biography* of Stalin:

> A commission of the Central Committee of the All-Union Communist Party (Bolsheviks), under the direction of Comrade Stalin and with his most active personal participation, prepared *The Short Course of the History of the All-Union Communist Party (Bolsheviks).*

But even this phrase did not satisfy Stalin: The following sentence replaced it in the final version of the *Short Biography*:

> In 1938 appeared the book, *History of the All-Union Communist Party (Bolsheviks), Short Course,* written by Comrade Stalin and approved by a commission of the Central Committee of the All-Union Communist Party (Bolsheviks).

Can one add anything more? *(Animation in the hall.)*

As you see, a surprising metamorphosis changed the work created by a group into a book written by Stalin. It is not necessary to state how and why this metamorphosis took place.

A pertinent question comes to our mind: If Stalin is the author of this book, why did he need to praise the person of Stalin so much and to transform the whole post-October historical period of our glorious Communist Party solely into an action of "the Stalin genius"?

Did this book properly reflect the efforts of the party in the socialist transformation of the country, in the construction of socialist society, in the industrialization and collectivization of the country, and also other steps taken by the party which undeviatingly traveled the path outlined by Lenin? This book speaks principally about Stalin, about his speeches, about his reports. Everything without the smallest exception is tied to his name.

And when Stalin himself asserts that he himself wrote *The Short Course of the History of the All-Union Communist*

Party (*Bolsheviks*) this calls at least for amazement. Can a Marxist-Leninist thus write about himself, praising his own person to the heavens?

Or let us take the matter of the Stalin prizes. *(Movement in the hall.)*

Not even the tsars created prizes which they named after themselves.

Stalin recognized as the best a text of the national anthem of the Soviet Union which contains not a word about the Communist Party; it contains, however, the following unprecedented praise of Stalin: "Stalin brought us up in loyalty to the people. He inspired us to great toil and acts." In these lines of the anthem the whole educational, directional and inspirational activity of the great Leninist party is ascribed to Stalin. This is, of course, a clear deviation from Marxism-Leninism, a clear debasing and belittling of the role of the party. We should add for your information that the Presidium of the Central Committee has already passed a resolution concerning the composition of a new text of the anthem, which will reflect the role of the people and the role of the party. *(Loud, prolonged applause.)*

And was it without Stalin's knowledge that many of the largest enterprises and towns were named after him? Was it without his knowledge that Stalin monuments were erected in the whole country—these "memorials to the living"? It is a fact that Stalin himself had signed on 2 July 1951 a resolution of the USSR Council of Ministers concerning the erection on the Volga-Don Canal of an impressive monument to Stalin; on 4 September of the same year he issued an order making 33 tons of copper available for the construction of this impressive monument.

Anyone who has visited the Stalingrad area must have seen the huge statue which is being built there, and that on a site which hardly any people frequent. Huge sums were spent to build it at a time when people of this area had lived since the war in huts. Consider, yourself, was Stalin right when he wrote in his biography that "he did not allow in himself . . . even a shadow of conceit, pride, or self-adoration"?

STALIN TURNS AGAINST LENIN

At the same time, Stalin gave proofs of his lack of respect for Lenin's memory. It is not a coincidence that, despite the decision taken over thirty years ago to build a Palace of Soviets as a monument to Vladimir Ilyich, this Palace was not built, its construction was always postponed and the project allowed to lapse.

We cannot forget to recall the Soviet Government resolution of 14 August 1925 concerning "the founding of Lenin prizes for educational work." This resolution was published in the press, but until this day there are no Lenin prizes. This, too, should be corrected. *(Tumultuous, prolonged applause.)*

During Stalin's life—thanks to known methods which I have mentioned, and quoting facts, for instance, from the *Short Biography* of Stalin—all events were explained as if Lenin played only a secondary role, even during the October Socialist Revolution. In many films and in many literary works the figure of Lenin was incorrectly presented and inadmissibly depreciated.

Stalin loved to see the film, *The Unforgettable Year 1919*, in which he was shown on the steps of an armored train and where he was practically vanquishing the foe with his own saber. Let Kliment Yefremovich [Voroshilov], our dear friend, find the necessary courage and write the truth about Stalin; after all, he knows how Stalin had fought. It will be difficult for Comrade Voroshilov to undertake this, but it would be good if he did. Everyone will approve of it, both the people and the party. Even his grandsons will thank him. *(Prolonged applause.)*

In speaking about the events of the October Revolution and about the civil war, the impression was created that Stalin always played the main role, as if everywhere and always Stalin had suggested to Lenin what to do and how to do it. However, this is slander of Lenin. *(Prolonged applause.)*

I will probably not sin against the truth when I say that

99 percent of the persons present here heard and knew very little about Stalin before the year 1924, while Lenin was known to all; he was known to the whole party, to the whole nation, from the children up to the graybeards. (*Tumultuous, prolonged applause.*)

All this has to be thoroughly revised so that history, literature, and the fine arts properly reflect V. I. Lenin's role and the great deeds of our Communist Party and of the Soviet people—the creative people. (*Applause.*)

Comrades! The cult of the individual has caused the employment of faulty principles in party work and in economic activity; it brought about rude violation of internal party and Soviet democracy, sterile administration, deviations of all sorts, covering up of shortcomings and varnishing of reality. Our nation gave birth to many flatterers and specialists in false optimism and deceit.

We should also not forget that, due to the numerous arrests of party, Soviet, and economic leaders, many workers began to work uncertainly, showed overcautiousness, feared all that was new, feared their own shadows, and began to show less initiative in their work.

Take, for instance, party and Soviet resolutions. They were prepared in a routine manner, often without considering the concrete situation. This went so far that party workers, even during the smallest sessions, read their speeches. All this produced the danger of formalizing party and Soviet work and of bureaucratizing the whole apparatus.

STALIN AND AGRICULTURE

Stalin's reluctance to consider life's realities and the fact that he was not aware of the real state of affairs in the provinces can be illustrated by his direction of agriculture.

All those who interested themselves even a little in the national situation saw the difficult situation in agriculture, but Stalin never even noted it. Did we tell Stalin about this? Yes, we told him, but he did not support us. Why? Because Stalin never traveled anywhere, did not meet city and *kolkhoz* workers; he did not know the actual situation in the provinces.

He knew the country and agriculture only from films. And these films had dressed up and beautified the existing situation in agriculture.

Many films so pictured *kolkhoz* life that the tables were bending from the weight of turkeys and geese. Evidently, Stalin thought that it was actually so.

Vladimir Ilyich Lenin looked at life differently; he was always close to the people; he used to receive peasant delegates and often spoke at factory gatherings; he used to visit villages and talk with the peasants.

Stalin separated himself from the people and never went anywhere. This lasted tens of years. The last time he visited a village was in January 1928, when he visited Siberia in connection with grain deliveries. How then could he have known the situation in the provinces?

And when he was once told during a discussion that our situation on the land was a difficult one and that the situation of cattle breeding and meat production was especially bad, a commission was formed which was charged with the preparation of a resolution called "Means toward Further Development of Animal Breeding in Kolkhozes and Sovkhozes." We worked out this project.

Of course, our propositions of that time did not contain all possibilities, but we did chart ways in which animal breeding on *kolkhozes* and *sovkhozes* would be raised. We had proposed then to raise the prices of such products in order to create material incentives for the *kolkhoz*, MTS [machine-tractor station] and *sovkhoz* workers in the development of cattle breeding. But our project was not accepted and in February 1953 was laid aside entirely.

What is more, while reviewing this project, Stalin proposed that the taxes paid by the *koklhozes* and by the *kolkhoz* workers should be raised by 40 billion rubles; according to him, the peasants are well off and the *kolkhoz* worker would need to sell only one more chicken to pay his tax in full.

Imagine what this meant. Certainly, 40 billion rubles is a

sum which the *kolkhoz* workers did not realize for all the products which they sold to the Government. In 1952, for instance, the *kolkhozes* and the *kolkhoz* workers received 26,280 million rubles for all their products delivered and sold to the Government.

Did Stalin's position, then, rest on data of any sort whatever? Of course not.

In such cases facts and figures did not interest him. If Stalin said anything, it meant it was so—after all, he was a "genius," and a genius does not need to calculate, he only needs to look and can immediately tell how it should be. When he expresses his opinion, everyone has to repeat it and to admire his wisdom.

But how much wisdom was contained in the proposal to raise the agricultural tax by 40 billion rubles? None, absolutely none, because the proposal was not based on an actual assessment of the situation but on the fantastic ideas of a person divorced from reality.

We are currently beginning slowly to work our way out of a difficult agricultural situation. The speeches of the delegates to the Twentieth Congress please us all; we are glad that many delegates deliver speeches to the effect that there are conditions for the fulfillment of the sixth Five-Year Plan for animal husbandry, not during the period of five years, but within two to three years. We are certain that the commitments of the new Five-Year Plan will be accomplished successfully. *(Prolonged applause.)*

Comrades!

If we sharply criticize today the cult of the individual which was so widespread during Stalin's life and if we speak about the so many negative phenomena generated by this cult which is so alien to the spirit of Marxism-Leninism, various persons may ask: How could it be? Stalin headed the party and the country for thirty years and many victories were gained during his lifetime. Can we deny this? In my opinion, the question can be asked in this manner only by those who are blinded and hopelessly hypnotized by the cult of the individual, only by those who do not understand the essence of the revolution and of the Soviet state, only by those who do not understand, in a Leninist manner, the role of the party and of the people in the development of Soviet society.

The Socialist Revolution was attained by the working class and by the poor peasantry with the partial support of middle-class peasants. It was attained by the people under the leadership of the Bolshevik Party. Lenin's great service consisted in the fact that he created a militant party of the working class, but he was armed with Marxist understanding of the laws of social development and with the science of proletarian victory in the fight with capitalism, and he steeled this party in the crucible of revolutionary struggle of the masses of the people.

During this fight the party consistently defended the interests of the people, became its experienced leader, and led the working masses to power, to the creation of the first socialist state.

You remember well the wise words of Lenin that the Soviet state is strong because of the awareness of the masses that history is created by the millions and tens of millions of people.

Our historical victories were attained thanks to the organizational work of the party, to the many provincial organizations, and to the self-sacrificing work of our great nation. These victories are the result of the great drive and activity of the nation and of the party as a whole; they are not at all the fruit of the leadership of Stalin, as the situation was pictured during the period of the cult of the individual.

If we are to consider this matter as Marxists and as Leninists, then we have to state unequivocally that the leadership practice which came into being during the last years of Stalin's life became a serious obstacle in the path of Soviet social development. Stalin often failed for months to take up some unusually important problems, concerning the life of the party and of the state, whose solution could not be postponed. During Stalin's leadership our peaceful relations with other nations were often threatened, because one-man decisions could cause and often did cause, great complications.

In recent years, when we managed to free ourselves of the

harmful practice of the cult of the individual and took several proper steps in the sphere of internal and external policies, everyone saw how activity grew before their very eyes, how the creative activity of the broad working masses developed, how favorably all this acted upon the development of the economy and of culture. *(Applause.)*

WHERE WERE THE MEMBERS OF THE POLITICAL BUREAU?

Some comrades may ask us: Where were the members of the Political Bureau of the Central Committee? Why did they not assert themselves against the cult of the individual in time? And why is this being done only now?

First of all, we have to consider the fact that the members of the Political Bureau viewed these matters in a different way at different times. Initially, many of them backed Stalin actively because Stalin was one of the strongest Marxists and his logic, his strength, and his will greatly influenced the cadres and party work.

It is known that Stalin, after Lenin's death, especially during the first years, actively fought for Leninism against the enemies of Leninist theory and against those who deviated. Beginning with Leninist theory, the party, with its Central Committee at the head, started on a great scale the work of socialist industrialization of the country, agricultural collectivization, and the cultural revolution.

At that time Stalin gained great popularity, sympathy, and support. The party had to fight those who attempted to lead the country away from the correct Leninist path; it had to fight Trotskyites, Zinovievites, and Rightists, and Bourgeois Nationalists. This fight was indispensable.

Later, however, Stalin, abusing his power more and more, began to fight eminent party and Government leaders and to use terroristic methods against honest Soviet people. As we have already shown, Stalin thus handled such eminent party and Government leaders as Kossior, Rudzutak, Eikhe, Postyshev, and many others.

Attempts to oppose groundless suspicions and charges resulted in the opponent falling victim of the repression. This characterized the fall of Comrade Postyshev.

In one of his speeches Stalin expressed his dissatisfaction with Postyshev and asked him, "What are you actually?"

Postyshev answered clearly, "I am a Bolshevik, Comrade Stalin, a Bolshevik."

This assertion was at first considered to show a lack of respect for Stalin; later it was considered a harmful act and consequently resulted in Postyshev's annihilation and branding without any reason as a "people's enemy."

In the situation which then prevailed, I talked often with Nikolai Aleksandrovich Bulganin. Once when we two were traveling in a car, he said, "It has happened sometimes that a man goes to Stalin on his invitation as a friend. And, when he sits with Stalin, he does not know where he will be sent next—home or to jail."

It is clear that such conditions put every member of the Political Bureau in a very difficult situation. And, when we also consider the fact that in the last years Central Committee plenary sessions were not convened and that sessions of the Political Bureau occurred only occasionally, from time to time, then we will understand how difficult it was for any member of the Political Bureau to take a stand against one or another unjust or improper procedure, against serious errors and shortcomings in the practices of leadership.

As we have already shown, many decisions were taken either by one person or in a roundabout way, without collective discussion.

The sad fate of Political Bureau member Comrade Voznesensky, who fell victim to Stalin's repressions, is known to all. It is a characteristic thing that the decision to remove him from the Political Bureau was never discussed but was reached in a devious fashion. In the same way came the decision concerning the removal of Kuznetsov and Rodionov from their posts.

The importance of the Central Committee's Political Bureau was reduced and its work disorganized by the creation within the Political Bureau of various commissions—the "quintets," "sextets," "septets" and "novenaries." Here is, for instance, a resolution of the Political Bureau of 3 October 1946:

Stalin's Proposal:
1. The Political Bureau Commission for Foreign Affairs ("Sextet") is to concern itself in the future, in addition to foreign affairs, also with matters of internal construction and domestic policy.
2. The Sextet is to add to its roster the Chairman of the State Commission of Economic Planning of the USSR Comrade Voznesensky, and is to be known as a Septet.
Signed: Secretary of the Central Committee, J. Stalin.

What a terminology of a card player! *(Laughter in the hall.)*

It is clear that the creation within the Political Bureau of this type of commissions—"quintets," "sextets," "septets," and "novenaries,"—was against the principle of collective leadership. The result of this was that some members of the Political Bureau were in this way kept away from participation in the decision of the most important state matters.

One of the oldest members of our party, Kliment Yefremovich Voroshilov, found himself in an almost impossible situation. For several years he was actually deprived of the right of participation in Political Bureau sessions. Stalin forbade him to attend the Political Bureau sessions and to receive documents. When the Political Bureau was in session and Comrade Voroshilov heard about it, he telephoned each time and asked whether he would be allowed to attend. Sometimes Stalin permitted it, but always showed his dissatisfaction.

Because of his extreme suspicion, Stalin toyed also with the absurd and ridiculous suspicion that Voroshilov was an English agent. *(Laughter in the hall.)*

It's true—an English agent. A special tapping device was installed in his home to listen to what was said there. *(Indignation in the hall.)*

By unilateral decision, Stalin also separated one other man from the work of the Political Bureau—Andrey Andreyevich

Andreyev. This was one of the most unbridled acts of willfulness.

Let us consider the first Central Committee plenum after the Nineteenth Party Congress when Stalin, in his talk at the plenum, characterized Vyacheslav Mikhailovich Molotov and Anastas Ivanovich Mikoyan and suggested that these old workers of our party were guilty of some baseless charges. It is not excluded that, had Stalin remained at the helm for another several months, Comrades Molotov and Mikoyan would probably have not delivered any speeches at this Congress.

Stalin evidently had plans to finish off the old members of the Political Bureau. He often stated that Political Bureau members should be replaced by new ones.

His proposal, after the Nineteenth Congress, concerning the selection of twenty-five persons to the Central Committee Presidium, was aimed at the removal of the old Political Bureau members and the bringing in of less experienced persons so that these would extol him in all sorts of ways.

We can assume that this was also a design for the future annihilation of the old Political Bureau members and, in this way, a cover for all the shameful acts of Stalin, acts which we are now considering.

ERADICATING THE CULT OF THE INDIVIDUAL

Comrades! In order not to repeat the errors of the past, the Central Committee has declared itself resolutely against the cult of the individual.

We consider that Stalin was excessively extolled. However, in the past, Stalin doubtlessly performed great services to the party, to the working class, and to the international workers' movement.

The question is complicated by the fact that all this which we have just discussed was done during Stalin's life under his leadership and with his concurrence; here Stalin was convinced that this was necessary for the defense of the interests of the working classes against the plotting of enemies and against the attack of the imperialist camp.

He saw this from the position of the interest of the working class, of the interest of the laboring people, of the interest of the victory of Socialism and Communism. We cannot say that these were the deeds of a giddy despot. He considered that this should be done in the interest of the party; of the working masses, in the name of the defense of the revolution's gains. In this lies the whole tragedy!

Comrades! Lenin had often stressed that modesty is an absolutely integral part of a real Bolshevik. Lenin himself was the living personification of the greatest modesty. We cannot say that we have been following this Leninist example in all respects.

It is enough to point out that many towns, factories and industrial enterprises, *kolkhozes* and *sovkhozes*, Soviet institutions and cultural institutions have been referred to by us with a title—if I may express it so—of private property of the names of these or those Government or party leaders who were still active and in good health. Many of us participated in the action of assigning our names to various towns, *raions*, undertakings and *kolkhozes*. We must correct this. *(Applause.)*

But this should be done calmly and slowly. The Central Committee will discuss this matter and consider it carefully in order to prevent errors and excesses. I can remember how the Ukraine learned about Kossior's arrest. The Kiev radio used to start its programs thus: "This is radio Kossior." When one day the programs began without naming Kossior, everyone was quite certain that something had happened to Kossior, that he probably had been arrested.

Thus, if today we begin to remove the signs everywhere and to change names, people will think that these comrades in whose honor the given enterprises, *kolkhozes*, or cities are named have met some bad fate and that they have also been arrested. *(Animation in the hall.)*

How is the authority and the importance of this or that leader judged? On the basis of how many towns, industrial enterprises and factories, *kolkhozes* and *sovkhozes* carry his name. Is it not about time that we eliminate this "private property" and "nationalize" the factories, the industrial enterprises, the *kolkhozes* and *sovkhozes*? (*Laughter, applause, voices: "That is right."*)

We should, in all seriousness, consider the question of the cult of the individual. We cannot let this matter get out of the party, especially not to the press. It is for this reason that we are considering it here at a closed Congress session. We should know the limits; we should not give ammunition to the enemy; we should not wash our dirty linen before their eyes. I think that the delegates to the Congress will understand and assess properly all these proposals. (*Tumultuous applause.*)

Comrades! We must abolish the cult of the individual decisively, once and for all; we must draw the proper conclusions concerning both ideological-theoretical and practical work.

It is necessary for this purpose:

First, in a Bolshevik manner to condemn and to eradicate the cult of the individual as alien to Marxism-Leninism and not consonant with the principles of party leadership and the norms of party life, and to fight inexorably all attempts at bringing back this practice in one form or another.

To return to and actually practice in all our ideological work the most important theses of Marxist-Leninist science about the people as the creator of history and as the creator of all the material and spiritual good of humanity, about the decisive role of the Marxist party in the revolutionary fight for the transformation of society, about the victory of Communism.

In this connection we will be forced to do much work in order to examine critically from the Marxist-Leninist viewpoint and to correct the widely spread erroneous views connected with the cult of the individual in the sphere of history, philosophy, economics, and of other sciences, as well as in literature and the fine arts. It is especially necessary that in the immediate future we compile a serious textbook of the history of our party which will be edited in accordance with scientific Marxist objectivism, a textbook of the history of Soviet society, a book pertaining to the events of the Civil War and the Great Patriotic War.

Secondly, to continue systematically and consistently the work done by the party's Central Committee during the last years, a work characterized by minute observation in all party organizations, from the bottom to the top, of the Leninist principles of party leadership, characterized, above all, by the main principle of collective leadership, characterized by the observation of the norms of party life described in the statutes of our party, and, finally characterized by the wide practice of criticism and self-criticism.

Thirdly, to restore completely the Leninist principles of Soviet Socialist democracy, expressed in the Constitution of the Soviet Union, to fight the arbitrariness of individuals abusing their power. The evil caused by acts violating revolutionary socialist legality which have accumulated during a long time as a result of the negative influence of the cult of the individual has to be completely corrected.

Comrades! The Twentieth Congress of the Communist Party of the Soviet Union has manifested with a new strength, the unshakable unity of our party, its cohesiveness around the Central Committee, its resolute will to accomplish the great task of building Communism. *(Tumultuous applause.)*

And the fact that we present in all their ramifications the basic problems of overcoming the cult of the individual which is alien to Marxism-Leninism, as well as the problem of liquidating its burdensome consequences, is an evidence of the great moral and political strength of our party. *(Prolonged applause.)*

We are absolutely certain that our party, armed with the historical resolutions of the Twentieth Congress, will lead the Soviet people along the Leninist path to new successes, to new victories. *(Tumultuous, prolonged applause.)*

Long live the victorious banner of our party—Leninism! *(Tumultuous, prolonged applause ending in ovation. All rise.)*

8

QUESTIONS ON STALINISM*

Palmiro Togliatti
(Interview in Nuovi Argomenti,
Rome 16 June 1956)

Khrushchev had endorsed the concept of different paths to socialism in his "Report to Party Congress XX" and had undermined the authority of the Russian party to a greater extent by his "Secret Speech." But the leadership of communist parties outside Russia, with the exception of the Yugoslavs, was too shocked and frightened—they were all tainted by Stalinism—to do much in response to the new permissiveness except hold their breaths, or to deny what Khrushchev had said about Stalin.

In the west, the communist parties all had a Stalinist tradition; none had raised its voice in 1948 and 1949 in support of Tito. Now, the French party, for example, defended Stalin against the accusations of Party Congress XX and insisted on the correctness of the previous positions and actions of the Soviet Union and its communist party.

But there were some exceptions to the generality, and primary among these was Palmiro Togliatti, co-founder of the Communist Party of Italy and its head in the post–

* Excerpts

World War II period. A decade earlier Togliatti had spoken of an "Italian road to socialism" and had stated his firm belief in democracy in the Western sense. But these remarks were made in the heat of a political campaign, and were apparently quickly forgotten in the CPI and forgiven in Moscow. But in June 1956, Togliatti, under the impact of the "Secret Speech" and the widespread ferment in the communist world, returned to his earlier ideas and elaborated on them.

He stated that the Soviet Union had gone astray and that all its mistakes could not be blamed on Stalin and the "cult of the individual." He warned of the stultifying effects of bureaucracy and emphasized that socialism is incomplete unless it is democratic.

Finally, Togliatti rejected the Soviet Union as the only, the "obligatory," model for the achievement of socialism and made his famous assertion that the communist world system had now become "polycentric." Togliatti's statement was a powerful one—in many ways a harbinger of the Eurocommunism of two decades later.

Q. What is the significance, in your opinion, of the condemnation of the personality cult in the USSR? What are the internal, external, political, social, economic, psychological, and historical reasons for it?
A. The condemnation of the personality cult declared by the communists of the Soviet Union and the criticisms of Stalin's work mean exactly, in my opinion, that which has been said and is being repeated by the Soviet communist leaders—neither more nor less than this. . . .

It is necessary therefore to get used to thinking that the criticisms of Stalin and of the cult of the individual mean, for our Soviet comrades, exactly that which up to now they have said. And what, precisely? That because of the errors of Stalin and of the cult of the individual, negative elements had come together, unfavorable and even clearly bad situations had been created in different sectors of Soviet life and society, in different parts of the activity of the party and of the state. However it is not simple to reduce all these negative circumstances under one general concept, because in this case too there is the risk of excessive, arbitrary, and false generalization—that is, the risk of judging the whole economic, social, and cultural Soviet reality as bad, to reject it, to critize it, which is a return to the usual reactionary idiocies. The least arbitrary of the generalizations is that which sees in the errors of Stalin the progressive superimposing of a personal power on the collective will of democratic origin and nature and, as a consequence of this, the amassing of phenomena of bureaucratization, of violation of legality, of stagnation, and even, partially, of degeneration, in different points of the social organism. However it must be immediately added that this superimposition was only partial and has probably had its most serious manifestations at the summit of the directive organs of the state and of the party. This was the point of departure toward a tendency to restrict democratic life, the initiative and liveliness of thought and action in numerous fields (technical and economic development, cultural activity, literature, art, etc.), but it absolutely cannot be said that the destruction of those fundamental features of Soviet society has derived from this —features from which this society derives its democratic and socialist character and which render it superior, for its quality, to the modern capitalistic societies. Soviet society could not condone such errors, as on the other hand the bourgeois capitalistic regime can condone much more serious errors and situations. Those errors could not become a stable and general element of civil, economic, and political life. If they had lasted longer, perhaps they would have brought matters to the breaking point, although this hypothesis should also be received with caution, because a rupture would certainly have brought to the popular masses and to the whole socialist movement more damge than advantages; not only the men who could have been the authors of the rupture, were aware of this, but very vast strata of society were aware of it.

With this I do not want to say that the consequences of Stalin's errors have not been very serious. They have been very serious, they have extended to many areas, and I do not believe that overcoming them will be a simple matter, nor that it will be possible to do it very rapidly. In substance, it can be said that a large part of the leadership cadres of Soviet society (party, state, economy, culture, etc.) had, in the Stalin cult, grown numb, losing or having reduced its own critical and creative ability to think and to act. For this reason, it was absolutely necessary that the denunciation of Stalin's errors be made, and made in such a way that it would stir minds and reactivate the whole life of the organisms on which the complex system of socialist society is based. In this way there will be a new democratic progress of this society, and this will be a powerful contribution to better understanding among all peoples, to international détente, to the advancement of socialism and to peace.

Q. Do you believe that the criticisms of the personality cult in the USSR must bring about institutional changes?

The legitimacy of power is the great problem of public law; and modern political thought tends to indicate the source of legitimacy in the will of the people. The Wester-type parliamentary democracies maintain that the will of the people, in order to express itself, requires a plurality of parties. Do you maintain that power in a one-party regime with elections without choice between government and opposition is legitimate?

A. I could be wrong, but in my opinion there are today no institutional changes to be foreseen in the Soviet Union, nor must such changes derive from the criticisms formulated in an open manner by Congress XX. This does not mean that sufficiently profound modifications do not have to be accomplished, some of which, in any case, are already under way.

First of all, what is intended by institutional changes? I believe that those who talk about them mean changes in the political structure that would bring the Soviet society to some, at least, of the forms of political organization characteristic of the so-called Western regimes, or else would give new importance to some of the institutions that are characteristic of these regimes. To the problem posed thusly, my answer is negative.

And let us indeed begin, if you wish, with an examination of the legitimacy of power and of its source, but let us try to free ourselves from the hypocritical formalism with which the apologizers of "Western civilization" treat this question. We have read *The State and Revolution*, nor, fortunately, have we forgotten the substance of that teaching. It is not the criticism of Stalin's errors that will make us forget it. In the reality of the so-called Western civilizations the source of the legitimacy of power is not at all the will of the people. The will of the people is, in the best of circumstances, one of the factors that contribute, expressing itself periodically through elections, to determining a part of the policies of the government. In the elections, however—and indeed let us use the example of Italy, typical in some respects—there enters into action a manifold system of pressures, intimidations, coercions, falsifications, legal and illegal tricks, through which the expression of the will of the people comes to be very seriously limited and falsified. This system is in the hands of (and works in favor of) not only he who in that moment is in the government, but also he who in the society holds the real power. And this power comes from wealth, from ownership of the means of production and exchange, and from that which derives from them, beginning with the actual direction of political life, to the inevitable protection of the religious authorities and of all the other nerve centers of power that exist in a capitalist society. We maintain that today, given the developments and the present force of the democratic and socialist movement, large rents can be torn in this system that impedes the free expression of the will of the people, and an increasingly large passageway can be opened toward the manifestation of this will. For this reason, we are moving on democratic terrain, and without leaving this terrain we maintain that continuing new developments are possible. That does not mean that we do not see things as they are and that from the way democratic life goes on in the Western world—beware, then, of going a little too far, in this world, to Spain, or Turkey, or South America, or Portugal, or the discriminatory electoral system of the United States of America, etc., etc.!—we should make a fetish, a universal and absolute model, of democracy! On the contrary, we continue to think that democracy of the Western type is a limited, imperfect, and in many ways false democracy that needs to be developed and perfected, through a series of economic and political reforms. Even if, therefore, we arrive at the conclusion that Congress XX opens a new process of democratic development in the Soviet Union, we are very far away from thinking, and we maintain that it is mistaken to think, that this development can or should be accomplished with a return to "Western"-type intitutions.

The legitimacy of power, in the Soviet Union, has its primary source in the revolution. This revolution has given power to the working class, which was a minority, but which succeeded, by resolving the great national and social problems before it, in steadily gathering around it all the popular masses, in transforming the economic structure of the country, in creating a new society constructed according to socialist principles, function, and progress. To forget the revolution, to not take into account the new social structure —to forget, that is, all that is characteristic of the Soviet Union and then to make a purely external comparison with the ways of political life in the capitalist countries—is a trick and nothing more.

But this first recall to reality is not sufficient. The Soviet society has had, since its beginning, its own democratic political structure, founded, precisely, on the existence and functioning of the soviets (councils of workers, peasants, laborers, and soldiers). The system of the soviets is, as such, much more democratic and advanced than any traditional democratic system, and this is for two reasons. The first is that it causes democratic life to penetrate into all constituent parts of the society, starting from the basic workers' units and going up, step by step, to the great city, regional, and national assemblies. The second is that it brings together the elementary cells of democratic life and the productive units, and therefore overcomes that negative aspect of the traditional democratic organizations which consists of the separation of the world of production from that of politics and therefore of the external, formal character of liberty. Is it possible that in the operation of the Soviet system there was an arrest, a stumbling-block, from which derived a limitation of Soviet democracy? Not only is it possible, but at Congress XX it was openly recognized. Soviet democratic life was limited, in part suffocated, by the coming to power of bureaucratic and authoritarian methods and by violations of the laws of the regime. Theoretically, this is indeed possible, because a socialist regime is not protected, in and of itself, from errors and dangers; whoever thinks so would be falling into a naïve infantalism. Socialist society is a society not only composed of men, but a society in the course of development, in which there continue to exist objective and subjective contrasts, and which is subject to the events of history. In fact, the question is to see how and why such a limitation of Soviet democratic life could happen, but whatever the answer to this question that we arrive at, for us there is no doubt that it will never be possible to conclude that it is necessary to return to the forms of organization of the capitalist societies.

The existence of more than one party or only one party cannot, in and of itself, be considered the distinguishing characteristic between the bourgeois societies and the socialist societies, just as it does not mark, in and of itself, the line of distinction between a democratic society and a nondemocratic socicty. In thc Sovict Union two parties shared power for a certain period of time, after the revolution, with a Soviet regime and a proletarian dictatorship. In today's China there exists a plurality of parties in power, and the regime is indeed defined as a democratic dictatorship. Also, in the people's democracies there still exist parties other than the communist party, although not everywhere. In the still capitalist countries where the workers' and people's movement is very strongly developed, the hypothesis of profound socialist transformations is realizable with the presence of a plurality of parties and through the initiative of some of them. In the Soviet Union of today, however, to think of a plurality of parties seems impossible to us. From where would they come? Through a decision from above? That would be a fine democratic process! It must be recognized that there exists not only a social homogeneity owing to the disappearance of the capitalist classes, and a political homogeneity that expresses itself through the alliance between workers and peasants, but there exists a form of unity between civil life and political leadership that is unknown and perhaps not even understood here in the "Western" world. The very notion of a party is, in the Soviet Union, something different from that which we understand with this term. The party works and fights for the realization and development of socialism, but its work is essentially of a positive and constructive nature, not of a polemic nature against a hypothetical internal political opponent. The "opponent" against which one fights is the objective difficulty to overcome, the conflict to resolve through working, the reality to dominate, the remnants of the old to be destroyed for the advancement of the new, etc. The dialectic of conflicts, which is essential for the development of society, no longer expresses itself in the competition between different parties, those of the government and its opposition, because there no longer exists either an objective base (in things), or a subjective base (in the minds of men) for such a competition. It is expressed right within the unitarian system that includes a whole series of organizations coordinated among themselves (party, soviets, unions, etc., etc.). The criticism that is made against Stalin is that he impeded this manifestation of the dialectic within this system. The correction lies not in the denial of the system or in the destruction of it, but rather in the restoration of normality.

But if I consider absurd the possibility that the system be destroyed in order to go backwards, I do believe however that modifications, even profound ones, can and must be introduced internally, on the basis of past experience, on the basis of successes achieved in every area, and on the very basis of the necessity of having more efficient guarantees against errors like those of Stalin. Attention must be concentrated on this point, and therefore the new measures that are gradually being taken in the Soviet Union, both by the party and the government, must be followed and studied. The most interesting and most important are those which are establishing an ever-increasing decentralization of economic leadership. Centralization, even in extreme forms, was a necessity of the periods in which profound changes had to be made rapidly, destroying the bases of capitalism, setting the foundations of the socialist economy, facing up to urgent economic, political, and military necessities. Even centralization, however, especially in its extreme forms, is not, in and of itself, an obligatory form of socialist economic leadership. A lesser or greater degree of centralization, and therefore of leadership from above, is dictated by the complex of objective conditions, but it determines a greater or lesser degree, respectively, of peripheral democratic life, of the activity and initiative of the masses—and for us the activity of the masses, their effective participation in the criticism, in the control, and hence in the direction of the entire social and economic organism, are the true signs of democracy. Here, in our regime of plurality of parties, of dialectic between government and opposition, etc., etc., this activity of the masses does not exist in any form nor in any measure, or at best, in very limited and very indirect forms and measures. For this reason we say that this is not yet a true democracy and we do not understand why, in order to correct the bad things done by Stalin, the Soviet peoples should fall back into it.

* * *

Q. Do you maintain that the personal dictatorship of Stalin came about against and outside historical and political Russian traditions or that, on the other hand, it was a development of such traditions?

In order to affirm and maintain itself, Stalin's personal dictatorship made use of a group of coercive measures that in the West, beginning with the French Revolution, are called "terrorism." Do you maintain that this "terrorism" was a necessity?

A. I will answer these two questions together because, aside from their concrete formulation, which would limit the inquiry to themes of a particular type, they do allow, if this limitation is overcome, a discussion of the problem that logically presents itself at this point, and that is how, in the Soviet society, the errors denounced by Congress XX could have been committed, and hence could have been created and could have lasted for so long a period of time, a situation in which democratic life and socialist laws underwent continuous, serious, and extensive violations. To this must be added, as is certainly understandable, the question of the coresponsibility for these errors of the political leadership group, including the comrades who today have taken the initiative both in the denunciation and the correction of the evil that had first been done, as well as the consequences of this evil.

* * *

And here it must be recognized, openly and without hesitation, that, while Congress XX made an enormous contribution to recognizing and solving many serious new problems of the democratic and socialist movement, while it marks a very important stage in the development of the Soviet society, the position that was taken at the congress and which today is being amply developed in the Soviet press regarding Stalin's errors and the causes and conditions that rendered them possible cannot on the other hand be considered satisfactory. The cause of everything is supposed to be the "personality cult," the cult of a person who had particular and serious defects, who lacked modesty, who was inclined toward personal power and who at times made mistakes out of incompetency, who was not loyal in his relations with the other leaders, who had a longing for greatness and an excessive love of himself, who was extremely suspicious, and who in the end, through the exercise of personal power, finally detached himself from the people, neglected his work, and even succumbed to an evident form of persecution mania. The present Soviet leaders knew Stalin much better than we—(perhaps on another occasion I will have a chance to talk about some contacts I had with him)—and we therefore have to believe them when today they describe him in this way. We can only think, to ourselves, that, since he was like that, aside from the impossibility of making a change, about which we have already spoken, they could at least have been more prudent in that public and solemn exaltation of the qualities of this man, to which they had accustomed us. It is true that today they criticize themselves, and this is to their great credit, but in this criticism a little of their prestige is without doubt lost. But aside from this, as long as one limits oneself, in substance, to denouncing, as the cause of everything, Stalin's personal defects, one remains in the sphere of the "personality cult." At first, all the good was due to the superhuman positive qualities of one man; now, all the bad comes to be attributed to his equally exceptional and even amazing defects. As much in the one case as in the other, we are outside the criterion of judgment characteristic of Marxism. The real problems, which are why and how Soviet society could reach and did reach certain forms so distant from democratic life and from the legal system it had set out for itself, even to the extent of degeneration, are avoided. The study will have to be made following the several stages of development of this society, and it is above all our Soviet comrades that must do it, because they know things better than we, who could be mistaken because of partial or incorrect knowledge of the facts.

We recall, first of all, that Lenin, in his last speeches and writings, had emphasized the danger of bureaucratization that was threatening the new society. It seems to us without doubt that Stalin's errors were tied to an excessive increase in the weight of the bureaucratic apparatus in Soviet economic and political life, and perhaps first of all in the life of the party. And here it is very difficult to say which was the cause, which the result. The one came, a little at a time, to be the expression of the other. Is this excessive weight of the bureaucracy also to be related to a tradition originating in the forms of political organization and in the customs of old Russia? Perhaps this cannot be excluded, and I believe that there are references by Lenin in this direction. However, it must be taken into account that after the revolution, the leadership personnel changed totally, or almost totally, and for us, then, it is not so important to evaluate the residue of the old, as to note the fact that a new type of bureaucratic leadership arose from the front ranks of the new leadership class, in the moment in which it was undertaking completely new tasks.

* * *

It is an error of principle to believe that, once the first great successes of socialism are achieved, socialist construction goes ahead on its own and not through the interplay of contradictions of a new type, that have to be resolved within the framework of the new society, by the action of the masses and of the party that leads them.

I believe that two principal consequences derived from this. The first was the sterilization of the activity of the masses, in the places and in the organisms (party, unions, factory, soviets) where the real and new difficulties of the situation should have been faced up to, and where instead there began to prevail writings and speeches full of pompous declarations, prepared statements, etc., which were all cold and ineffective, because devoid of contact with life, the true creative debate slowly disappeared, and hence the very activity of the masses was reduced, moving more by directive from above than by its own intiative. But the second consequence was even more serious, and it is that when reality started showing through and the difficulties started coming out (as a consequence of the imbalance and the conflicts that remained in everything), the tendency to think that always and in every case, evil—an interruption in the application of a plan, difficulty in supplying provisions, in the flow of raw materials, in the development of various parts of industry and agriculture, etc., etc.—was due to sabotage, to the work of class enemies, to counterrevolutionary groups operating clandestinely, and so forth, manifested itself and little by little ended up by prevailing. It is not that there were not these things. There were these things too. The Soviet Union was surrounded by ruthless enemies, ready to resort to any means for bringing damage to it and to stop its advancement; but that mistaken sense of judgment of the objective situation caused a loss of the sense of limitation, caused confusion in the notion of the borderline that separates good from bad, friend from enemy, inability or weakness from conscious hostility and from treason, the conflict and the difficulties that sprang out of things from the hostile act of him who conspires to destroy you. Stalin gave a pseudoscientific formulation to this fearful confusion with his mistaken thesis that enemies increase and the class struggle becomes increasingly bitter with the progress of socialist construction. This aggravated the confusion and rendered it permanent. It was at this time that the incredible violations of socialist doctrine began that today have been publicly denounced. However, it is necessary to search even deeper to understand how these positions could have been accepted and could have become popular, and one of the directions of the inquiry will have to be that which has been indicated by us, if you wish to understand everything. Stalin was at one time the expression and the author of a situation, and he was these things as much because he had demonstrated himself to be the most expert organizer and leader of a bureaucratic-type apparatus at the moment when it was gaining supremacy over democratic forms of life, as for having given a doctrinaire justification for what was in reality a mistaken policy, upon which then he based his personal power to the point that it assumed degenerate forms. All this explains the consensus that existed around him, which lasted until his death and perhaps is still in some degree preserved.

It must not be forgotten, then, that even when this power of his was established, the successes of the Soviet society were not lacking. There were successes in the economic field, in the political field, in the cultural field, in the military field, and in the field of international relations. No one will be able to deny that the Soviet Union in 1953 was incomparably stronger, more developed in every sense, more solid internally, and more authoritative in its foreign relations than it was, for example, at the time of the first Five-

Year Plan. How come so many errors did not impede so many successes? Here too, it is the Soviet leaders that must give the answer, understanding that this is today one of the problems that assail the sincere militants of the international workers' movement. Up to what point, from when and within what limits did Stalin's errors compromise the party's political line, create subsidiary problems? And what weight did these difficulties have, and how, despite those errors, was it possible to make progress? On the basis of what we know, we are only able to make some general affirmations, and we are disposed to review them if necessary. It seems to us that it must be recognized that the line followed in socialist construction continued to be the right one, even if the errors that are being denounced are such that it is not possible for them not to have seriously limited the successes of its implementation. This is, however, one of the points for which the largest explanations will be required, because the restriction, and in some cases even the disappearance, of democratic life is something essential for the validity of a political line. It seems to us, in any case, incontrovertible that the bureaucratization of the party, of the state organs, of the unions, and, above all, of the peripheral organs, which are the most important, must have slowed down, limited, compressed the creative political thought of the party, the activity of the masses, the democratic functioning of the state and the constructive enthusiasm of the entire society, with real evident damages. On the other hand, the successes achieved both in peace and in war (and after the war), are the proof of an impressive capacity for work, for enthusiasm, and for sacrifice on the part of the popular masses, in any situation, and of their continuing adhesion to the goals that party policy placed before the whole country, and which through their work were achieved. It is difficult to say, for example, what other people would have been capable of resisting, recovering, and then winning, with Hitler in the suburbs of Moscow and then on the Volga, and with the terrible living conditions of the war period. Hence it must be concluded that the substance of the socialist regime was not lost, because none of the preceding conquests was lost, nor, above all, the adhesion to the regime of the masses of workers, peasants, intellectuals that form the Soviet society. This same adhesion goes to prove that, in spite of everything, this society maintained its fundamental democratic character.

We have said a number of times that it falls to our Soviet comrades to face up to some of the questions posed by us and to supply the elements for a complete answer. Until now they have developed criticisms of the "personality cult," above all correcting mistaken historical and political judgments of facts and persons, destroying myths and legends created for the purpose of exalting one single person. This is very good, but it is not all that should be expected of them. What is more important today is to respond justly, using a Marxist criterion, to the question of how the errors denounced today may have been intertwined with the development of a socialist society, and hence whether in the very development of this society there may not have been introduced, at a certain point, disturbing elements, mistakes of a general type, against which the entire socialist camp must be put on guard—and I mean all those who are already building socialism in their own way, and those who are still searching for a way of their own. It is certainly possible to agree that the central problem is the safeguarding of the democratic characteristics of socialist society, how to relate the questions of political democracy, and economic democracy, internal democracy, and the leadership function of the party with the democratic functioning of the state, and how a mistake that has entered into one area can make its effects felt on the entire system—this is what must be studied in depth and explained.

* * *

Q. Do you believe that the criticism of the personality cult will bring about a change in the relationship between the USSR and the people's democracies, between the Russian Communist Party and the communist parties of other countries, and in general between the USSR and the international workers' movement?

A. I hope that there is no one, at least in Italy, who still gives credence to the stupid legend about the communist parties that receive step-by-step instructions, directives, and orders from Moscow. If such a person still exists, it is useless to address our remarks to him, because it is evident that he is too much of a thickhead, that he is absolutely incapable of even coming close to understanding the problems of the international workers' movement of today. Therefore we are writing for the others.

In the first years after World War I, when the Communist International was formed, there is no doubt that the principal questions of political policy for the workers' movement and then for the communist movement in the individual countries, were amply debated at the center, in Moscow, in the congresses and other international meetings, from which were drawn precise policies. In this period it can be said that a centralized directorship of the communist movement existed, and the principal responsibility for it fell upon our Russian comrades, assisted by comrades coming from other countries. Very soon, however, the movement began to move ahead on its own, above all where it had good leaders. In 1924, for example, the decision by our party to leave the Aventine Assembly of the opposition parties and to go back to Parliament, was made by us in clear conflict with the advice that was coming to us from the leaders of the International, which was to do the opposite. At the time of Congress VII (1935), the parties that had grown strong, which were united and well led, already felt that an international center could only elaborate general judgments of the situation and of the duties of our movement, but the decision-making process and practical political implementation had to be the work of the individual parties, had to be fully entrusted to their initiative and responsibility. They went ahead in this way, in France and in Spain, above all, in the period of the great struggles between 1934 and 1939, then during the war, and still more after it. If they moved ahead in the great wake of the Soviet Union's international politics, it is because they were convinced that they were the right politics, and such they were, in fact.

The Information Bureau, constituted in 1947 with very

different duties than those that the International had had, did, essentially, two things, the first good, the second bad. The first was to correctly orient the entire workers' movement in the resistance and struggle against the war plans of imperialism. The second was the unfortunate intervention against the Yugoslav communists. Other than a public bulletin useful only for information purposes, it did nothing. It never happened, for example, that we Italians had to discuss our politics in an international meeting except at the founding meeting of the Cominform. Every initiative taken by us after the war was exclusively our work, perhaps not even always fully understood by our comrade leaders of the other communist parties, because they were dictated by the conditions under which we work in Italy and which are completely peculiar to us. Today, what's more, the Information Bureau has been dissolved, for reasons which have been amply shown.

The errors committed by Stalin in the leadership of the Soviet Communist Party certainly contributed, since they limited debating and democratic life at the summit of that party, to rendering somewhat exterior and formal the relations between the Soviet communists and those of other countries, to creating between them a certain detachment, without however diminishing their reciprocal trust, because we did not have and could not have any notion of the facts that are being revealed today. At least regarding us this is so. In other countries, above all in the countries of people's democracy, some of Stalin's errors were repeated in a mechanical way after the war, just as, in these countries, there was probably the tendency to transfer and implement, in a mechanical way, the entire Soviet experience and practice, without always giving the necessary consideration to the particular conditions that required and require individual ways of developing, correcting, and implementing the Soviet experience.

The criticism of Stalin made at Congress XX, which for the most part reached us unexpectedly, certainly struck a blow at the cadres of the international communist movement and even, to a lesser degree, at its masses. The manner in which our enemies threw themselves on these criticisms to make of them an instrument for the struggle against us has caused a tightening of ranks of the party militants around the party. Apart from that it must be said that there was not only surprise among them. There was grief, and here and there, confusion. Doubts about the past and so forth came out. These things were unavoidable, given the seriousness of the accusations against Stalin and the manner of the denunciation, since our Soviet comrades, limiting themselves in substance to revealing the facts and undertaking the proper correction, have until now neglected the task, as yet not accomplished, of confronting the difficult subject of complete political and historical justice.

I do not believe that a lessening of the reciprocal trust and solidarity between the various parts of the communist movement will result from all this. However it does undoubtedly indicate not only the necessity, but the desire for an increasingly greater autonomy of judgment, and this can only work to the benefit of our movement. The internal political structure of the worldwide communist movement is changed today. What the Communist Party of the Soviet Union has done remains, as has been said, the first great model of the construction of a socialist society for which a profound, decisive, revolutionary break opened the way. Today the socialist construction front in countries where the communists are the leading party is so enlarged (it comprises a third of the human race!), that even for this part the Soviet model can no longer and must no longer be obligatory. In every country governed by communists, the objective and subjective conditions, the traditions, and the organizational forms of the movement can and must be influential in various ways. In the rest of the world there are countries where it is desirable to move toward socialism without the communists being the leading party. In still other countries, the march toward socialism is a goal for which the efforts of several movements are concentrated, but which often have not reached either an agreement or a reciprocal understanding. The whole system becomes polycentric and in the communist movement itself one cannot speak of a single guide, but rather of a progress that is achieved often following different roads. One general problem, common to the entire movement, arises from the criticisms of Stalin—the problem of the dangers of bureaucratic degeneration, of the suffocation of democratic life, of confusion between constructive revolutionary force and the destruction of revolutionary legality, of the detachment of the economic and political leadership from the initiative, the criticism, and the creative activity of the masses. We will salute the fact that among the communist parties in power a competition is being established concerning the best way to avoid this danger. And it will be our job to work out our way and our method, so that we too will be guaranteed against the dangers of stagnation and bureaucratization, and will know how to resolve together the problems of liberty for the working masses and of social justice, and hence how to win for ourselves an increasingly greater following and prestige among the same masses.

9

SOCIALISM AND WAR*

Eduard Kardelj
(Belgrade, August 1960)

With Stalin's death, Yugoslav–Russian animosity, which had flared in the aftermath of the ouster of Yugoslavia from the Cominform in 1948, quieted down, although not entirely, for it still smoldered.

In the late 1950s, however, a full-scale propaganda onslaught against the Yugoslav communists resumed within the communist world; this time it originated not in Moscow but in Peking. The Chinese communists, though discouraging "socialism in one country" and encouraging the concept of "many paths to socialism" in the wake of 1956, had now turned conservative. Their own domestic and international experiences since 1956 had convinced Mao that the permissiveness of the many-paths approach constituted a danger within his own and other communist countries, and had weakened the international movement, which, with increasing signs of what he interpreted as Soviet lack of will, Mao had hopes of leading in the near future. Mao's bone of contention was actually not so much with Yugoslavia as with Moscow, but he was not yet prepared to attack the Russians frontally and so took aim at the Yugoslavs instead.

* Excerpts

At first the Yugoslavs did not respond to Mao's attacks, for he was really striking at the weak-kneed Khrushchev, not at them, they knew. It was Moscow's fight, not theirs. But, at length, the Yugoslavs felt called upon to defend themselves, and in August 1960 a series of articles began appearing in Borba, *the official Belgrade organ, under the name of Kardelj, vice-president of the People's Republic of Yugoslavia and the leading Yugoslav communist theoretician. The articles, later collected together in a lengthy pamphlet,* Socialism and War, *lashed out at the Chinese for their contention that war between capitalism and communism was inevitable and for their attempt to resurrect "socialism in one country" with its stress on a single model. But at the same time that the Chinese were attacked for being pro-Stalinist for their insistence on the single path, they were, almost bizarrely, attacked for being pro-Trotskyite, for their emphasis on the spread of the revolution.*

CHINESE IDEOLOGY AND CHINESE REALITY

If from a mass of empty words, slanders, verbalist dialectics, and general political slogans we extract the real substance of the Chinese charges against Yugoslav foreign policy, they boil down to the following basic arguments.

The first argument asserts: the Yugoslav communists are revisionists and their revisionism derives from their fear of imperialism and war. This cowardice of theirs has persuaded them to pursue an opportunist policy of compromise with the bourgeoisie and with imperialism. Thereby, they have sunk from the position of a revolutionary settlement of accounts with capitalism to that of reformism and now accept the theory of the peaceful growing of capitalism into socialism. To conceal this, the Yugoslav communists embellish imperialism. Consequently, they assist American imperialism. To that end they have even invented the policy of active coexistence, which is nothing less than a device for the concealment of their opportunist policy.

The second argument says: in contradistinction to this Yugoslav "opportunism," Chinese communists are not afraid either of imperialism or of war. They are for a radical settlement of accounts between the world of socialism and that of imperialism by means of a revolutionary clash. If this is war, it will be a just war and one should not be afraid of it or renounce it, because the sacrifices will soon be recompensed.

Further, the Chinese communists say that the assertion of the possibility of any lasting coexistence between the world of socialism and the world of capitalism and imperialism is illusory and harmful.

They consider that sooner or later a conflict between these two worlds is inevitable. As these Chinese authors see it, there can be talk of coexistence, disarmament, the policy of agreement, and so forth, solely for the purpose of unmasking imperialism. On the other hand, to take the principle of coexistence to be a lasting and essential principle of socialist international policy would, according to these conceptions, be tantamount to renouncing the revolutionary method of resolution of the social contradictions of the present-day world. To speak today about peaceful means of struggle for a transition from capitalism to socialism, that is, to the rule of the working-class, is, according to those conceptions, not only unrealistic—as the proletariat can never overcome counterrevolutionary violence otherwise than by means of revolutionary violence—but also senseless and opportunist, for at a time when the strength of the socialist countries is growing so rapidly, these countries should not renounce the possibility of settling accounts with imperialism in a revolutionary way, and should not run away from war.

If we reduce these arguments to what is fundamental—as seen through Chinese spectacles—we get the following picture: the Yugoslav communists are opportunists, whereas the Chinese communists are radical revolutionaries. It goes without saying that both these contentions are proved from the point of view of "genuine Marxism"—from a pedestal, so to speak, of infallibility—and so quotations are made to fit and the classics of Marxism are interpreted arbitrarily. In fact, both arguments are equally false: their aim is equally to distort the true picture of things and to cloud the real essence of the difference of opinion.

* * *

THE OLD WITHIN THE NEW

Even though the Chinese theories discussed in this paper are in their actual political content in a certain sense a new phenomenon, produced by the Chinese Revolution, in their ideological form they are not quite new. Internal contradictions similar to those characteristic of present-day Chinese society gave rise to similar theories in the first period after the October Revolution.

I have no intention of asserting that the ruling theory of the Chinese communists is Trotskyite, but yet the extraordinary similarity which does exist between those two theories once again is convincing evidence that like circumstances breed like ideologies.

Trotsky did not believe in the possibility of the maintenance or rather, of the development of socialism in the Soviet Union, unless the revolution were extended to Western Europe. To a mind so superficial, static, and so given to abstract schemes as Trotsky's was, it was impossible to accept the fact that before them then stood a long-drawn-out day-to-day struggle, full of hardships, against tremendous difficulties, both in the internal and in the foreign policy of the young Soviet republic.

And indeed, those difficulties were exceptionally great. The new Soviet state was being built up in circumstances of great economic backwardness, with a numerically very small working class and with a very limited number of skilled cadres loyal to the revolution, with very extensive breeding centers of counterrevolution, and with serious conservative vestiges in the mentality of a large part of the nation. The internal sources of economic advancement were relatively very weak and undeveloped and indicated that there would be an arduous and relatively slow development of the material foundations—anyway, much slower than the hopes which had inspired the revolution could allow. The world which surrounded the first socialist state was a hostile one, firmly determined to liquidate it on the first occasion, and powerful enough to make that threat real. That it was unable to realize those threats at once, in the first years of the revolution, was above all the merit of the world working class, which tied its hands. But it had never renounced that aim, and indeed made every effort by economic and political blockade to drown the revolution in its own difficulties and contradictions. In addition, not only did the hopes of a European revolution not materialize, but it became clear that it would be necessary to be reconciled to the fact that before the first socialist country stood a long period of isolated existence as an island surrounded by an ocean of a hostile world.

To Trotsky this seemed a completely blind alley, a total defeat of the world revolution, the Russian Revolution being the last unit of that world revolution, now encircled, which must either break out of the encirclement or die gloriously. This outlook resulted in his putting his hopes in an adventure, which would have been condemned in advance to failure, namely, war. His theories of permanent revolution, his proofs of the impossibility of building up socialism in the isolated Soviet Union, his dogmatic envisagement of the inevitability of a war of united imperialism against the Soviet Union, his faulty assessment of the internal factors of social development in other countries, all expressed in an unrealistic expectation—which for that matter was so cruelly shown to be false outside Warsaw in 1920—that the European proletariat would at the first step of the Red Army automatically rise against its own bourgeoisie—all this was a reflection of the psychotic state into which Trotsky had fallen in his blind alley.

For that matter, quite apart from this, Trotsky's whole mental outlook was one of simple expectation of elemental revolutionary impulses, for he was incapable of perceiving the social factors which prepare and drive revolutionary impulses, or of distinguishing the paths or the means by which conscious revolutionary socialist thought can influence the movement and strength of such factors. He saw the revolution as a fact in isolation, that is, as an abstract historical inevitability, and could not see it as something interconnected with a multitude of other forms of social movement, could not see the revolution which needed to be prepared by the internal development of every country. Precisely for this reason he felt a blind alley just when the Russian Revolution was not in a blind alley at all, but on the contrary, on the threshold of a victory in the field of world history.

In contradistinction to Trotsky, Lenin saw all these phenomena from a different angle. Whereas to Trotsky the defeat of the European revolution was the blind alley of the Russian Revolution, to Lenin it was merely a signal for a change of political tactics. The defeat of the European revolution was not absolute. Though it had not succeeded in handing power to the working class, it had succeeded in preventing the European bourgeoisie from making any effective intervention in the Soviet Union. Further, it had produced a number of other advantageous results, which strengthened the social-political role of the working class. To Lenin this meant not merely the feasibility of warding off war for a considerable time, but also, at least theoretically, the possibility of avoiding war altogether. Thereby was opened up the prospect, not merely of building up socialism in the Soviet Union, but also the possibility of economic cooperation between the Soviet state and the capitalist world, which would facilitate and speed up the building of a material base in the USSR. The strengthening of the workers' movement, its revolutionary victories in certain countries, the further expansion of the national liberation movements in the colonies, internal changes in the capitalist world—all this could not but gradually improve, not worsen, the situation of the first socialist country in the world. The fact that the Soviet Union did maintain its position against intervention during the several years of the civil war was for it a victory of significance on the level of world history and at the same time yet another proof of the feasibility of building socialism in one country. Indeed, it is precisely in the integral nature, the interconnectedness, interweaving and all the mutual impacts of all those processes and contradictions that we have the true process of the socialist revolution, not a "victorious march" of the Red Army through Europe, but a never-ceasing process of internal social developments in every country and their interconnecting on the international, worldwide scale.

With those views as basis, Lenin in both theory and practice assumed a stand of opposition to the theory of permanent world revolution, which as formulated by Trotsky had lost its Marxist character and had been transformed into an ideological program of a policy of war adventure, calling for the European communist parties to adopt a sectarian and dogmatic policy. Counter to this he drew up a new policy for the Soviet state, one based on a lengthy period of coexistence of the states of the capitalist system and those of the socialist system—a policy, that is, of peace and peaceable coexistence and of economic and other cooperation with the capitalist countries. Together with this, Lenin considered that the socialist state should offer whatever support to the progressive and revolutionary movements and forces in other countries was in the given circumstances feasible, provided it did not threaten the existence of socialism and the socialist state.

The criticism of Lenin's thesis of the feasibility of the victory of socialism in a single country was for Trotsky merely the starting point and argument of his basic theory, that of permanent world revolution, which in the last resort would have boiled down to a war of the Soviet Union against the capitalist world, in the hope of that war instigating revolution in Western Europe and the world as a whole. One should add that Trotsky did not clearly formulate this consequence of his theory, but by the internal logic of his theory this follows automatically.

History has cast Trotsky's theses to oblivion, for in every aspect practice has shown them to be false. Yet the vital elements of those theories have now reappeared on the world stage in these Chinese theories.

* * *

WAR AND SOCIALISM

* * *

It is customary to say that foreign policy is a reflection of home policy. The contrary, however, is also true. Foreign policy has definite consequences in both internal social developments and in political developments. This holds good both for capitalist and socialist countries, although these processes unfold in varied ways in these fields. But above all, both one and the other policy have a great influence on the development of socialism as a world system, which in its very nature is the product of the interlocking of very complex processes, forms and paths. *This very complexity is at the same time socialism's wealth, that is, that internal force which makes it possible for those processes to interlock and mutually criticize each other, which ensures the most adequate vigor and rapidity of development. Anything that damps down that vigor, that tends to uniformity and monopolism, acts as a brake on these developments.*

"Proletarian revolutions," wrote Marx in *The 18th Brumaire of Louis Bonaparte*,

> constantly criticize themselves, constantly interrupt their own course, returning to what had seemed to be finished, to begin it all over again, turning the frightful basic shortcomings, weaknesses, and timidities of their initial essays to ridicule.

At the present time the problem of a free choice of paths and forms of socialist development is certainly gaining in importance. Considered as a social-economic category in the course of history, there is of course in principle only one socialism. Feudalism, capitalism, and other social systems are also quite precise categories, but nonetheless the paths and forms by which they arose and developed were most multifarious. The same applies to socialism all the more, since here we have a process of inception and development of a classless society, consequently the process is so much more complex.

What is more, *the problems of the contradictions between the world of socialism and the world of capitalism will gradually acquire a secondary significance, while the problems of the further development of socialist social relations will increasingly become the real history of our age.* True, it would be a mistake today to underestimate the importance of these contradictions, since the forces of capitalism are still powerful, but it would be a still greater mistake to think that by saying that this or that country is a socialist country we have said everything. The same battle is fought out on the socialist ground too, even though in different forms, and this at the same time is all interlocked with the internal contradictions of socialist development itself, and it is precisely this that in the transitional stage makes it possible for hegemonistic trends, national egoisms, bureaucratic monopolism and so forth, to appear.

The contradictions between the world of socialism and the world of capitalism, it goes without saying, are with all the inevitability of a natural process—parallel with the economic consolidation of socialism—bound to acquire the character of a gradual overcoming of the remnants of the old world. That development will be realized through manifold internal processes, political and social, both in the capitalist and in the socialist countries, by processes which will be further speeded up by the influence exerted by the international role of socialism, as this finds expression in various forms of cooperation and division of labor among the nations, as also in all forms of influence by example and experience.

The very variety of both objective and human factors, which go to make the concrete forms or paths of socialism so multifarious, further, the varied nature of the starting-points of socialist development in the various countries, which results in there being a great variety of modes and intensities of the interweaving of elements of the new and the old, and finally, the political and social-economic indispensability of every country—independently of the level of its material starting point—uninterruptedly further developing socialist relationships if it wishes to maintain the unity of the working class and the people—all this means that *the maximum of liberty in the selection of paths and forms of socialist development—on the basis of scientific socialist theory and the totality of the practical experience of socialism—is the first and the most significant condition of the healthy and rapid development of socialism as a world system,* and at the same time the first and most important condition for the suppression of that conservatism which accompanies any monopoly, in the political system of a socialist country just as much as in any other social system.

It is precisely for this reason that the dilemma between a course based on coexistence and a course based on the inevitability of war becomes of such great importance for all the socialist forces in the world. A policy which in its final consequences bears in itself any element of Bonapartism is harmful not merely from the standpoint of that reaction which it is likely to excite in the non-socialist countries, which we have already discussed, but above all from the standpoint of the further development of socialism. In itself this policy would be a reflection of definite deformations of socialist development in any country in which such trends appeared, and, further, if such a policy did appear, it would also begin to play its own independent role in the sense of a further deepening of those deformations in the world socialist system.

* * *

CAUSES AND CONSEQUENCES

As we emphasized at the outset, the Chinese policy is not merely a consequence of "a deviation from the line of Marxism," nor merely an accident, but constitutes a law-conditioned political fruit of the structure and contradictions of the world today. Precisely for this reason it will tend to appear for some considerable period of time, in this form or that, with this or with that intensity, as a trend of international political relationships in our time, till at least to a certain degree the conditions which create it change. As those conditions are not immutable or insuperable, the hope is justified that sooner or later Chinese socialism will indeed overcome its present oscillations and get over them.

The peoples of China, whom imperialist pressure and the internal feudal regimes kept under fierce exploitation and in long-lasting backwardness, found their own way out of their internal contradictions in revolution and with the prospect of socialism before them. The Chinese Revolution has been one of the greatest revolutionary epics in the history of mankind. But the revolutionary war which in China lasted all but twenty-five years, against the united forces of China's own reactionaries and of international imperialism, does not speak merely of its profundity or of the sharpness of the contradictions which made that revolution indispensable, but also of the great responsibilities of that revolution to its own people. One of the main factors which had made the revolution indispensable, namely, the relative economic backwardness of the country, has however now become the main obstacle to any speed in internal development, and the principal source of the danger of internal reactionary forces rising again and undermining the unity of the country. The settlement of this question now brings into question the sheer existence of the revolution as such. The people which has shed so much blood in the long-drawn-out revolution, now with justice expects that victorious revolution to open up new prospects precisely in this sphere.

In a report on the work of the Government made in May 1957, Liu Shao-ch'i declared that the "speed of building up the country constitutes the most important question of all those with which we have had to contend since the victory of the socialist revolution."

In these words we have the clearest expression of the essence of the principal internal contradiction in the development of Chinese society.

The struggle against those problems is an exceptionally hard one. China has received and is still receiving a certain amount of economic aid from the socialist countries. But however great that aid, and no matter in what it consists, it cannot be sufficient to ensure the speeded-up economic expansion of a country which is a continent in itself. For the economic development of China to be normal, it needs to be an integral part of world industry.

On the other hand, China was exposed, and still is exposed, to the long-drawn-out pressure of the capitalist world, in particular of thc United States of America, which vainly hopes that this will weaken the revolution and strengthen the counterrevolutionary forces. When open intervention proved infeasible, an economic blockade of China was organized and efforts were made to secure the country's complete political isolation. The door to the United Nations Organization and to other organizations of international cooperation was closed. Apart from this, a constant threat is maintained against China by the artificial maintenance of the counterrevolutionary regime on Formosa and the establishment of military bases all around China. As a result, not only is it made impossible for China to find a place in world trade which would contribute to a more normal internal economic development, and not only does China receive no support whatsoever from world industry, but pressure is additionally exerted to increase the country's material burdens.

All these facts have very greatly increased the strains to which the peoples of China are subjected in their efforts to overcome backwardness and build up new social relationships, and that increase in the necessary effort has had as a consequence an increased sense that only self-reliance and extreme sacrifices on the part of the Chinese peoples and forces themselves can give any results. It was all the easier for such a feeling to arise since we have here a huge country, with hundreds of millions of inhabitants. It is perfectly natural under such conditions that there should have arisen a tendency to the view that the encircling ring imposed on China by the capitalist states by pressure and force must be broken by counterpressure and—if necessary—by force. Under such circumstances, to many Chinese, unable to take an integral view of social developments in the whole world, a policy based on coexistence not only does not look like practical politics, but is even felt to be likely to contribute to the maintenance of this state in which the peoples of China are now situated—that is, they see it as a brake on Chinese progress.

* * *

. . . [T]he leading factors in China have adopted the course of an all-out mobilization of their internal forces, even at the cost of the greatest hardships for the people. This mobilization is so all-embracing and so intensive that it has made the whole system of internal economic and political relations subordinate to it. In certain fields this mobilization has undoubtedly given significant material results. But as one of the phases of development of the revolution it is on the point of exhausting itself. Not only that, that historic effort which in itself is progressive, nevertheless, as it begins in a certain sense to become an end in itself—since dogmatic and conservative thought imposes it as a permanent essence of socialism, and because it begins to become a brake on the advance of socialist economic relations precisely in the most advanced sector of production—gives rise to the germ of a new contradiction, which in course of time cannot but begin to undermine precisely that great revolutionary effort. Here I have in mind the contradiction between the centralized administrative management of production and distribution on the one hand, which unquestionably gives rise to a conservative bureaucratism and a trend to the petrifaction of state-employment relations, and on the other hand the demands of the workers for distribution according to work done, which inevitably gives rise to a need for an appropriate system of industrial management that would liberate labor from the pressure of state-employment relations.

Of course, this process requires a rather long evolution. We would be sterile idealist and abstract dream-spinners, were we to expect or want to see this contradiction decided overnight by a subjective decision of the Chinese leadership. However, the problem is not that of the "final" solution, but whether the conditions exist for an unhindered evolution in that direction. Today the paths of such an evolution in China are by reason of the policy under discussion closed or at least seriously blocked; therefore contradictions cannot but grow worse and tend to produce certain deformations both in economic and political life. One of the first reactions under such conditions is unquestionably a weakening of subjective incentives to greater productivity of labor, which calls for an increased application of administrative supervision and thereby leads straight to all sorts of bureaucratic deformations of socialist development. Such a situation gives rise to a powerful political monopoly of the center, while with lack of economic strength and under the influence of internal contradictions such a center, based on strong political authority, may well fall a victim to the illusion that by its political power alone it can tackle and solve problems which in reality can only be settled by material evolution.

Since such efforts are impractical, every further step of material advancement finds expression in an increase in the material efforts and sacrifices of the people. To justify such sacrifices, or in other words, to keep the mass of the people mobilized for those sacrifices, the Chinese theoreticians have without any need or advantage invented a whole ideology. Humanism has been declared to be petty-bourgeois hypocrisy. The aspiration for "personal happiness" has been condemned as anti-socialist individualism. Democratic tendencies have been represented as ridiculous philistine prejudices. The criticism of bureaucratic-state-management monopolism has been attacked as revisionism of the worst kind.

It goes without saying that ideological tendencies of this sort could not but also come to expression in Chinese international policy. Such great sacrifices can certainly only be called for and justified if it is a matter not only of a program for a brighter future but also one of national independence and a definite position for the Chinese nation in international relations, one to which China has a right, but which the United States of America and other capitalist countries dispute. Hence, the policy of the cold war and of frightening people by threat of war not only does not hinder these Chinese efforts on the home front, but even makes them easier to bear.

Here, unquestionably, we have some of the main sources and causes of the Chinese criticism of the policy of coexistence and of their adopting the policy of cold war. Of course there are also others, but in the framework of the subjects of this discussion there is no need for me to enter into an analysis of factors which have no direct connection with those subjects.

However, under present-day conditions to adopt the cold war policy does not only mean "frightening," "bringing pressure to bear," and so on—it also means directly strengthening, even creating and organizing the forces of war in the capitalist countries; in other words, like it or not, it means preparing war. Herein precisely lies the danger of the present Chinese policy.

From the standpoint of any "tactical aims" or methods whatsoever it is senseless to talk of peace and coexistence, yet threaten war. The struggle for peace has its own language and its own means, but neither threats of war nor pressure on others, neither menacing others or the cold war are among them. Whoever wants to seem convincing in the struggle for peace and coexistence should first and foremost struggle precisely against such phenomena and methods.

In the West there are circles which are for a policy called "neither war nor peace." It would seem that the authors of some Chinese press-articles support a similar international policy. But both these and those are very myopic politicians. Even at the time of the October Revolution these sort of "tactics," which Trotsky and others supported, proved untenable, and Lenin decisively rejected them. But above all today, when opposed one to the other we have two huge concentrations of weapons of war, every sober-minded man should know that tactics of "neither war nor peace" do not mean anything else but—preparation for war, even instigation of war.

Precisely for this reason there is no real distinction at all between the threat or menace of war and the preparation and instigation of war.

Of course, *it is one thing to draw up one's aims and demands properly, and another to discover effective means and weapons for the realization of those aims appropriate to the given conditions of struggle.* It is in this that lies the contradictoriness of the Chinese policy, and this not only the foreign policy but also a considerable field of home policy. Examining their own problems within their national frontiers which, extensive as they are, are still cramped from the standpoint of socialism as a world system, and lack sufficient confidence in the strength of world socialism, precisely because the internal forces of Chinese socialism are weak the Chinese politicians have decided on a policy which not only is not capable of solving the problems which it was invented to solve, but one which on the contrary will merely go to increase the difficulties which the Chinese Revolution has to overcome. And not only have they come out against the policy of coexistence, which would have been the quickest path to breaking the blockade which encloses China, but the leading circles of China have also decided on all sorts of international acts which have excited the unanimous resistance precisely of those peoples who were the closest and most natural allies of China in the struggle for the final liberation of Asia from the vestiges of imperialist rule and for the overcoming of the backwardness of the Asian peoples. This policy has gone so far that that great country has even begun to stir up undecided, but very trifling, frontier problems, which certainly is not at all in harmony with the spirit of a socialist foreign policy. In this way, instead of confidence, the Chinese policy is creating fear all along its frontiers, and fear gives new strength to the policy of the blockade, just when this had begun to be compromised and markedly weakened.

What is more, by her insistence on subordinating the interests and views of world socialism to her own interests and views, China has come into conflict with the socialist forces as well. It is completely clear that such a policy cannot make it any easier for China to resolve her own internal problems, but even more is it clear that it is doing serious harm to the further expansion of socialism in the world.

Such a foreign policy will undoubtedly have its repercussions also on the internal development of China, in the sense of a further political and economic centralization, an extreme strengthening of the apparatus of the state and the control by this of the whole of internal life. And such phenomena will be not merely an inexhaustible source of bureaucratic-étatist distortions of socialist development—that is, of conservative aspirations for the preservation and strengthening of the state—but also a cause of new economic difficulties, and first and foremost of a still slower growth of productivity of labor and of a still lower profitability of investments. Such development will impose on the people still greater sacrifices and will still further exacerbate the contradictions of material developments. This is in fact a spiral which inevitably leads the whole conception up a blind alley. Social development has its own insuperable laws, which will not subject themselves to any man's philosophizing, not even that of the Chinese. Everybody who has essayed ignoring those laws, by following a course of subjective elaborations of policy, instead of remaining solidly on the ground of a real analysis of the actual conditions, has suffered defeat. Nor will the Chinese communists be able sooner or later to avoid feeling the consequences of their policy of scorning the objective laws governing things. We can only hope that those failures, which even now have begun to draw the attention of the communists of China to the dangers facing them, will, in Lenin's words, be that factor which in the end will persuade them to abandon a sterile political course by which it is plain that they cannot find a lasting solution to any one of their problems.

THE CHINESE-YUGOSLAV DIFFERENCES OF OPINION

History itself creates the cure for every ailment. The phenomena of contradictions which have so clearly come to expression in the development of the socialist world, and which perhaps trouble and frighten some short-sighted people, will at the same time help those who fight for socialism better to understand the problems of present-day socialism and not be contented with the interpretation of certain phenomena in the course of development by a simple repetition of stereotyped dogmatic phrases.

This also applies to the Chinese-Yugoslav differences of opinion. Today it must be clear to every Marxist that these differences of opinion are not the fruit of any abstract ideological-theoretical disputes about the interpretation of Marxism. Nor are they the fruit of any sort of Yugoslav "national communism," nor of any Yugoslav infringement of the principles of socialist internationalism or so forth, as has so often been maintained in the attacks on the communists of Yugoslavia. *They are in their essence the reflection of real contradictions of socialist development which arise from the fact that in its forms, its paths, and its means, socialism is not a process which is repeated every time and everywhere in the same way, but is one which never appears anywhere in a "pure" form, that is, free from all the influences of the material and ideological elements of the given period, environment, and conditions.*

Under such conditions the right of the people freely to decide on the ways and means of socialist development is a principle which guarantees not only equality among the peoples but, still more important, also the most rapid and painless development and advance of world socialism. Precisely for this reason we have always fought for that principle, and today still fight, in regard to the Chinese anti-Yugoslav campaign.

This also applies to the principle of socialist solidarity. That principle too finds expression in varied ways, in varied acts and organizations; but what is essential is that it unites the socialist forces on basic questions of the defense of the socialist achievements and the consolidation of these. The essence of this principle is not in any formal unity nor is it in any mechanical discipline, but in a real and profound sense of the identity of the elementary interests of the socialist forces in all quarters of the world. But this sense is possible only on the basis of the complete equality of rights and of self-government of all the peoples on the socialist road.

In his time Engels wrote:

> The international movement of the European and American proletariat has today grown so strong that not only its first narrow form—a secret association—but also its second, infinitely vaster form—the public International Workers' Association—has become a fetter, and the simple feeling of solidarity, based on the consciousness of identity of class position, is enough to create and maintain among the workers of all countries and languages one and the same great party of the proletariat.

What then is to be said about the present-day strength of the international workers' movement? Are we to consider that the sense of identity of the basic class interests of the socialist forces is less developed today than it once was? It is clear that we should not look at things in that way, for that would be to negate not only the experience of our time but also the very teachings of Marxism about the class struggle. However, for precisely this sense to be the real basis of socialist solidarity, the principle of solidarity should never be set in opposition to the principle of the independent determination and testing in practice of the varied forms and ways of socialist development, including here the international policy of socialism. In other words, the concrete forms of solidarity should not blot out the possibility of a democratic clearing up of the problems of socialist advancement by a testing out of them through varied implementation and through democratic forms of the struggle of ideas.

For these reasons, we Yugoslav communists not only have never avoided open discussion between the communists of the various countries about the problems of present-day realities and the advancement of socialism, but have considered it useful and indispensable, of course on condition that it does not destroy the sense of mutual responsibility in matters concerning the solidarity of the progressive forces. This also holds as regards the difference between our views and the Chinese conceptions of a socialist international policy. If the Chinese communists really wished in basic principle to clear up any of the problems of present-day prospects of the further development of socialism, and if such discussion were kept within the limits and forms of discussion appropriate between equal partners, this might be advantageous, even were it impossible to make both sides' views fit each other. In the last resort, we have never held that the aim of discussions of this sort is the removal of all differences of opinion, for today that is becoming an impossibility, when communists are no longer merely a revolutionary movement struggling for power, but are at the head of a number of states and are becoming the expression of the most varied material developments. Differences of opinion as to various questions of tactics, methods of struggle and how to approach the resolution of this or that problem cannot fail to exist under present-day conditions. Such discussions, however, have their purpose precisely in the fact that despite differences of opinion they could ensure that indispensable solidarity of the socialist and the progressive forces which strengthens socialism and the progress of mankind as a whole and is their defense against reactionary attacks.

To attain this sort of discussion between communists, the methods introduced by Stalin, who pronounced anybody who had his own opinion about socialist policy to be this or that sort of traitor to socialism, must be rejected. In other words, now that at last the cult of personality and the political methods which arose from that cult have been condemned, discussion between communists should also be freed from the methods of slander, interruption, lies, distortions, insinuations, the attachment of all manner of ideological labels, and this precisely in order, quite apart from the differences of opinion, to ensure socialist solidarity also regarding questions of common interests, on the basis of complete equality.

In this framework, what is both feasible and necessary is also international criticism conducted in democratic forms. The Yugoslav communists do not consider themselves proof against error, or infallible, but they cannot admit anybody else, whoever it may be, to have a monopoly right to the determination of the truth or the paths of socialist practice either in internal or external politics. For this reason, criticism is an indispensable instrument for the clearing up of points of dispute. But as Lenin has already said, criticism can take two forms, which are always dependent on the purpose of the criticism; one is the method of criticism which aims at destroying, the other the method of criticism which desires to assist. Among communists and all socialist and progressive forces, even when very profound differences of opinion exist over matters of principle, the methods of the latter type of criticism should prevail. And such criticism also has its own language, methods, and democratic forms.

In contradistinction to the Chinese anti-Yugoslav propaganda, and despite insults, we have always striven in our criticism of Chinese policy to remain on the level of this latter kind of criticism. This we intend to go on doing. We have no desire to impose our views on the Chinese communists, not merely because we have neither the will to do so nor the possibility of doing so, but also because precisely such acts would be most profoundly counter to those democratic principles for which we stand and on which the mutual relations of the peoples and of the movements in the world of socialism should be built and developed. Differences of opinion which cannot be brushed aside here should be settled by evolution and by experience, not by antagonistic exacerbation of ill feeling.

But, it goes without saying, we also cannot allow anybody to force their views on us by pressure, political or otherwise. Mutual criticism is one thing, but the introduction of force into mutual relations is another. And any political pressure —outside the framework of a democratic criticism—in the framework of the relations between the socialist countries we consider to be a hegemonistic exercise of force. This is precisely why we also cannot accept the line of argument of the Chinese critics of Yugoslavia according to which it is the duty of the Yugoslav communists to stand in line with Chinese socialism, though the Chinese communists have no similar obligation to Yugoslav socialism.

The current Chinese anti-Yugoslav campaign has taken over the thoroughly discredited legacy of the Stalin campaign of 1948 and subsequent years. Clearly here we have not to do with the criticism or the discussion of which I spoke above, but with an act of political pressure, one which is precisely aimed at silencing such criticism and discussion. Thus savagely attacking the Yugoslav communists, the Chinese leaders obviously would like to create an atmosphere in which anybody who did not mechanically repeat the ultra-radical and sectarian phrases of the Chinese lexicon would thereby automatically declare himself to be an adherent of "Yugoslav revisionism." And this of itself is a proof that we have to do here not with socialist solidarity but with a struggle for an ideological and political monopoly, for the realization of certain fixed notions about the international and internal policy of socialism.

Perhaps in some countries men will be found who will condemn our polemicizing with the Chinese authors of the anti-Yugoslav campaign, considering it detrimental to the general interests of socialism. Perhaps such people think that silence would be more advantageous. But socialist Yugoslavia also has its own interests and it cannot allow anybody in the name of a false "socialism" to trample on those interests in the most crude manner. But that is not the most important thing. It would be more harmful than any polemicizing to allow anybody to fish in muddied waters—that is, in conditions where the working masses do not really know what it is all about. The Yugoslav communists are under an obligation to tell their own people—and not only their own people, but also the international proletariat as a whole—what the real essence of the Chinese-Yugoslav differences of opinion really is.

And finally, to assume an attitude regarding the tackling of the large and decisive problems of present-day socialism is certainly an unavoidable historical task of today's generation of revolutionary socialists; and for this reason we Yugoslav communists are firmly convinced that frank replies to these Chinese attacks, equally openly pronounced and published, can only be of advantage to the cause of socialism, for they will bring more clarity into the problems under discussion.

The forces of reaction, let me add, hope in vain to extract some advantage for themselves from this. Everything that leads to the consolidation of a line of policy based on coexistence will also build up the confidence of the people in the possibility of maintaining lasting peace; it will increase the number and the strength of the adherents of coexistence in the capitalist world as well, and this not only inside the working-class and the anti-imperialist movements in that world, but also in other sober circles of society which do not want mankind to be exposed to the catastrophe of a fresh world war—that is, those who are beginning to grasp that what is historically unavoidable in the development of society cannot be escaped.

In conclusion, it is necessary once again to emphasize that it would be very mistaken to look at the totality of the role and development of the Chinese Revolution through the prism of the differences of opinion under discussion here. We must not forget the epoch-making role which the Chinese Revolution has played in our age. It is precisely this revolution which dealt the system of imperialism and colonialism in Asia and in the other continents a fateful blow, thereby playing a decisive part in changing the whole relationship of forces in the present-day world from the foundations upward. The men who under the most arduous conditions led that revolution and by their abilities proved one of the significant factors in its victory are today still largely at the head of China. Consequently, whatever the transitory deformations in Chinese policy, we are sure that Chinese socialism will master them. But precisely for this reason it is so much the more necessary to criticize these phenomena openly, and this the more so since it is they that are the source of the Chinese anti-Yugoslav campaign.

Throughout its development the Yugoslav communists afforded the Chinese Revolution active political support. And when the revolutionary Government of the new China was installed, Yugoslavia was one of the first to recognize it and give it her support, both in the United Nations Organization and outside this. At that time the Chinese Government, carrying out Stalin's anti-Yugoslav line, did not consider it necessary even to reply to the Yugoslav proposals for the establishment of normal relations between the two countries. But this nevertheless in no way changed the attitude of approval of revolutionary China which we had adopted, nor did it weaken our support of the justified Chinese demands in international politics.

This is how today we still look on the new China and our relations with her. We wish that the Chinese peoples may see their efforts to build the material basis for socialism crowned with the greatest success. In addition, we desire Chinese-Yugoslav relations to be based on the principle of mutual aid to one of the other in the building of socialism, without either imposing any ready-made ideological or political schemes on the other. In that spirit we shall continue further stubbornly doing all that lies in our power to secure an improvement of our relations with China and the Chinese communists, for in our view it is solely on such a basis that cooperation between two socialist countries can develop with success.

If the price of such cooperation has to be renunciation of the principles of our independent socialist home and foreign policies—independent not of the interests of socialism but of anybody else's particular subjectively concocted notions—in this case those of the Communist Party of China—it must be said outright that this is a price we are not prepared to pay, for it would mean the renunciation under pressure from without of precisely those basic and most essential principles which should rule in the relations between socialist countries.

10

OPEN LETTER ON RELATIONS WITH CHINA*

The Central Committee of the Communist Party of the Soviet Union
(Moscow, 14 July 1963)

Following the disarray in the communist world in 1956, the Chinese took the lead in trying to reconstitute communist unity. They reasserted the role of the CPSU as the leading party and attempted to augment Soviet authority. They so acted because they believed that the movement required it; in return they expected appreciation and a strengthening of their voice in the movement.

In late 1957 and early 1958, however, Khrushchev made it clear that even though the Chinese acknowledged the USSR as being the senior partner, he was unwilling to share leadership with them. What's more, he was not concerned whether they liked his position or not. He also made it clear that they could not expect additional economic aid.

After 1958, the difficulties between the Russians and the Chinese increased. In 1961 there were fierce differences over the renewed downgrading of Stalin. In 1962 there were seri-

* Excerpts

ous disagreements over Khrushchev's handling of the Cuban missile crisis.

Throughout this period there were biting exchanges between Moscow and Peking, but an attempt was made to maintain a certain decorum. The Russians lashed out at the Albanians when they meant the Chinese; and the Chinese flayed away at the Yugoslavs when they meant the Russians. Even when this was no longer done, the names of rival leaders were not specifically mentioned, though the individuals were readily identifiable. But in 1963 all such restraints were removed; Mao and Khrushchev were identified by name, with the former being called, among other things, a Trotskyite and a racist, and the latter being labeled as a cowardly, traitorous bedfellow of imperialism.

One of the high—or low—points in the exchange between Russia and China was the "Open Letter" of July 14, 1963, in which Moscow used more than 15,000 words to set forth its complaints against the Chinese comrades.

Dear comrades:

The Central Committee of the CPSU deems it necessary to address this open letter to you to set out our position on the fundamental questions of the international Communist movement in connection with the letter of the Central Committee of the Communist party of China of June 14, 1963.

The Soviet people are well aware that our party and Government, expressing as they do the will of the entire Soviet people, spare no effort to strengthen fraternal friendship with the peoples of all Socialist countries, with the Chinese people. We are united by a common struggle for the victory of communism; we have the same aim, the same aspirations and hopes.

For many years the relations between our parties were good. But some time ago, serious differences came to light between the CPC on the one hand the CPSU and other fraternal parties on the other. At the present time, the Central

Committee of the CPSU feels increasingly concerned over statements and actions by the leadership of the Communist party of China undermining the cohesion of our parties, the friendship of our peoples.

* * *

I.
HISTORY OF THE DIFFERENCES

For nearly half a century the Soviet country, under the leadership of the Communist party, has been leading a struggle for the triumph of the ideas of Marxism-Leninism in the name of the freedom and happiness of the working people in the whole world. From the very first days of the existence of the Soviet state, when the great Lenin stood at the helm of our country, until the present day, our people have rendered—and are rendering—tremendous, disinterested aid to all the peoples fighting for their liberation from the yoke of imperialism and colonialism, for the building of a new life.

World history has known no example of one country's rendering such extensive aid to other countries in developing their economy, science and technology.

* * *

Comrade Mao Tse-tung said in 1957:

"In the course of the struggle for national liberation, the Chinese people enjoyed the fraternal sympathy and support of the Soviet people. After the victory of the Chinese Revolution, the Soviet Union is also rendering tremendous all-round assistance to the cause of the construction of Socialism in China. The Chinese people will never forget all this."

* * *

In April 1960, the Chinese comrades openly disclosed their differences with the world Communist movement by publishing a collection of articles called "Long Live Leninism!"

This collection, based on distortions—truncated and incorrectly interpreted theses of the well-known works of Lenin—contained propositions actually directed against the foundations of the declaration of the Moscow meeting of 1957, which was signed on behalf of the CPC by Comrade Mao Tse-tung, against the policy of peaceful coexistence of states with different social systems, against the possibility of preventing a world war in the present day, against the use of both peaceful and nonpeaceful roads of the development of Socialist revolutions.

* * *

Deepening their ideological differences with the fraternal parties, the leaders of the CPC began carrying them over to international relations. The Chinese organs began curtailing economic and trade relations of the PRC [People's Republic of China] with the Soviet Union and other Socialist countries. On the initiative of the PRC Government, the volume of China's trade with the Soviet Union was cut almost 67 percent in the last three years; deliveries of industrial plants dropped 40 times. This reduction took place on the initiative of the Chinese leaders.

We regret that the PRC leadership has embarked on such a road. We have always believed, and believe now, that it is necessary to go on developing Soviet-Chinese relations to develop cooperation. This would have been beneficial for both sides, and above all to People's China, which had received great assistance from the Soviet Union and other Socialist countries.

The Soviet Union developed extensive relations with China before, and it comes out today, too, for their expansion and not curtailment. It seems that the CPC leadership should have displayed primary concern for the development of economic relations with the Socialist countries. However, it began acting in the opposite direction, disregarding the damage caused by such actions to the PRC economy.

The Chinese leaders did not tell their people truthfully through whose fault these relations were curtailed. Broad propaganda aimed at discrediting the foreign and domestic policy of the CPSU, at stirring up anti-Soviet sentiment, was started among the Chinese Communists and even among the general population.

The CPSU Central Committee called the attention of the Chinese comrades to these incorrect actions. We told the Chinese comrades that the people should not be prompted to praise or anathematize this or that party, depending on the arising disputes or differences. It is clear to every Communist that disagreements among fraternal parties are nothing more than a temporary episode, whereas relations among the peoples of the Socialist countries are being established for all times to come.

But the Chinese leaders, every time, ignored the comradely warnings of the CPSU, further exacerbating Chinese-Soviet relations.

Since the end of 1961, the Chinese representatives at international democratic organizations began openly imposing their erroneous views. In December 1961, at the Stockholm session of the World Council of Peace, the Chinese delegation came out against the convocation of the World Congress for Peace and Disarmament.

In the course of 1962, the activities of the World Federation of Trade Unions, the World Movement of Peace Champions, the Afro-Asian Solidarity Movement, the World Federation of Democratic Youth, the Women's International Democratic Federation, and many other organizations were endangered as a result of the splitting activities of the Chinese representatives.

They came out against the participation of representatives of the Afro-Asian Solidarity Committees of the European Socialist countries in the third Solidarity Conference of the peoples of Asian and African countries in Moshi [Tanganyika].

The leader of the Chinese delegation told the Soviet representatives that "whites have nothing to do here." At the Journalists Conference in Jakarta [Indonesia], the Chinese representatives followed a line toward preventing Soviet journalists from participating as full-fledged delegates on the plea that the Soviet Union is not an Asian country.

It is strange and surprising that Chinese comrades accused the overwhelming majority of the recent World Congress of Women of splitting activities and an erroneous political line while, during the adoption of the appeal to the women of all continents, only representatives of two countries—China and Albania—out of 110 countries represented at the congress, voted against it. Well, indeed, the entire multimillion-member army of freedom-loving women is marching out of step, and only two are marching in step—keeping in line!

Such, in brief, is the history of the differences of the Chinese leadership with the CPSU and other fraternal parties. It shows that the CPC leaders counterpose their own special line to the general course of the Communist movement, trying to impose on it their own dictate, their deeply erroneous views on the key problems of our time.

II.
QUESTIONS OF WAR AND PEACE

What is the gist of the differences between the CPC on the one hand, and the CPSU, the international Communist movement on the other hand?

* * *

[F]irst of all, the question of war and peace.

In the appraisal of problems of war and peace, in the approach to their solution, there can be no uncertainties or reservations, for this involves the destinies of peoples, the future of all mankind.

The CPSU Central Committee believes its duty is to tell the party and the people with all frankness that in questions of war and peace the CPC leadership has cardinal, based-on-principle differences with us, with the world Communist movement.

The essence of these differences lies in the diametrically opposite approach to problems so vital as the possibility of averting world thermonuclear war, peaceful coexistence of states with different social systems, interconnection between the struggle for peace and the development of the world revolutionary movement.

* * *

To prevent a new world war is quite a real and feasible task. Congress XX of our party formed the extremely important conclusion that in our times there is no fatal inevitability of war between states.

This conclusion is not a fruit of good intentions but the result of a realistic, strictly scientific analysis of the balance of class forces on the world arena; it is based on the gigantic might of world Socialism. Our views on this question are shared by the entire world Communist movement.

* * *

Socialism and peace are now inseparable in the minds of the broad masses!

The Chinese comrades obviously underestimate all the danger of thermonuclear war. "The atomic bomb is a paper tiger; it is not terrible at all," they contend.

The main thing, don't you see, is to put an end to imperialism as quickly as possible; but how—with what losses—this will be achieved seems a secondary question.

To whom, it is right to ask, is it secondary? To the hundreds of millions of people who are doomed to death in the event of the unleashing of a thermonuclear war? To the states that will be erased from the face of the earth in the very first hours of such a war?

No one, including big states, has the right to play with the destinies of millions of people. Those who do not want to exert efforts to exclude world war from the life of the peoples—to avert a mass annihilation of people and the destruction of the values of human civilization—deserve condemnation.

* * *

Such posing of the question by the Chinese comrades may engender well-justified suspicion that this is no longer a class approach in the struggle for the abolition of capitalism but for some entirely different aims. If both the exploiters and the exploited are buried under the ruins of the old world, who will build the "bright future?"

In this connection, it is impossible not to note that instead of the class-internationalist approach expressed in the call "Workers of the world, unite!" the Chinese comrades stubbornly propagate a slogan devoid of any class meaning: "The wind from the East prevails over the wind from the West."

In the questions of the Socialist Revolution, our party firmly adheres to the Marxist-Leninist class petitions, being of the opinion that revolutions in every country are carried out by the working class, the working people, without military interference from outside.

* * *

The deep difference—in the views of the CPSU and other Marxist-Leninist parties on the one hand and the CPC leaders on the other hand—on the questions of war, peace and peaceful co-existence, was manifested with particular clarity during the 1962 crisis in the Caribbean Sea. It was a sharp international crisis; never before had mankind come so close to the brink of a thermonuclear war as it did in October of last year.

The Chinese comrades allege that in the period of the Caribbean crisis we made an "adventurist" mistake by introducing rockets in Cuba, and then "capitulated" to American imperialism when we removed the rockets from Cuba. (Such allegations were made in the leading article in *Jenmin Jihpao* on March 8, 1963, "On the Statement of the Communist Party of the U.S.A.") Such assertions utterly contradict the facts.

What was the actual state of affairs? The CPSU Central Committee and the Soviet Government possessed trustworthy information that an armed aggression of United States imperialism against Cuba was about to start. We realized with sufficient clarity that the most resolute steps were needed to rebuff aggression, to defend the Cuban Revolution effectively.

Curses and warnings—even if they are called "serious warnings" and are repeated two and a half hundred times over—have no effect on the imperialists.

Proceeding from the need for defending the Cuban Revolution, the Soviet Government and the Government of Cuba reached agreement on the delivery of missiles to Cuba, because this was the only effective way of preventing aggression on the part of American imperialism.

The delivery of missiles to Cuba signified that an attack on her would meet resolute rebuff, with the employment of rocket weapons against the organizers of the aggression. Such a resolute step on the part of the Soviet Union and Cuba was a shock to the American imperialists, who felt for the first time in their history that in case they undertook an armed invasion on Cuba, a shattering retaliatory blow would be dealt on their own territory.

Inasmuch as the point in question was not simply a conflict between the United States and Cuba, but a clash between two major nuclear powers, the crisis in the area of the Caribbean Sea would have turned from a local one into a world one. A real danger of world thermonuclear war arose.

There were two alternatives in the prevailing situation: either to follow in the wake of the "madmen" (this is how the most aggressive and reactionary representatives of American imperialism are dubbed) and embark upon the road of unleashing a world thermonuclear war, or, profiting from the opportunity offered by the delivery of the missiles, to take all measures to reach an agreement on the peaceful solution of the crisis and to prevent aggression against the Cuban Republic.

We have chosen, as is known, the second road, and are convinced that we have done the right thing. We are confident that all our people are unanimous on this score. The Soviet people have proved more than once that they know how to stand up for themselves, how to defend the cause of the revolution, the cause of Socialism. And nobody knows better than they do how much sorrow and suffering a war brings, what difficulties and sacrifices it costs the people.

Agreements on the removal of missile weapons, in reply to the United States Government's commitment not to invade Cuba and to keep its allies from doing this, the heroic struggle of the Cuban people, the support rendered to them by the peace-loving nations, have made possible the frustration of the plans of the extreme adventuristic circles of American imperialism, which were ready to go whole hog.

As a result, it was possible to defend revolutionary Cuba and save peace.

The Chinese comrades regard as "embellishment of imperialism" our statement that the Kennedy Government has also displayed definite reasonableness, a realistic approach in the course of the crisis around Cuba. Do they really think that all bourgeois governments lack all reason in everything they do?

Thanks to the courageous and farsighted position of the USSR, the staunchness and restraint of the heroic Cuban people and their government, the forces of Socialism and peace have proved that they are able to curb the aggressive forces of imperialism, to impose peace on the war advocates. This was a major victory of the policy of reason, of the forces of peace and Socialism; this was a defeat of the forces of imperialism, of the policy of military ventures.

* * *

But it should not be forgotten that we have also given a commitment to the Cuban people: If the United States imperialists break their promise and invade Cuba, we shall come to the assistance of the Cuban people. Every sober-minded person understands well that in case of an act of aggression by the American imperialists we shall come to the assistance of the Cuban people from Soviet territory, just as we would have helped them from Cuban territory, too.

* * *

III. DIFFERENCES ON THE PERSONALITY CULT

There are serious difficulties between the CPC and the CPSU and other Marxist-Leninist parties on the question of struggle against the consequences of the Stalin personality cult.

The CPC leaders took upon themselves the role of the defenders of the personality cult, the propagators of Stalin's faulty ideas. They are trying to thrust upon other parties the practices, the ideology and morals, the forms and methods of the leadership that were flourishing in the period of the personality cult. We must say outright that this is an unenviable role that will bring them neither honor nor glory. No one will succeed in drawing the Marxist-Leninists, the progressive people, onto the road of defending the personality cult.

The Soviet people, the world Communist movement duly appreciated the courage and the boldness, the truly Leninist firmness of principle demonstrated in the struggle against the consequences of the personality cult by our party, by its Central Committee, headed by Comrade Nikita Khrushchev.

Everybody knows that our party did so in order to remove the heavy burden that fettered the powerful forces of the working people and thus in order to speed the development of the Soviet society. Our party did so in order to free the ideals of Socialism, bequeathed to us by the great Lenin, from the stigma of abuses of personal power and arbitrariness.

Our party did so in order to prevent a recurrence of the tragic events that accompanied the personality cult, to make all fighters for socialism derive lessons from our experience.

The entire Communist movement correctly understood and supported the struggle against the personality cult alien to Marxism-Leninism, against its harmful consequences. At one time it was approved by the Chinese leaders, too. They spoke about the tremendous international significance of the CPSU's Congress XX.

* * *

Any unbiased person who compares these pronouncements of the Chinese leaders with what is said in the letter of the CPC Central Committee of June 14 will become convinced that they have made a 180-degree turn in evaluating our party Congress XX. But are any vacillations and waverings permissible on such questions of principle? Of course they are not. Either the Chinese leaders then had no differences with the CPSU Central Committee on these questions of principles, or all these statements were false.

It is well known that practice is the best measure of truth.

It is practice, precisely, that proves convincingly the wonderful results in the life of our country brought about by the realization of the line of party Congresses XX, XXI, and XXII. In the course of the ten years that have passed since our party made a sharp turn toward restoration of Leninist principles and norms in party life, Soviet society has achieved truly majestic results in developing economy, in promoting culture and science, in raising the people's welfare, in consolidating the defense potential, and in the successes of foreign policy.

The atmosphere of fear, suspicion, and uncertainty that poisoned the life of the people in the period of the personality cult is gone, never to return.

It is impossible to deny the fact that the Soviet people now live better, enjoy the benefits of Socialism.

* * *

Alluding to the fact that our party proclaims for its task the struggle for a better life for the people, the CPC leaders hint at some sort of "bourgeoisation" and "regeneration" of the Soviet society. According to their logic, if a people walks in shoes made out of rags and eats thin cabbage soup from a common bowl, that is communism. And if a workingman lives well and wants to live still better tomorrow—that is almost the restoration of Capitalism! And they want to present this philosophy to us as the latest revelation in Marxism-Leninism! This fully discloses the authors of such "theories" as people who do not believe in the strength and capabilities of the working class, which took power into its own hands and created its own Socialist state.

If we turn to the history of our country, the CPSU program, we will easily see from what we began—when under the leadership of Lenin we took power into our hands—and what summits the Soviet people have achieved.

* * *

IV.
PROBLEMS OF CONDUCTING THE REVOLUTIONARY STRUGGLE

The next important question on which we differ is that of the ways and methods of the revolutionary struggle of the working class in the countries of capitalism, the struggle for national liberation, the ways of the transition of all mankind to Socialism.

* * *

Everyone who has pondered the meaning of the present struggle for peace, against thermonuclear war, realizes that by their policy of peace the Soviet Communists, and the fraternal parties of the other Socialist countries, give inestimable aid to the working class, the working people of the capitalist countries. And this is not because averting nuclear war means saving from death the working class, the peoples of whole countries and even continents—though this alone is enough to justify all our policy.

. . . This policy is the best way to help the international revolutionary working-class movement achieve its principal class aims; is it not a tremendous contribution to the struggle of the working class when the countries of Socialism, in the conditions of peace they themselves have won, score magnificent successes in the development of economy, score ever new victories in science and technology, constantly improve the living and working conditions of the people, develop, and improve Socialist democracy?

Looking at these successes and victories, every worker in a capitalist country will say: "Socialism proves by deeds that it is superior to capitalism. This system is worth fighting for."

In the present conditions, socialism wins the hearts and minds of the people not only through books but primarily by its deeds, by its living example.

* * *

[The Chinese comrades] want to achieve the revolution sooner, by other—what seem to them shorter—ways. But victorious revolution can consolidate its successes and prove the superiority of Socialism over capitalism by the work and only by the work of the people.

True, this is not easy, especially if the revolution is accomplished in countries that have inherited an underdeveloped economy. But the example of the Soviet Union and many other Socialist countries proves convincingly that in these conditions, too—if correct leadership is provided—it is possible to score great successes and to demonstrate to the entire world the superiority of Socialism over Capitalism.

* * *

The Chinese comrades have disagreed with the world Communist movement also concerning the forms of the transition of different countries to Socialism.

It is common knowledge that the CPSU and the other Marxist-Leninist parties, as is clearly pointed out in the documents of the Moscow meetings and in the program of the CPSU, proceed from the possibilities of both a peaceful and a non-peaceful transition to Socialism. Despite this, the Chinese comrades stubbornly ascribe to our party and to the other fraternal parties the recognition of the peaceful method alone.

In its letter of March 30, 1963, the CPSU Central Committee has again outlined its position on this score:

> The working class and its vanguard, the Marxist-Leninist parties, endeavor to carry out socialist revolution in a peaceful way with-

out civil war. The realization of such a possibility is in keeping with the interests of the working class and all the people, and with the national interests of the country.

At the same time, the choice of the means of developing the revolution depends not only on the working class. If the exploiting classes resort to violence against the people, the working class will be forced to use non-peaceful means of seizing power. Everything depends on the particular conditions and on the distribution of class forces within the country and in the world arena.

Naturally, no matter what forms are used for the transition from capitalism to Socialism, such a transition is possible only by means of a Socialist revolution and of the dictatorship of the proletariat in various forms.

Appreciating highly the selfless struggle of the working class headed by the Communists in the capitalist countries, the CPSU considers it its duty to render them every kind of aid and support.

We have repeatedly explained our viewpoint, and there is no need to outline it in greater detail here.

And what is the position of the Chinese comrades on this question? It key-notes all their statements and the letter of the CPC Central Committee of June 14.

The Chinese comrades regard as the main criterion of revolutionary spirit the recognition of an armed uprising always, in everything, everywhere. Thereby the Chinese comrades actually deny the possibility of using peaceful forms of struggle for the victory of the Socialist revolution, whereas Marxism-Leninism teaches that the Communists must master all forms of revolutionary class struggle—both violent and nonviolent.

Yet another important question is that of the relationship between the struggle of the international working class and the national-liberation movement of the peoples of Asia, Africa, and Latin America. The international revolutionary working-class movement represented today by the world system of Socialism and the Communist parties of the capitalist countries, and the national-liberation movement of the peoples of Asia, Africa, and Latin America—these are the great forces of our epoch. The correct coordination among them constitutes one of the main requisites for victory over imperialism.

How do the Chinese comrades solve this question? This is seen from their new "theory," according to which the main contradiction of our time is, you see, contradiction not between Socialism and imperialism, but between the national-liberation movement and imperialism. The decisive force in the struggle against imperialism, the Chinese comrades hold, is not the world system of Socialism, not the struggle of the international working class, but again the national-liberation movement.

In this way the Chinese comrades, apparently, wish to win in the easiest way popularity among the peoples of Asia, Africa, and Latin America. But let nobody be deceived by this "theory."

Whether the Chinese theoreticians want it or not, this theory essentially means the isolation of the national-liberation movement from the international working class and its offspring—the world system of Socialism. But this would have constituted a tremendous danger to the national-liberation movement itself.

* * *

The question arises: what is the explanation for the incorrect propositions of the CPC leadership on the basic problems of our time? It is either the complete divorce of the Chinese comrades from actual reality, a dogmatic, bookish approach to problems of war, peace, and the revolution, their lack of understanding of the concrete conditions of the modern epoch or the fact that behind the rumpus about the "world revolution" raised by the Chinese comrades are other goals that have nothing in common with revolution.

All this shows the erroneousness, the disastrous nature, of the course that the CPC leadership tries to impose on the world Communist movement. What the Chinese leaders propose under the guise of a "general line" is nothing but an enumeration of the most general tasks of the working class, made without due consideration for time and the concrete correlation of class forces, without due consideration for the peculiarities of the modern stage of history.

* * *

V.
THE DIVISIVE NATURE OF CHINESE ACTIVITIES

The erroneous views of the CPC leaders on the cardinal political and theoretical questions of our time are inseparably linked with their practical activities directed toward undermining the unity of the world Socialist camp and the international Communist movement.

The Chinese comrades recognize in oratory that the unity of the USSR and the Chinese People's Republic is a mainstay of the entire Socialist community, but in fact they are undermining contacts with our party, with our country in all directions.

The CPC leadership often speaks of its loyalty to the commonwealth of the Socialist countries, but the attitude of the Chinese comrades to this commonwealth refutes their high-sounding declarations.

The statistics show that in the course of the last three years the People's Republic of China cut the volume of its trade with the countries of the Socialist community by more than 50 percent. Some Socialist countries felt the results of this line of the Chinese comrades with particular sharpness.

The acts of the Chinese leadership stand in glaring contradiction not only to the principles of mutual relations between Socialist countries but in many cases even to the generally recognized rules and norms that should be observed by all states.

The flouting of the agreements signed earlier inflicted serious damage on the national economy of some Socialist states. It is quite understandable that the economy of China also suffers tangibly from the curtailment of its economic contacts.

In an effort to justify its actions in the eyes of the popular masses, the CPC leadership recently advanced a theory of "reliance on one's own forces." Generally speaking, the correct way of creating a material and technical basis for Socialism is to build socialism in every country relying primarily on the efforts of its people, with the best utilization of the internal resources of the country. The construction of Socialism in every country is primarily a matter of concern for the people of that country, its working class, and the Communist party.

The Soviet Union, which was the first country of Socialism had to build Socialism relying only on its own forces and using its internal resources. And although there is now a system of Socialist countries, this in no way means that the people of some country may sit with folded arms and rely exclusively on the assistance of other countries of Socialism. The Communist party of every Socialist country regards it as its duty to mobilize all internal reserves for successful economic development. Therefore the statement of the CPC Central Committee about the construction of Socialism mainly by its own forces would, in its direct meaning, give rise to no objections.

However, as shown by the whole text of the letter of the CPC Central Committee and the numerous statements in the Chinese press, this thesis is actually given an interpretation with which it is impossible to agree.

The formula of the "Socialist construction mainly by our own forces" conceals the concept of creating self-sufficient national economies for which the economic contacts with other countries are restricted to trade only. The Chinese comrades are trying to impose this approach on other Socialist countries, too.

The proclamation of the course of "reliance on our own forces" was apparently needed by CPC leadership in order to weaken the bonds of close friendship between the Socialist countries. This policy of course, has nothing in common with the principles of Socialist internationalism. It cannot be regarded otherwise than as an attempt to undermine the unity of the Socialist commonwealth.

Parallel to the line toward curtailment of economic contacts, the CPC leadership took a number of measures aimed at aggravating the relations with the Soviet Union.

The Chinese leaders are undermining the unity not only of the Socialist camp but also of the entire world Communist movement, trampling under foot the principles of proletarian internationalism and grossly violating the norms of relations between fraternal parties.

* * *

In their attacks on the CPSU and other Marxist-Leninist parties, the CPC leaders assign a special place to the Yugoslav question. They try to present matters in such a way as though difficulties in the Communist movement were caused by an improvement of relations between the Soviet Union (and other Socialist countries) and Yugoslavia. Contrary to the facts, they stubbornly contend that Yugoslavia allegedly is not a Socialist country.

As is known, in 1955 the CPSU together with other fraternal parties displayed initiative in normalizing relations with Yugoslavia so as to overcome the protracted conflict, the main guilt for which lies with Stalin. At that time the CPC leaders had no doubts as to the nature of the Socialist system in Yugoslavia. Thus the newspaper *Jenmin Jihpao* noted that "Yugoslavia has already achieved notable successes in the construction of Socialism."

An objective analysis of the socioeconomic processes in Yugoslavia shows that the positions of Socialism have consolidated there in the following years. If in 1958 the Socialist sector in industry amounted to 100 percent, in agriculture to 6 percent, and in trade to 97 percent, now the Socialist sector in industry amounts to 100 percent, in agriculture to 15 percent, and in trade to 100 percent. A rapprochement of Yugoslavia's positions with the position of the Soviet Union and other Socialist states in foreign policy questions took place in the period since the beginning of the normalization of relations.

Why, then, have the Chinese leaders changed so drastically their position on the Yugoslav question? It is hard to find an explanation other than that they saw in this one of the, in their opinion, advantageous pretexts to discredit the policy of the CPSU and other Marxist-Leninist parties.

Soviet Communists know that differences on a number of ideological questions of principle continue to remain between the CPSU and the Yugoslav Communist League. We have openly stated and continue to state this to the Yugoslav leaders. But it would be wrong to "excommunicate" Yugoslavia on these grounds from Socialism, to sever her from Socialist countries and to push her into the camp of imperialism, just as the CPC leaders are doing. This is precisely what the imperialists want.

At present there are fourteen Socialist countries in the world. We are profoundly convinced that in the near future their number will be considerably greater. The range of questions encountered by the fraternal parties, which stand at the helm of state, is increasing; besides, each of the fraternal parties is working under different conditions.

It is not surprising that under these circumstances the fraternal parties may develop different approaches to the solution of this or that problem. How should Marxists-Leninists act in this case? Declare that this or that Socialist country whose leaders do not agree with them is no longer a Socialist country? This would be real arbitrariness. This method has nothing in common with Marxism-Leninism.

If we were to follow the example of the Chinese leaders, then, because of our serious differences with the leaders of the Albanian party of Labor, we should have long proclaimed Albania to be a non-Socialist country. But this would be an erroneous, subjectivist approach. Despite our differences with the Albanian leaders, the Soviet Communists regard Albania as a Socialist country and, for their part, do everything to prevent Albania from splitting away from the Socialist community.

We watch with regret how the leaders of the CPC undermine the traditional Soviet-Chinese friendship, weaken the unity of the Socialist countries.

The CPSU stands, and will stand, for the unity and cohesion of the Socialist community of the entire world Communist movement.

* * *

The Central Committee of the Communist Party of the Soviet Union

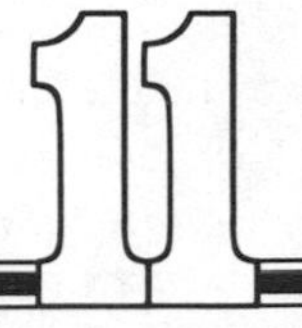

COMMENT ON THE OPEN LETTER OF THE CENTRAL COMMITTEE OF THE COMMUNIST PARTY OF THE SOVIET UNION*

Editorial Departments of
Jenmin Jihpao and Hong Chi
(Peking, 6 September 1963 to 31 March 1964)

In early 1958, Mao embarked on the "Great Leap Forward." One of its chief purposes was to speed the Chinese effort to catch up with the Soviet Union. But halfway through the year it became apparent that the Great Leap was a flop. Not that it did not succeed in some of its goals, but it aspired to too much, and it had too little with which to do it.

At the plenum of the Central Committee in November and December 1959, the blame for the failures of the Great Leap was placed at Mao's doorstep. He was not renominated for another term as chairman of the PRC; he was let out to

* Excerpts

pasture. As he later described it, he was treated "as a dead man at his own funeral." Mao was not purged: that was not the style of the PRC. But he was not given any responsibility.

However, Mao was not ready to retire—then or ever. The one area in which he was still allowed to function was ideology. Here a major subject of contention was the Soviet Union, to whose party Mao, as well as the leaders of the CPC currently in the saddle, was opposed. Mao concentrated much of his effort on the increasingly strident anti-Moscow polemics which began eminating from Peking in the early 1960s. He did so not only because he was opposed to what he saw the Russians doing—and because he was allowed to do little else—but also because he saw his Chinese opposition, with their emphasis on production and the building up of the bureaucracy, behaving like the Russians. A blow against the Russians then became a blow against his domestic opponents.

There is reason to believe that Mao was the principal author of the eight responses to the Open Letter of the CC CPSU.

I.
THE ORIGIN AND DEVELOPMENT OF THE DIFFERENCES BETWEEN THE LEADERSHIP OF THE CPSU AND OURSELVES (6 SEPTEMBER 1963)

* * *

There is a saying, "It takes more than one cold day for the river to freeze three feet deep." The present differences in the international communist movement did not, of course, begin just today.

The open letter of the Central Committee of the CPSU spreads the notion that the differences in the international communist movement were started by the articles which we published in April 1960, under the title of *Long Live Leninism!* This is a big lie.

What is the truth?

The truth is that the whole series of differences of principle in the international communist movement began more than seven years ago.

To be specific, it began with Congress XX of the CPSU in 1956.

Congress XX of the CPSU was the first step along the road of revisionism taken by the leadership of the CPSU. From Congress XX to the present, the revisionist line of the leadership of the CPSU has gone through the process of emergence, formation, growth, and systematization. And by a gradual process, too, people have come to understand more and more deeply the revisionist line of the CPSU leadership.

* * *

The facts of the past seven years have amply proved that the present differences within the international communist movement are differences between the line of adhering to Marxism-Leninism and the line of clinging to revisionism, between the revolutionary line and the nonrevolutionary and counterrevolutionary line, between the anti-imperialist line and the line of capitulation to imperialism. They are differences between proletarian internationalism and great-power chauvinism, sectarianism and splittism.

The facts of the past seven years have amply proved that the road taken by the leadership of the CPSU is the course of allying with imperialism against socialism, allying with the United States against China, allying with the reactionaries of all countries against the people of the world, and allying with the renegade Tito clique against fraternal Marxist-Leninist parties. This erroneous line of the leadership of the CPSU has led to a revisionist flood on an international scale, brought the international communist movement face to face with the danger of a split of unprecedented gravity, and brought serious damage to the peoples' cause of world peace, national liberation, people's democracy, and socialism.

The facts of the past seven years have also amply proved that the Communist Party of China has constantly striven to prevent the situation from deteriorating and to uphold principle, eliminate differences, strengthen unity, and wage a common struggle against the enemy. We have exercised great restraint and done our very best.

The Communist Party of China has always stressed the importance of the unity of the Chinese and Soviet parties and the two countries. It has always held in respect the Communist Party of the Soviet Union created by the great Lenin. We have always cherished deep proletarian affection for the great CPSU and the great Soviet people. We have rejoiced over every achievement of the CPSU and the Soviet people, and we have been saddened by every error of the leadership of the CPSU that has harmed the socialist camp and the international communist movement.

It is not just today that the Chinese Communists have begun to discover the errors of the CPSU leadership. Ever since Congress XX of the CPSU, we have watched with concern as the leadership of the CPSU took the road of revisionism.

Confronted with this grave situation, our party has scores of times and for a long period considered: What should we do?

We asked ourselves, should we follow the leadership of the CPSU and suit all our actions to its wishes? In that case, the leadership of the CPSU would of course rejoice, but would not we ourselves then turn into revisionists?

We also asked ourselves, should we keep silent about the errors of the leadership of the CPSU? We believed that its errors were not just accidental, individual and minor errors, but rather a whole series of errors of principle, which endanger the interests of the entire socialist camp and international communist movement. As a member in the ranks of the international communist movement, how could we be indifferent and keep silent about these errors? If we should do that, would not we be abandoning our duty to defend Marxism-Leninism and proletarian internationalism?

We foresaw that if we criticized the errors of the leaders of the CPSU, they would certainly strike at us vindictively and thus inevitably cause serious damage to China's socialist construction. But should communists take a stand of national egoism and not dare to uphold truth for fear of vindictive blows? Should communists barter away principles?

We took into consideration the fact that the CPSU was built by Lenin, that it is the party of the first socialist state, and that it enjoyed high prestige in the international communist movement and among the people of the whole world. Therefore, over a considerable period of time, we were particularly careful and patient in criticizing the leaders of the CPSU, trying our best to confine such criticism to inter-party talks between the leaders of the Chinese and Soviet parties and to solve the differences through internal discussion without resorting to open polemics.

But all the comradely criticism and advice given to the leaders of the CPSU by responsible comrades of the Central Committee of the CPC in scores of inter-party talks did not succeed in enabling them to return to the correct path. The leaders of the CPSU went farther and farther down the road of revisionism and splittism. In return for the advice we gave in goodwill, they applied a succession of political, economic and military pressures against us and launched increasingly violent attacks.

The leaders of the CPSU have a bad habit: they indiscriminately stick labels on anyone who criticizes them.

They say, "You are anti-Soviet!" No, friends! The label "anti-Soviet" cannot be stuck on us. Our criticism of your errors is precisely for the sake of defending the great CPSU and the great Soviet Union and preventing their prestige from being badly damaged by you. To put it plainly, it is you, and not we, who are really anti-Soviet and who are defaming and discrediting the CPSU and the Soviet Union. Ever since the complete negation of Stalin at Congress XX of the CPSU, you have committed innumerable foul deeds. Not all the water in the Volga can wash away the great shame you have brought upon the CPSU and upon the Soviet Union.

* * *

II.
ON THE QUESTION OF STALIN (13 SEPTEMBER 1963)

* * *

Khrushchev has abused Stalin as a "murderer," a "criminal," a "bandit," a "gambler," a "despot of the type of Ivan the Terrible," "the greatest dictator in Russian history," a "fool," an "idiot," etc. When we are compelled to cite all this filthy, vulgar, and malicious language, we are afraid it may soil our pen and paper.

Khrushchev has maligned Stalin as "the greatest dictator in Russian history." Does not this mean that the Soviet people lived for thirty long years under the "tyranny" of "the greatest dictator in Russian history" and not under the socialist system? The great Soviet people and the revolutionary people of the whole world completely disagree with this slander!

Khrushchev has maligned Stalin as a "despot of the type of Ivan the Terrible." Does not this mean that the experience the great CPSU and the great Soviet people provided over thirty years for people the world over was not the experience of the dictatorship of the proletariat but that of life under the rule of a feudal "despot?" The great Soviet people, the Soviet Communists and Marxist-Leninists of the whole world completely disagree with this slander!

Khrushchev has maligned Stalin as a "bandit." Does not this mean that the first socialist state in the world was for a long period headed by a "bandit?" The great Soviet people and the revolutionary people of the whole world completely disagree with this slander!

Khrushchev has maligned Stalin as a "fool." Does not this mean that the CPSU which waged heroic revolutionary struggles over the past decades had a "fool" as its leader? The Soviet Communists and Marxist-Leninists of the whole world completely disagree with this slander!

Khrushchev has maligned Stalin as an "idiot." Does not this mean that the great Soviet Army which triumphed in the anti-fascist war had an "idiot" as its supreme commander? The glorious Soviet commanders and fighters and all anti-fascist fighters of the world completely disagree with this slander!

Khrushchev has maligned Stalin as a "murderer." Does not this mean that the international communist movement had a "murderer" as its teacher for decades? Communists of the whole world, including the Soviet communists, completely disagree with this slander!

Khrushchev has maligned Stalin as a "gambler." Does not this mean that the revolutionary peoples had a "gambler" as their standard-bearer in the struggles against imperialism and reaction? All revolutionary people of the world, including the Soviet people, completely disagree with this slander!

Such abuse of Stalin by Khrushchev is a gross insult to the Soviet people, a gross insult to the CPSU, to the Army, to the dictatorship of the proletariat and to the socialist system, to the international communist movement, to the revolutionary people, the world over and to Marxism-Leninism.

* * *

The "combat against the personality cult" launched by Khrushchev is a despicable political intrigue. Like someone described by Marx, "He is in his element as an intriguer, while a nonentity as a theorist."

The open letter of the Central Committee of the CPSU states that "while debunking the personality cult and fighting against its consequences" they "put high the leaders who . . . enjoy deserved prestige." What does this mean? *It means that, while trampling Stalin underfoot, the leaders of the CPSU laud Khrushchev to the skies.*

They describe Khrushchev, who was not yet a communist at the time of the October Revolution and who was a low-ranking political worker during the Civil War, as the "active builder of the Red Army."

They ascribe the great victory of the decisive battle in the Soviet Patriotic War entirely to Khrushchev, saying that in the Battle of Stalingrad "Khrushchev's voice was very frequently heard" and that he was "the soul of the Stalingraders."

They attribute the great achievements in nuclear weapons and rocketry wholly to Khrushchev, calling him "cosmic father." But as everybody knows, the success of the Soviet Union in manufacturing the atom and hydrogen bombs was a great achievement of the Soviet scientists and technicians and the Soviet people under Stalin's leadership. The foundations of rocketry were also laid in Stalin's time. How can these important historical facts be obliterated? How can all credit be given to Khrushchev?

* * *

III.
IS YUGOSLAVIA A SOCIALIST COUNTRY?
(26 SEPTEMBER 1963)

Is Yugoslavia a socialist country?

This is not only a question of ascertaining the nature of the Yugoslav state, but it also involves the question of which road the socialist countries should follow: whether they should follow the road of the October Revolution and carry the socialist revolution through to the end or follow the road of Yugoslavia and restore capitalism. In addition, it involves the question of how to appraise the Tito clique: whether it is a fraternal party and a force against imperialism or a renegade from the international communist movement and a lackey of imperialism.

On this question there are fundamental differences of opinion between the leaders of the CPSU on the one hand, and ourselves and all other Marxist-Leninists, on the other.

All Marxist-Leninists hold that Yugoslavia is not a socialist country. The leading clique of the League of Communists of Yugoslavia has betrayed Marxism-Leninism and the Yugoslav people and consists of renegades from the international communist movement and lackeys of imperialism.

In Khrushchev's opinion, Yugoslavia is not only a socialist country but an "advanced" socialist country. There, one finds not "idle talk about revolution" but "actual construction of socialism," and the development of Yugoslavia is "a concrete contribution to the general world revolutionary workers' movement," which Khrushchev rather envies and wishes to emulate.

* * *

One would like to ask:

Can a country be socialist when . . . it is guided by a variety of international opportunism, a variety of modern revisionist theories?

Can a country be socialist when . . . it has betrayed Marxism-Leninism and sets itself against the international communist movement as a whole?

Can a country be socialist when . . . it carries on subversive work against the socialist camp and the world communist moment?

Can a country be socialist when . . . it engages in activities which prejudice the unity of all the peace-loving forces and countries?

Can a country be socialist when the imperialist countries headed by the United States have nurtured it with several billions of U.S. dollars?

* * *

IV.
APOLOGISTS OF NEO-COLONIALISM
(22 OCTOBER 1963)

A great revolutionary storm has spread through Asia, Africa, and Latin America since World War II. Independence has been proclaimed in more than fifty Asian and African countries. China, Vietnam, Korea, and Cuba have taken the road of socialism. The face of Asia, Africa, and Latin America has undergone a tremendous change.

* * *

The storm of the people's revolution in Asia, Africa, and Latin America requires every political force in the world to take a stand. This mighty revolutionary storm makes the imperialists and colonialists tremble and the revolutionary people of the world rejoice. The imperialists and colonialists say, "Terrible, terrible!" The revolutionary people say, "Fine, fine!" The imperialists and colonialists say, "It is rebellion, which is forbidden." The revolutionary people say, "It is revolution, which is the people's right and an inexorable current of history."

An important line of demarcation between the Marxist-Leninists and the modern revisionists is the attitude taken toward this extremely sharp issue of contemporary world politics. The Marxist-Leninists firmly side with the oppressed nations and actively support the national-liberation movement. The modern revisionists in fact side with the imperialists and colonialists and repudiate and oppose the national-liberation movement in every possible way.

In their words, the leaders of the CPSU dare not completely discard the slogans of support for the national-liberation movement, and at times, for the sake of their own interests, they even take certain measures which create the appearance of support. But if we probe to the essence and consider their views and policies over a number of years, we see clearly that their attitude toward the liberation struggles of the oppressed nations of Asia, Africa, and Latin America is a passive or scornful or negative one, and that they serve as apologists for neo-colonialism.

In the open letter of the Central Committee of the CPSU of July 14, 1963, and in a number of articles and statements, the comrades of the CPSU have worked hard at defending their wrong views and attacking the Chinese Communist Party on the question of the national-liberation movement. But the sole outcome is to confirm the anti-Marxist-Leninist and anti-revolutionary stand of the leaders of the CPSU on the subject.

* * *

In line with their erroneous theories the leaders of the CPSU have sedulously worked out a number of nostrums for all the ills of the oppressed nations. Let us examine them.

The first prescription is labeled peaceful coexistence and peaceful competition.

* * *

The second prescription is labeled aid to backward countries.

* * *

The third prescription is labeled disarmament.

* * *

The fourth prescription is labeled elimination of colonialism through the United Nations.

* * *

It is apparent that what he [Khrushchev] really means by looking to United Nations for help is looking to the imperialists for help. The facts show that the United Nations, which is still under the control of the imperialists, can only defend and strengthen the rule of colonialism but can never demolish it.

In a word, the nostrums of the leaders of the CPSU on the national-liberation movement have been concocted to make people believe that the imperialists will give up colonialism and bestow freedom and liberation upon the oppressed nations and peoples and that, therefore, all revolutionary theories, demands, and struggles are outmoded and unnecessary and should and must be abandoned.

Although they talk about supporting the movements and wars of national liberation, the leaders of the CPSU have been trying by every means to make the people of Asia, Africa and Latin America abandon their revolutionary struggle, because they themselves are sorely afraid of the revolutionary storm.

The leaders of the CPSU have the famous "theory" that "even a tiny spark can cause a world conflagration" and that a world war must necessarily be a thermonuclear war, which means the annihilation of mankind. Therefore, Khrushchev roars that " 'local wars' in our time are very dangerous," and that "we will work hard . . . to put out the sparks that may set off the flames of war." Here Khrushchev makes no distinction between just and unjust wars and betrays the communist stand of supporting just wars.

The history of the eighteen years since World War II has shown that wars of national liberation are unavoidable so long as the imperialists and their lackeys try to maintain their brutal rule by bayonets and use force to suppress the revolution of oppressed nations. These large-scale and small-scale revolutionary wars against the imperialists and their lackeys, which have never ceased, have hit hard at the imperialist forces of war, strengthened the forces defending world peace and effectively prevented the imperialists from realizing their plan of launching a world war. Frankly speaking, Khrushchev's clamor about the need to "put out" the sparks of revolution for the sake of peace is an attempt to oppose revolution in the name of safeguarding peace.

* * *

Having used up all their wonder-working weapons for opposing the national-liberation movement, the leaders of the CPSU are now reduced to seeking help from racism, the most reactionary of all imperialist theories. They describe the correct stand of the CPC in resolutely supporting the national-liberation movement as "creating racial and geographical barriers," "replacing the class approach with the racial approach," and "playing upon the national and even racial prejudices of the Asian and African peoples."

* * *

When they peddle the "theory of racism," describing the national-liberation movement in Asia, Africa, and Latin America as one of the colored against the white race, the leaders of the CPSU are clearly aiming at inciting racial hatred among the white people in Europe and North America, at diverting the people of the world from the struggle against imperialism and at turning the international working-class movement away from the struggle against modern revisionism.

The leaders of the CPSU have raised a hue and cry about the "Yellow Peril" and the "imminent menace of Genghis Khan." This is really not worth refuting. We do not intend in this article to comment on the historical role of Genghis Khan or on the development of the Mongolian, Russian, and Chinese nations and the process of their formation into states. We would only remind the leaders of the CPSU of their need to review their history lessons before manufacturing such tales. Genghis Khan was a Khan of Mongolia, and in his day both China and Russia were subjected to Mongolian aggression.

* * *

V.
TWO DIFFERENT LINES ON THE QUESTION OF WAR AND PEACE (19 NOVEMBER 1963)

The whole world is discussing the question of war and peace.

The criminal system of imperialism has brought upon the people of the world numerous wars, including two disastrous world wars. Wars launched by imperialism have caused the people heavy suffering, but have also educated them.

Since World War II, people everywhere have been vigorously demanding world peace. More and more people have come to understand that to defend world peace it is imperative to wage struggles against the imperialist policies of aggression and war.

Marxist-Leninists throughout the world are duty-bound to treasure the peace sentiments of the people and to stand in the forefront of the struggle for world peace. They are duty-bound to struggle against the imperialists' policies of aggression and war, to expose their deceptions and defeat their plans for war. They are duty-bound to educate the people, raise their political consciousness and guide the struggle for world peace in the proper direction.

In contrast to the Marxist-Leninists, the modern revisionists help the imperialists to deceive the people, divert the people's attention, weaken and undermine their struggle against imperialism, and cover up the imperialists' plans for a new world war, thus meeting the needs of imperialist policy.

The Marxist-Leninist line on the question of war and peace is diametrically opposed to the revisionist line.

The Marxist-Leninist line is the correct line conducive to the winning of world peace. It is the line consistently upheld by all Marxist-Leninist parties, including the Communist Party of China, and by all Marxist-Leninists.

The revisionist line is a wrong line which serves to increase the danger of a new war. It is the line gradually developed by the leaders of the CPSU since Congress XX.

* * *

[It] is clear that the thesis on the possibility of preventing a third world war was advanced by Marxist-Leninists long ago; it was not first put forward at Congress XX of the CPSU, nor is it Khrushchev's "creation."

Is it then true that Khrushchev has created nothing at all? No. He has created something. Unfortunately, these "creations" are by no means Marxist-Leninist, but revisionist.

First, Khrushchev has willfully interpreted the possibility of preventing a new world war as the only possibility, holding that there is no danger of a new world war.

Marxist-Leninists hold that while pointing to the possibility of preventing a new world war, we must also call attention to the possibility that imperialism may unleash a world war. Only by pointing to both possibilities, pursuing correct policies, and preparing for both eventualities can we effectively mobilize the masses to wage struggles in defence of world peace. Only thus will these socialist countries and people and other peace-loving countries and people not be caught unawares and utterly unprepared should imperialism force a world war on the people of the world.

However, Khrushchev and others are against exposing the danger of a new war which the imperialists are plotting.

According to them, imperialism has actually become peace-loving. This is helping the imperialists to lull the masses and sap their fighting will so that they will lose their vigilance against the danger of the new war the imperialists are plotting.

Second, Khrushchev has willfully interpreted the possibility of preventing a new world war as the possibility of preventing all wars, holding that the Leninist axiom that war is inevitable so long as imperialism exists is outmoded.

The possibility of preventing a new world war is one thing; the possibility of preventing all wars, including revolutionary wars is another. And it is completely wrong to confuse the two.

There is soil for wars so long as imperialism and the system of exploitation of man by man exist.

* * *

VI. PEACEFUL COEXISTENCE—TWO DIAMETRICALLY OPPOSED POLICIES (12 DECEMBER 1963)

Since Congress XX of the CPSU, Khrushchev and other comrades have talked more about the question of peaceful coexistence than about anything else.

Again and again the leaders of the CPSU claim that they have been faithful to Lenin's policy of peaceful coexistence and have creatively developed it. They ascribe to their policy of "peaceful coexistence" all the credit for the victories won by the peoples of the world in prolonged revolutionary struggles.

They advertise the notion that imperialism, and US imperialism in particular, supports peaceful coexistence, and they wantonly malign the Chinese Communist Party and all Marxist-Leninist parties as being opponents of peaceful coexistence. The open letter of the Central Committee of the CPSU even slanders China as favoring "competition in unleashing war" with the imperialists.

They describe the words and deeds by which they have

betrayed Marxism-Leninism, the proletarian world revolution, and the revolutionary cause of the oppressed peoples and nations as being in conformity with Lenin's policy of peaceful coexistence.

But can the words "peaceful coexistence" really serve as a talisman for the leaders of the CPSU in their betrayal of Marxism-Leninism? No, absolutely not.

We are now confronted with two diametrically opposed policies of peaceful coexistence.

One is Lenin and Stalin's policy of peaceful coexistence, which all Marxist-Leninists, including the Chinese Communists, stand for.

The other is the anti-Leninist policy of peaceful coexistence, the so-called general line of peaceful coexistence advocated by Khrushchev and others.

* * *

Lenin advanced the policy of peaceful coexistence as a policy to be pursued by the proletariat in power toward countries with different social systems. He never made it the sum total of a socialist country's foreign policy. Time and again Lenin made it clear that the fundamental principle of this foreign policy was proletarian internationalism.

* * *

Lenin consistently held that it was impossible for the oppressed classes and nations to coexist peacefully with the oppressor classes and nations.

* * *

The heart and soul of the general line of peaceful coexistence pursued by the leaders of the CPSU is Soviet-U.S. collaboration for the domination of the world.

* * *

We would like to ask the leaders of the CPSU: Since the 1957 Declaration and the 1960 Statement say clearly that U.S. imperialism is the sworn enemy of the people of the world and the main force making for aggression and war, how can you "unite" with the main enemy of world peace to "safeguard peace"?

We would like to ask them: Can it be that more than a hundred countries and over three thousand million people have no right to decide their own destiny? Must they submit to the manipulations of the two "giants," the two "greatest powers," the Soviet Union and the United States? Isn't this arrogant nonsense of yours an expression of great-power chauvinism and power politics pure and simple?

We would also like to ask them: Do you really imagine that if only the Soviet Union and the United States reached agreement, if only the two "great men" reached agreement, the destiny of mankind would be decided and all international issues settled? You are wrong, hopelessly wrong. From time immemorial, things have never happened in this way, and they are much less likely to do so in the 1960s.

* * *

All too often have the leaders of the CPSU said fine things about the U.S. imperialists and begged favors from them; all too often have they lost their temper with fraternal countries and parties and put pressure on them; all too many are the tricks and deceptions they have practised on the revolutionary people in various countries—solely in order to beg for "friendship" and "trust" from U.S. imperialism. But "while the drooping flowers pine for love, the heartless brook babbles on." All that the leaders of the CPSU have received from the U.S. imperialists is humiliation, again humiliation, always humiliation!

* * *

There is mutual deception and rivalry even between the United States and the other imperialist powers, and the United States will not be satisfied until it has trampled them underfoot. How then can you imagine that the imperialist United States will live in harmony with the socialist Soviet Union?

* * *

VII.
THE LEADERS OF THE CPSU ARE THE GREATEST SPLITTERS OF OUR TIMES (4 FEBRUARY 1964)

Never before has the unity of the international communist movement been so gravely threatened as it is today when we are witnessing a deluge of modern revisionist ideology. Both internationally and inside individual parties, fierce struggles are going on between Marxism-Leninism and revisionism. The international communist movement is confronted with an unprecedentedly serious danger of a split.

It is the urgent task of the communists, the proletariat, and the revolutionary people of the world to defend the unity of the socialist camp and of the international communist movement.

The Communist Party of China has made consistent and unremitting efforts to defend and strengthen the unity of the socialist camp and the international communist movement in accordance with Marxism-Leninism and the revolutionary principles of the 1957 Declaration and the 1960 Statement. It has been and remains the unswerving position of the Communist Party of China to uphold principle, uphold unity, eliminate differences and strengthen the struggle against our common enemy.

* * *

While presenting themselves as champions of unity, the leaders of the CPSU are trying to pin the label of splittism on the Communist Party of China. In its open letter the Central Committee of the CPSU says:

> The Chinese leaders are undermining the unity not only of the socialist camp but of the entire world communist movement, trampling on the principles of proletarian internationalism and grossly violating accepted standards of relations between fraternal parties.

And the subsequent articles published in the Soviet press have been condemning the Chinese Communists as "sectarians" and "splitters."

But what are the facts? Who is undermining the unity of the socialist camp? Who is undermining the unity of the international communist movement? Who is trampling on the principles of proletarian internationalism? And who is grossly violating the accepted standards of relations between fraternal parties? In other words, who are the real, out-and-out splitters?

* * *

The events of recent years show that the leaders of the CPSU headed by Khrushchev have become the chief representatives of modern revisionism as well as the greatest splitters in the international communist movement.

Between Congresses XX and XXII of the CPSU, the leaders of the CPSU developed a rounded system of revision. They put forward a revisionist line which contravenes the proletarian revolution and the dictatorship of the proletariat, a line which consists of "peaceful coexistence," "peaceful competition," "peaceful transition," "a state of the whole people," and "a party of the entire people." They have tried to impose this revisionist line on all fraternal parties as a substitute for the common line of the international communist movement which was laid down at the meetings of fraternal parties in 1957 and 1960. And they have attacked anyone who perseveres in the Marxist-Leninist line and resists their revisionist line.

The leaders of the CPSU have themselves undermined the basis of the unity of the international communist movement and created the present grave danger of a split by betraying Marxism-Leninism and proletarian internationalism and pushing their revisionist and divisive line.

Far from working to consolidate and expand the socialist camp, the leaders of the CPSU have endeavored to split and disintegrate it. They have thus made a mess of the splendid socialist camp.

* * *

We would like to advise the leaders of the CPSU to think matters over calmly: what will your clinging to revisionism and splittism lead to? Once again, we would like to make a sincere appeal to the leaders of the CPSU: We hope you will be able to return to Marxism-Leninism and proletarian internationalism, to the revolutionary principles of the 1957 Declaration and the 1960 Statement and to the principles guiding relations among fraternal parties and countries as laid down in these documents, so that the differences will be eliminated and the unity of the international communist movement and the socialist camp and unity between China and the Soviet Union will be strengthened on these principled bases.

Despite our serious differences with the leaders of the CPSU, we have full confidence in the vast membership of the CPSU and in the Soviet people, who grew up under the guidance of Lenin and Stalin. As always, the communists and the people of China will unswervingly safeguard the unity between China and the Soviet Union, and consolidate and develop the deep-rooted friendship between our two peoples.

Communists of the world, unite on the basis of Marxism-Leninism!

VIII.
THE PROLETARIAN REVOLUTION AND KHRUSHCHEV'S REVISIONISM (31 MARCH 1964)

* * *

In the history of the international communist movement the betrayal of Marxism and of the proletariat by the revisionists has always manifested itself most sharply in their opposition to violent revolution and to the dictatorship of the proletariat and in their advocacy of peaceful transition from capitalism to socialism. This is likewise the case with Khrushchev's revisionism. On this question, Khrushchev is a disciple of Browder and Tito as well as of Bernstein and Kautsky.

* * *

Khrushchev's revisionism is modern Bernsteinism and Kautskyism, pure and simple. As with Bernstein and Kautsky, Khrushchev's betrayal of Marxism is most sharply manifested in his opposition to revolutionary violence, in what he does "to expunge revolutionary violence." In this respect, Kautsky and Bernstein have now clearly lost their title to Khrushchev who has set a new world record. Khrushchev, the worthy disciple of Bernstein and Kautsky, has excelled his masters.

The entire history of the working-class movement tells us that the acknowledgment or non-acknowledgment of violent revolution as a universal law of proletarian revolution, of the necessity of smashing the old state machine, and of the necessity of replacing the dictatorship of the bourgeoisie by the dictatorship of the proletariat has always been the watershed between Marxism and all brands of opportunism and revisionism, between proletarian revolutionaries and all renegades from the proletariat.

According to the basic teachings of Marxism-Leninism, the key question in every revolution is that of state power. And the key question in the proletarian revolution is that of the seizure of state power and the smashing of the bourgeois state machine by violence, the establishment of the dictatorship of the proletariat, and the replacement of the bourgeois state by the proletarian state.

Marxism has always proclaimed the inevitability of violent revolution. It points out that violent revolution is the midwife to socialist society, the only road to the replacement of the dictatorship of the bourgeoisie by the dictatorship of the proletariat, and a universal law of proletarian revolution.

Marxism teaches us that the state itself is a form of violence. The main components of the state machine are the army and the police. History shows that all ruling classes depend upon violence to maintain their rule.

The proletariat would, of course, prefer to gain power by peaceful means. But abundant historical evidence indicates that the reactionary classes never give up power voluntarily and that they are always the first to use violence to repress the revolutionary mass movement and to provoke civil war, thus placing armed struggle on the agenda.

* * *

The idea of the "parliamentary road" which was publicized by the revisionists of the Second International was thoroughly refuted by Lenin and discredited long ago. But in Khrushchev's eyes, the parliamentary road seems suddenly to have acquired validity after World War II.

Is this true? Of course not.

Events since World War II have demonstrated yet again that the chief component of the bourgeois state machine is armed force and not parliament. Parliament is only an ornament and a screen for bourgeois rule. To adopt or discard the parliamentary system, to grant parliament greater or less power, to adopt one kind of electoral law or another —the choice between these alternatives is always dictated by the needs and interests of bourgeois rule. So long as the bourgeoisie controls the military-bureaucratic apparatus, either the acquisition of a "stable majority in parliament" by the proletariat through elections is impossible, or this "stable majority" is undependable. To realize socialism through the "parliamentary road" is utterly impossible and is mere deceptive talk.

About half the communist parties in the capitalist countries are still illegal. Since these parties have no legal status, the winning of a parliamentary majority is, of course, out of the question.

* * *

Even if in certain circumstances a communist party should win a majority of the seats in parliament or participate in the government as a result of an electoral victory, it would not change the bourgeois nature of parliament or government, still less would it mean the smashing of the old and the establishment of a new state machine. It is absolutely impossible to bring about a fundamental social change by relying on bourgeois parliaments or governments. With the state machine under its control the reactionary bourgeoisie can nullify elections, dissolve parliament, expel communists from the government, outlaw the Communist Party and resort to brute force to suppress the masses and the progressive forces.

* * *

While the leaders of the CPSU and their followers talk about the use of all forms of struggle, in reality they stand for legalism and discard the objective of the proletarian revolution on the pretext of changing forms of struggle. This is again substituting Kautskyism for Leninism.

The leaders of the CPSU often make use of Lenin's great work, *"Left-Wing" Communism, An Infantile Disorder*, to justify their erroneous line and have made it a "basis" for their attacks on the Chinese Communist Party.

This is of course futile. Like all his other works this book of Lenin's can only serve as a weapon for Marxist-Leninists in the fight against various kinds of opportunism and can never serve as an instrument of revisionist apologetics.

When Lenin criticized the "Left-wing" infantile disorder and asked the party of the proletariat to be skillful in applying revolutionary tactics and to do better in preparing for revolutions, he had already broken with the revisionists of the Second International and had founded the Third International.

Indeed, in *"Left-Wing" Communism* he stated that the main enemy of the international working-class movement at the time was Kautsky's type of opportunism. He repeatedly stressed that unless a break was made with revisionism there could be no talk of how to master revolutionary tactics.

Those comrades whom Lenin criticized for their "Left-wing" infantile disorder all wanted revolution, while the latter-day revisionist Khrushchev is against it, has therefore to be included in the same category as Kautsky and has no right whatsoever to speak on the question of combating the "Left-wing" infantile disorder.

It is almost absurd for the leadership of the CPSU to pin the label of "Trotskyism" on the Communist Party of China. In fact, it is Khrushchev himself who has succeeded to the mantle of Trotskyism and who stands with the Trotskyites of today.

Trotskyism manifests itself in different ways on different questions and often wears the mask of "ultra-Leftism," but its essence is opposition to revolution, repudation of revolution.

As far as the fundamental fact of their opposition to the proletarian revolution and the dictatorship of the proletariat is concerned, Trotskyism and the revisionism of the Second International are virtually the same. This is why Stalin repeatedly said that Trotskyism is a variety of Menshevism, is Kautskyism and social democracy, and is the advanced detachment of the counter-revolutionary bourgeoisie.

In its essence, the present-day revisionism of Khrushchev also opposes and repudiates revolution. Therefore, the only logical conclusion is that Khrushchev's revisionism is not only cut from the same cloth as Kautskyism, but also converges with Trotskyism to oppose revolution. Khrushchev had better pin the label of Trotskyism on himself.

* * *

The whole history of the dictatorship of the proletariat tells us that peaceful transition from capitalism to socialism is impossible. However, there is already the Yugoslav precedent for the "peaceful evolution" of socialism back into capitalism. Now Khrushchev's revisionism is leading the Soviet Union along this road.

This is the gravest lesson in the history of the dictatorship of the proletariat. All Marxist-Leninists, all revolutionaries and the generations to come must under no circumstances forget this great lesson.

Only eight years have elapsed since Congress XX of the CPSU. In this extremely short period of history, Khrushchev's revisionism has inflicted very great and grave damage on the Soviet Union and the revolutionary cause of the international proletariat.

Now is the time—now it is high time—to repudiate and liquidate Khrushchev's revisionism!

Here, we would give the leading comrades of the CPSU a

piece of advice: Since so many opportunists and revisionists have been thrown on to the rubbish heap of history, why must you obdurately follow their example?

Here too, we express the hope that those leading comrades of other fraternal parties who have committed revisionist errors will think this over: What have they gained by following the revisionist line of the leaders of the CPSU? We understand that, excepting those who have fallen deep into the revisionist quagmire, quite a number of comrades have been confused and deceived, or compelled to follow the wrong path. We believe that all those who are proletarian revolutionaries will eventually choose the revolutionary line and reject the anti-revolutionary line, will eventually choose Marxism-Leninism and reject revisionism. We entertain very great hopes in this regard.

Revisionism can never stop the wheel of history, the wheel of revolution. Revisionist leaders who do not make revolution themselves can never prevent the genuine Marxists and the revolutionary people from rising in revolution.

* * *

12

SPEECH TO PARTY CONGRESS V OF THE POLISH UNITED WORKERS' PARTY*

L. I. Brezhnev
(Warsaw, 12 November 1968)

On the night of August 20, 1968, 400,000 Soviet and a smattering of troops from four other Warsaw Pact nations invaded reform-minded Czechoslovakia and quickly put down the little resistance they met. There were protests in the West, in China, in Yugoslavia, and there was even a small demonstration in Red Square. But no concrete action was taken against the USSR, unless President Johnson's cancelation of an impending trip to Moscow is considered as such.

The Soviet Union had not been eager to call out the troops. It had a multitude of reasons for hesitating to act. But fears of the consequence of not acting—that the virus of Czech reform would infect Poland and East Germany and even the USSR itself—won out. Invasion had been ordered.

In the aftermath of the invasion, the Kremlin was never defensive about its action. But it did think it necessary to

* Excerpts

give a rationale for its decision, so as to drive the lesson home. This was done in what came to be known in the West as the "Brezhnev Doctrine," which was first released in bits and pieces and then received a fuller treatment in the speech which Brezhnev made at the Polish party congress in November.

In it, Brezhnev asserted the right, the responsibility, of the Soviet Union to step in whenever it saw socialism being "threatened" in a country where the revolution had already triumphed.

This was not a new theory. It was the clear implication under Stalin's "socialism in one country." Khrushchev had reiterated it in 1958. But since 1956, the USSR had begun to appear as a softer, more permissive power. Brezhnev and company now felt that it was necessary to restate that in Eastern Europe, at least, where it could control the situation, the Soviet Union would not permit the existence of any force that it chose to consider inimical to its own interests, which it defined as the same as the interests of socialism.

Honored delegates to the Congress!

Dear Comrades!

With great satisfaction, our delegation, in the name of the Central Committee of the CPSU, in the name of thirteen and a half million Soviet communists, brings warm, fraternal greetings to Congress V of the Polish United Workers' Party, to all Polish communists! (*Applause*). We wish your Congress successful and fruitful work.

* * *

We are living, comrades, in complex, stormy, and interesting times. The world revolutionary process, in the center of which is the struggle of the two basic social systems of our century, socialism and capitalism, is developing irrepressibly.

In this multifaceted struggle, we have already accomplished much. The world system of socialism has brought forth, affirmed, and defended its own right to life. It has developed the economies of the socialist countries, strengthened their defenses, perfected their social relations, improved the life of the workers. Simultaneously, cooperation among the countries of socialism has deepened, and unity with the revolutionary forces throughout the world has strengthened. The relationship of forces in the world scale continues to change to the advantage of socialism and its allies.

The might of the socialist camp is now such that the imperialists fear military destruction in the event of a direct clash with the basic forces of socialism. It is evident that, as long as imperialism exists, the danger of war that imperialist policy carries cannot on any count be disregarded. Indeed, it is a fact that in the new conditions the imperialists make increasingly frequent use of different and more cunning tactics. They are seeking the weak links in the socialist front, pursue a course of subversive ideological work inside the socialist countries, attempt to influence the economic development of these countries, strive to sow dissension, drive wedges between them, to encourage and inflame nationalist feelings and tendencies, attempt to isolate individual socialist states so that they can seize them by the throat one at a time. In a word, imperialism is trying to undermine socialism's solidarity specifically as a world system.

The experience of the development and struggle of the socialist countries in these new conditions during the past few years, including the recently increased activity of forces hostile to socialism in Czechoslovakia, reminds the communists of socialist countries with renewed force how important it is not to forget for one moment certain highly important, time-tested truths.

If we do not want to impede our movement along the path of socialist and communist construction, if we do not want to weaken out general positions in the struggle against imperialism, it is necessary that, in resolving any questions of our domestic and foreign policy, we always and everywhere maintain unbreakable loyalty to the principles of Marxism-Leninism, display a clear-cut class and party approach to all social phenomena and deal a stiff rebuff to imperialism on the ideological front without making any concessions to bourgeois ideology.

Precisely on a principled Marxist-Leninist foundation, great successes have been achieved in the social, political, economic, and cultural development of the socialist countries—successes the equal of which have not previously been known to history in tempo, depth, and scale.

Attempting to compromise socialism, the ideologists of the bourgeoisie speculate on the difficulties and errors in the development of one or another socialist country. What can be said on this matter? Yes, difficulties have occurred in the development of socialist countries, they occur now, and probably will occur in the future; every stage has its difficulties.

Some of these have an objective nature, conditioned by historical, natural, and other factors. Others have a subjective nature, attributable to the fact that particular problems of development have failed to receive the most successful solutions—i.e., some miscalculations, mistakes were made—and by the fact that people have not yet learned to use fully the potentials that, objectively speaking, underlie the socialist system.

The question is how to react to the difficulties and the mistakes that have been made.

Petit-bourgeois leaders, encountering difficulties, fall into hysterics, and begin to doubt absolutely everything. The revisionists, because of the emergence of difficulties, are ready to cross out all existing achievements, repudiate everything that has been gained, and surrender all their principled positions.

Real communists confidently clear the path ahead, and seek the best solutions to the problems that have arisen, based on socialist gains. They honestly acknowledge the mistakes made in one or another question, analyze and correct them, so as to strengthen the positions of socialism further, so as to stand firm and refrain from giving the enemies of socialism one iota of what has already been won, what has already been achieved through the efforts and struggle of the popular masses. (*Prolonged applause.*)

In a word, it can confidently be said that, if the party stands firmly on communist positions, if it is faithful to Marxism-Leninism, all difficulties will be overcome.

* * *

It is not for nothing that the enemies of socialism always choose precisely the communist party as the prime target for their attacks. It is not for nothing that revisionists of every stripe—who are conductors of influence in the workers' movement—invariably seek to vitiate, to weaken the party, to undermine its organizational basis, the Leninist principle of democratic centralism; that they preach weakening of party discipline. It is not for nothing that they circulate "theories" according to which the party should "separate itself" from guidance over the development of society in the areas of economics, state life, culture, and so forth. Such a situation would, of course, be very satisfactory for those who dream of turning development in all these areas backward—in the direction of capitalism.

In the present conditions, even more importance attaches to such highly important aspects of party activity as its ideological work, formation of the world view of man in socialist and communist society, exposure of bourgeois ideology.

From all this, the Soviet communists—and, we are confident, the communists of other fraternal countries—are drawing for themselves the clear conclusion that it is necessary to make every effort to strengthen the unity and solidarity of the party, to do everything possible to enhance its leadership role in the development of society and to perfect the forms of its activity.

* * *

Socialist states stand for the strict respect of the sovereignty of all countries. We determinedly oppose interference in the affairs of any states, the violation of their sovereignty.

At the same time, affirmation and defense of the sovereignty of states that have embarked on the path of socialist construction have special significance to us communists. The forces of imperialism and reaction are seeking to deprive the people of first one, then another socialist country of the sovereign right they have earned to ensure development for their country and well-being and happiness for the broad working masses by means of building a society free from all oppression and exploitation. But when encroachments on this right receive a joint rebuff from the socialist camp, the bourgeois propagandists raise the cry of "defense of sovereignty" and "noninterference." It is clear that this is the purest deceit and demagoguery on their part. In fact, these loudmouths are concerned not about saving socialist sovereignty but about its destruction.

It is well known that the Soviet Union has done a good deal for the real strengthening of the sovereignty, the autonomy of the socialist countries. The CPSU has always advocated that each socialist country determine the concrete forms of its development along the path of socialism by taking into account the specifics of their national conditions. But it is well known, comrades, that there exist general laws of socialist construction, deviation from which could lead to deviation from socialism as such. And when external and internal forces hostile to socialism try to turn the development of any socialist country in the direction of the restoration of the capitalist order, when a threat arises to the cause of socialism in that country—a threat also to the security of the socialist commonwealth as a whole—this has already become a problem not only for that country's people, but a common problem, the concern of all socialist countries. (*Applause.*)

It is understood that an action such as military help to a fraternal country to eliminate a threat to the socialist system is a measure of extreme necessity; it can be called forth only by the overt actions of enemies of socialism within the country and beyond its borders, actions that create a threat to the common interests of the camp of socialism.

Experience states that the triumph of the socialist system in one country or another under present conditions will be regarded as final, but the restoration of capitalism can be considered excluded only in that case where the communist party, as the leading force in society, steadfastly pursues a Marxist-Leninist policy in the development of all spheres of the life of society; only in that case where the party ceaselessly strengthens the defense of the country and the protection of its revolutionary gains, and where it is itself vigilant and instills within the people vigilance with respect to the class enemy, implacability toward bourgeois ideology; only where the principle of socialist internationalism is held sacred, and unity and fraternal solidarity with the other socialist countries are strengthened. (*Prolonged applause.*)

It can be said with confidence that the policy pursued by the Polish Workers' Party is a good example of a principled Marxist-Leninist policy, true to the principles of Marxism-Leninism. (*Applause.*)

Comrades! World imperialism, primarily U.S. imperialists and their chief European ally—Federal Republic of Germany ruling circles—continues its aggressive policy and takes many steps that contribute to the deterioration of the international atmosphere.

The imperialists are creating hotbeds of tension in various parts of the world, intensifying the arms race, seeking to return the world to the times of the "cold war." Revanchist sentiments which threaten the peace and security of the European people, are being openly ignited in the Federal Republic of Germany.

To this reactionary, aggressive policy line the countries of the socialist commonwealth oppose their own policy—flexible and realistic, but irreconcilable with respect to aggressors and revanchists. This policy is pervaded by the spirit of determined class support for revolutionary forces and the forces of socialism and progress throughout the world. (*Applause.*) At the same time, this policy supports the principles of peaceful coexistence, advocates the renunciation of attempts to settle questions of relations between the two opposed social systems by military means, and consistently supports a course of reducing international tensions.

In our struggle for peace and the security of peoples, for mutually advantageous cooperation among states with different social systems, we have achieved many successes, especially when the socialist countries have projected a coordinated, united front.

But the situation demands for all to exercise a high level of vigilance with respect to our class adversary in the world arena. This is why there is great importance to the work the Warsaw Pact states are now doing, in response to NATO's military preparations, to strengthen and perfect the military mechanism of our alliance of fraternal countries.

Let those who are inclined to forget the lessons of history and want to be occupied again in recarving the map of Europe, know that the borders of Poland, the German Democratic Republic, and Czechoslovakia, as well as any other countries who are members of the Warsaw Pact, are unshakable and inviolable. (*Stormy, prolonged applause.*) These borders are protected by all the armed might of the socialist commonwealth. We advise all those who like to encroach on foreign borders to remember this well!

* * *

The ranks of the allies of the working class in the struggle against imperialism are growing throughout the world. This brings closer the hour of social and national liberation for the oppressed peoples. At the same time various other levels of the population that are participating in the revolutionary movement along with the working class inject their own views and ideas, which differ from proletarian ideology and at times nurture right-wing opportunism and "leftist" adventurism in certain sectors of the communist movement.

It would be wrong to underestimate the danger and harmfulness of such tendencies. It is well known that both right wing and "leftist" revisionists, despite their seeming differences, come together where it is most important: both distort Lenin's theory of socialist revolution and denigrate the role of the working class and its vanguard, the Marxist-Leninist party, in socialist revolution and socialist construction. Both deviate from the principles of proletarian internationalism, in this way weakening the struggle against imperialism, and hamper the development of the revolutionary process. Both are characterized by a national narrowness in evaluating many highly important problems of the revolutionary struggle that sometimes carry over to outright chauvinism. How far the revisionists, acting under cover of "leftist phrases," can go in this respect is demonstrated by the policy of the group of Mao Tse-tung.

Needless to say, all these distortions are deeply foreign to real communists, who are faithful to Marxism-Leninism. Internationalism has always been an important source of the strength of the communist movement. The interests of the working class and its struggle against capitalism, V. I. Lenin taught, demand total solidarity and extremely close unity among the workers of all nations, demand the rejection of nationalistic policies. These interests stubbornly demand that communists rally to the defense of our militant ideological weapon—the revolutionary teaching of Marx and Lenin. (*Applause.*)

Communist parties operating in different conditions can take varying approaches to particular questions. We would be acting incorrectly, if we did not see that there are those who hold divergent opinions on certain questions. Some of these divergencies, in our opinion, have a strictly temporary character, and will disappear as the course of events brings clarity to the essence of these controversial questions. Others, obviously, might prove to be more lasting, but they should not, we believe, interfere with the joint struggle against the common adversary for our great common goals.

What is most important is that communist and workers' parties, despite disagreement on one or another question, should seek ways and means of developing international ties, strive to strengthen the unity of their ranks on the basis of Marxism-Leninism. We, for our part, have always considered comradely exchanges of opinion helpful, and are prepared for frank discussion of questions that have arisen among the fraternal parties. We are confident that it is precisely on the path of strengthening our ties and cooperation that the problems that arise will be settled in the interest of the unity of the international movement. And this is natural, for we have a common ideological basis—Marxism-

Leninism; a common enemy—imperialism; and a common goal—the triumph of communism (*Prolonged applause.*)

* * *

The situation requires unity among the fraternal parties in order to launch an even more powerful offensive against imperialism. For communists, the immortal slogan of our movement rings out challengingly today with fresh force: "Proletarians of all countries, unite!" (*Stormy, prolonged applause.*)

* * *

13

SPEECH TO PARTY CONGRESS XXII OF THE COMMUNIST PARTY OF FRANCE*

Georges Marchais
(Ile-Saint-Denis, 4 February 1976)

In the wake of the Soviet invasion of Czechoslovakia, there was an understanding in Eastern Europe that only limited and slowly evolving variations in the Soviet model would be permitted by the CPSU. But among Western European communists, the invasion of Czechoslovakia encouraged independence, and led to a search for a new socialist model.

Increasingly in the 1970s, particularly in Italy, where there was a limited tradition of communist independence and appreciation for the values of western democracy, it became clear that if the CPI was to have a chance of coming to power, there had to be the demonstration of a different melding of socialism and democracy than was represented by the Soviet experience—one more favorable to democracy and suitable to the West. The CPI sought to establish a dialogue with noncommunist elements, including the Vati-

* Excerpts

can. It took up the cudgel for human rights, particularly in the Soviet Union. It castigated the coercive methods of Soviet policy and called for the establishment of a multiparty political system.

Gradually the French party, whose background was more Stalinist than that of the CPI, also came to the conclusion that if power was to be achieved, it was going to have at least to give the appearance of being both independent and democratic.

In 1975 and 1976 the new line it had adopted—and circumstances—seemed to offer the CPF good prospects for the future, and it therefore accelerated its "liberalization."

At Congress XXII of the CPF, Georges Marchais, its secretary general, in his address to the congress, assured his comrades and all others who were listening that the CPF would seek power only through democratic means. He reemphasized the independence of the CPF from outside decision making and rejected as outmoded the principle—fundamental to Marx and cherished by Soviet ideology—of the dictatorship of the proletariat.

* * *

If the "dictatorship of the proletariat" does not figure in the draft document [of the party], to designate the political power in the socialist France for which we fight, it is because it does not capture the reality of our politics, the reality of what we propose to the country.

What do we say in the draft document? We say this:

"The power that will lead the socialist transformation of society will be the power of the working class and of other categories of workers, manual workers, and intellectuals, from the city and from the countryside—that is, the great majority of the people!

"This power will be established and will act on the basis of choice, freely expressed by universal suffrage, and will have as its task to bring to fruition the most advanced democratization of the whole economic, social, and political life of the country.

"It will have as its duty to respect and cause to be respected the democratic choices of the people."

Contrary to all that, "dictatorship" automatically evokes the fascist regimes of Hitler, Mussolini, Salazar, and Franco, that is, the negation of democracy. This is not what we want.

As for the proletariat, today it evokes the nucleus, the heart of the working class. While its role is essential, it does not represent the whole of the working class, nor, even more so, the whole of the workers from whom the socialist power that we envision will emanate.

It is therefore evident that what we propose to the workers, to our people, cannot be qualified as "dictatorship of the proletariat."

What is the basis for our definition of our position on this question? We stand upon the principles of scientific socialism elaborated by Marx, Engels, and Lenin.

At stake, in the first place, is the necessity for the working class to exercise a leading political role in the struggle for the socialist transformation of society.

If the workers, the popular masses, can today begin the fight, extract from the powerful certain urgent social measures and even conquer certain new freedoms, the real and durable satisfaction of their economic, social and political rights is totally impossible without a change in the class nature of power. The participation of the workers and their representatives in the management of the affairs of the country and their access to the leadership of society, constitute the key problem of the struggle for socialism. Among the whole of the workers, the working class is the largest, the most combative, the most experienced in the fight for social progress and—it is necessary to underscore this—for the national interest. It must then have its place in the socialist state and play a determining role in it.

In this regard, the draft document indicates: "The working class is the only class that can lead the revolutionary struggle to success. Its vital interests, its numerical strength, its concentration, its experience in the class struggle and its organization make it, for today and for tomorrow, the leading force in the struggle for a new society."

Secondly, at stake is the necessity for revolutionary struggle by the masses in order to cause the failure of the grand bourgeoisie's control.

The draft document emphasizes this point: "Thc cxploiting grand bourgeoisie will never renounce of its own will its domination and its privileges. It will always have a propensity to utilize all possible means to preserve them or to reconquer them." I will even add that this is particularly true of the French bourgeoisie. For if there exists in our country a democratic tradition, there exists also a tradition of Versailles which, the behavior of the men in power reminds us daily, is not dead.

That is why the draft document shows that workers, the popular masses, must "at each step gather together their forces and work actively to cause the failure of the reactionary maneuvers, . . . to paralyze or defeat the eventual attempts of the reactionary forces to resort to illegality, subversion, and violence."

With that said, in conformity with the spirit of our doctrine, we carefully take into account the "real process," in other words the conditions of our times and of our country. These conditions permit and require us to envision, in order to move toward socialism in France, other roads than those followed by the people who have already realized the socialist transformation of their countries.

* * *

The convergence of the primary interests of . . . social forces offers . . . possibilities without precedent for winning the majority of the people to the cause of the transformation of society, for constituting a broad movement of the majority of the people around the powerful pole that the working class represents. Is this a new historic theme? Yes. Must we seize this possibility? Without any doubt. . . .

Socialism must, in our country, identify itself—or otherwise suffer the penalty of remaining only within the domain of language—with the safeguarding and full flowering of the democratic experiences that broad and unyielding struggles have permitted our people to obtain. . . .

In the fight for socialism, nothing, absolutely nothing, can, in our time and in a country like ours, replace the popular majority will expressing itself democratically through the struggle and by means of universal suffrage. Whatever be the forms in which the march to socialism will be accomplished in our country, forms which cannot be foreseen in detail, it is necessary to be convinced that, at each step, political majority and arithmetical majority must coincide. They can. . . .

[Numerous] examples can be taken which show that our behavior today draws its inspiration from the living source of revolutionary theory and practice of our movement.

Such are the foundations of our position, the reasons that lead us to propose the democratic road defined by the draft document.

This is also why the "dictatorship of the proletariat" does not appear in the draft document.

Consequently, and as was demanded by all the federal conferences, we propose that the congress decide to abandon this notion. We propose equally that the congress charge the central committee that we are going to elect to submit at the next party congress necessary modifications to be made in the preamble of the rules.

* * *

Perhaps, certain people think, we communists, once having reached power, would have the intention of eliminating the others? Nothing in our experience can justify such a fear. We have never eliminated anyone, neither in the government in which we have participated, nor in the numerous municipalities that we direct, and where we have made room for our partners although we were not obliged to do so, since we possessed alone the absolute majority. What other party can say as much? None.

* * *

[The idea of diverse roads to socialism of which we have spoken] does not lead to any withdrawal into ourselves, any weakening of our solidarity with other communist parties, among them, in particular, those several which have already successfully led their countries to socialism.

* * *

We will be on the lookout to fight with determination—whoever be the instigators or the bearers—against anti-Sovietism, the lie and the slander of which the socialist countries are, without exception, the object.

It is with the same will to aid the progress of socialism, its influence, and its authority that we express frankly our point of view on what appears to us to be erroneous in the conduct of one or another socialist countries. It is not within our purpose to sermonize nor to indulge in demands in the affairs of brother parties. . . .

It is natural that we express our disagreement with repressive measures which attempt to eliminate freedoms of opinion, expression, or creation wherever they be made. We have been led to do so concerning certain occurrences in the Soviet Union. We cannot admit, in effect, that the communist ideal, whose object is man's happiness and for which we summon the workers to fight, can be tainted by unjust and unjustified acts. Such acts are not at all a necessary consequence of socialism. We can permit them even less, when it concerns a country whose people are solidly and definitively united around several decades of socialist work.

The existence of divergence on this subject with the Communist Party of the Soviet Union will not of itself lead us, no more so than in the past, to weaken our will to co-operate with it in the common struggle against imperialism and for our great common objectives. . . . [Our movement] is not, and cannot be, a church or a centralized organization subjecting each party to constraining decrees, to a uniform law.

* * *

14

EUROCOMMUNISM AND THE STATE*

Santiago Carrillo
(Published in Barcelona, 1977)

Eurocommunism developed primarily under Italian and French auspices. It was in those countries that a communist victory through the ballot box seemed most possible and that the CPI and CPF came under pressure to increase their acceptability to the electorate, which they did by criticizing Soviet practice and indicating their strong support for political pluralism.

In April 1977, the Communist Party of Spain (CPE) was legalized, and as it prepared for elections scheduled in June, it, too, followed the path of Eurocommunism.

The secretary general of the CPE, Santiago Carrillo, had never been Moscow's man. A socialist before he had been a communist, he had opted to spend the years of exile from Franco-dominated Spain in Paris, not in Moscow. In 1968, he had opposed the Soviet march into Czechoslovakia. The following year, the USSR, as evidence of its mistrust of him, attempted unsuccessfully to destroy his leadership by found-

* Excerpts

ing a rival Spanish communist party. Carrillo was, over the years, sympathetic to the idea of "many roads to socialism." But, early in 1977, seeking to make Spanish communism acceptable to an electorate that had been systematically taught to despise it and its Stalinist masters in Moscow, Carrillo went beyond the language of the CPI and CPF in setting forth the necessity for a democratic, pluralistic communism and particularly in evaluating the USSR, going so far as to state that the Soviet Union was not a socialist country.

Moscow reacted heatedly against both Carrillo and the CPE. Under pressure from other parties, the Kremlin retracted its charges against the Spanish party but not those against Carrillo. However, despite Moscow's hostility, or because of it, Carrillo's book Eurocommunism and the State, *which had been released in time for the Spanish elections, received abundant publicity and became widely read in Eastern Europe, where it was circulated clandestinely.*

SOCIALIST CRITICISM AND FORMS OF THE DEMOCRATIC STRUGGLE

To achieve . . . [universal suffrage] entails unfolding an energetic political, social, cultural, and theoretical fight against the dominant bourgeois ideology—that is, to develop all the action we have been discussing in order to turn the ideological machinery of the state against the dominant classes and progressively gain comprehension and support, at least in part, from that part of the state's strength which, up to now, has permitted those dominant classes to guarantee their own domination. This is equivalent to fighting for the democratization of economic, social, political, and cultural life by means of the democratization of the state's organization and machinery.

For this enterprise, we need to recoup intellectual and moral values for the forces that fight for socialism. Hypocritically, the system of monopolistic capital of the state tries to identify these values as its own. The bourgeoisie used to personify these values in a different era—when it was a revolutionary class—but it no longer personifies them today.

It is a necessity and an obligation *to open a breech, to achieve a real differentiation*, between those who sincerely cultivate the values of democracy and political liberalism, and those for whom democracy and liberalism mean the exclusive maintenance of the property of monopolistic capital and its economic privileges. The latter are democrats and liberals only so long as democracy and liberty do not question the ruling economic system; as soon as it changes, they become fascists and can coldly kill, torture, and persecute their own children.

At times, the one group and the other become jumbled, seeming to mix together. The political base of the center or left-center, which has sustained the European political system of this period, has been based on this intermingling.

Today, what distinguishes an authentic democrat or liberal from a rabid defender of the system of monopolistic capital is the acceptance or not of the right of socialist forces to govern and apply their program, if the majority of the population, by means of free elections, gives them that mandate. It also means the recognition of the right of communists to play on democratic territory without restrictions.

I would say, at the same time, that what distinguishes those European communist parties which have assimilated the experience of this period, and which grant democracy all of its worth, is their attitude toward those criticisms—made in good faith—of the defects of the established socialist systems, particularly toward its forms which are totalitarian in a certain sense (but let us not ever confuse them with fascist regimes), subverting democracy [and] individual human rights, [imposing] bureaucratism, etc. This critical attitude is radically different from the attitude of those who are enemies of these countries, not because of the defects of their political system, but because private capitalist property has been supressed in them and new possibilities have been opened for the promotion of the exploited classes. But our critical attitude can coincide in many aspects with the attitude of sincere democrats and liberals.

This distinguishing attitude on our side means, obviously, that we do not believe that *all* men are defined politically and socially by purely *economic* reasons. This is not in contradiction with historic materialism, nor with the general truth that classes are defined by their social placement and their relation to the means of production. In this age of transition, in the same manner that numerous Christians join the progressive movement, basing this on the revolutionary origins of Christianity, a whole series of people, agnostics or not, live in a similar evolution, basing themselves on conceptions which have their origin in the times in which the bourgeoisie was a revolutionary class which raised up the motto of "Equality, Liberty, Fraternity." If we do not understand this phenomenon, we run the risk of automatically classifying as adversaries of socialism people who objectively are not adversaries.

To criticize real or supposed errors of the communists, to criticize the negative aspects of established socialist regimes is not, in and of itself, either counterrevolutionary or anti-Soviet. We are referring here to serious criticism and not to calumny. Certainly, criticism of socialist countries, in order to be objective, has to distinguish the objective circumstances of different countries. In such criticism, one must take into account the history, the traditions, the development, and the culture of each people One cannot apply the same measurement standard to the Czechoslovakia or the Soviet Union of today as to the peoples of Indochina, Korea, or Cuba. But serious criticism can only strengthen socialism and contribute to its development.

It is clear that in these same established socialist regimes, especially in those which have achieved a certain level of economic development, such criticism must have internal channels of expression, and not be repressed by intolerable methods.

Socialism, in order to be extended and transformed into a world economic system—which does not mean either being the sole model nor the subordination to a state or a group of states, nor loss of the independence and originality of each country, nor even the disappearance of the differences in interests among different states—has to recoup for itself democratic and liberal values, the defense of human rights, including respect for differing minorities.

At the same time, and at the same level, the prizing of free elections as a rule, the criterion by which the government of society should be judged, does not mean reducing the role of the popular masses merely to a vote for their representatives every "X" number of years. The masses must possess the right to remove their elected officials when these do not deliver, and to elect new ones. They must possess the possibility of constantly intervening at all levels of power: political, economic, social, and cultural. This underscores the worth of the forms of self-developing democracy and popular control.

But the popular masses and the political forces should also keep other rights of intervention in political life, beyond the classical liberties of press, assembly, association, etc. For example, demonstrations and political strikes are democratic rights which cannot be abandoned in a truly democratic society. All that a profoundly democratic regime should eliminate is terrorism and physical violence as instruments of political action, and the use of calumny and defamation of people and groups.

In specific circumstances, including existing democratic institutions, when an elected government in a concrete moment acts by damaging the interests of the majority of the country and favoring the privileges of a minority, a political strike is a democratic right, as an element of protest and pressure against unjust means.

* * *

WHY THE CONCEPT OF THE DICTATORSHIP OF THE PROLETARIAT?

* * *

Lenin described the bureaucracy and permanent army as "a parasite clinging to the body of the bourgeois society, a parasite engendered by internal contradictions which rend this society, but precisely a parasite which closes up the vital pores."

Nonetheless, the state created by the October Revolution had to organize a bureaucracy and a permanent army; it gave that bureaucracy privileges which were more than the simple salary of a worker, and made it practically as immobile as the functionaries of a capitalist state.

Lenin himself later wrote the most acerbic criticisms against that same bureaucracy and against the dangers of bureaucratization.

The ideal proletarian state which Lenin dreamed of—that is, a state in which an armed proletariat, a popular militia, and functionaries considered replaceable and simple "countables" paid the same as workers, would replace the bureaucracy, the permanent army, and special organs of repression—after more than fifty years in power is not seen anywhere. In their place a powerful state machinery has grown up, dominating the society, which is still less than the "minimal state" that Lenin dreamed of.

If all states are instruments of domination of one class by another, and in the USSR there are no antagonistic classes, so that there does not objectively exist any necessity for repressing certain classes, whom does that state dominate?

The Stalinist phenomenon has grown and acted in that State with a series of formal features similar to those of fascist dictatorships. I emphasize the *formal* features because the essence of the Soviet social regime was and is radically opposed to the essence of fascism; this is not only a theoretical appreciation, but a truth manifested in the blood of the peoples of the USSR during World War II. And the revolutionary essence of the Soviet social regime has been repeatedly affirmed by solidarity with peoples who have fought against fascism and imperialism.

For a long time, we have attributed these phenomena to the personal characteristics of Stalin, using the formula of "the cult of personality," and it is true that Stalin's personal characteristics have weighed seriously in this question. We Marxists do not deny the role of personalities in history. But how could a personality with the characteristics of Stalin manage to impose itself, despite the fact that Lenin denounced them? It is true that Stalin knew how to play off—with supreme ability—the existing contradictions among the diverse groups forming the directorate of the Communist Party of the Soviet Union, and was able to make his own place as a unifier, getting rid of various persons, including all of those who could interfere with his own accession. But one must wonder if the practical sense of Stalin was not more in harmony with the *type of state* which was being formed in reality, with what Togliatti called the *system*, with the objective realities which surrounded him, than was his opposition, especially after sickness reduced the possibilities of action by Lenin and finally caused his premature death.

It is evident that the Stalinist phenomenon, which was a form of totalitarianism and abundantly exploited by capitalist propaganda, has weakened the democratic trustworthiness of the communist parties among a part of the population of our countries.

The denunciation which Khrushchev made of the Stalinist horrors momentarily broke the entire system set up by Stalin, as much in the USSR as in the socialist countries of Eastern Europe. There were happenings like those of Hungary and Poland where heterogeneous "national fronts" were spontaneously and tacitly formed against the Stalinist system of domination. While in Poland this system found a communist opposition capable of rectifying the situation, the Hungarians were not allowed their opposition. It was Soviet troops that reestablished "order"—a new blow against the international prestige of communism, a blow which has had repercussions in our parties.

For a few years, Khrushchev personified a new spirit of openness in the USSR toward the outside, as well as a new spirit of greater internal liberty. These coincided with successes like the launching of the first "Sputnik," Gagarin's climb into the cosmos, new currents in Soviet literature and cinema, and a cleansing and greater control of the special organs of repression—a type of springtime.

It was a period which raised the international prestige of the USSR. But that period ended quickly. A type of palace coup deposed Khrushchev, discovering his "errors" when all of us believed that there was, finally, a collective directorate co-responsible for the good and the bad. Certainly, under Khrushchev's direction there had sprung up the conflicts with China which he treated—as shown by what has come to light—with undoubtable lightness and torpidity, using methods which gave off a passably Stalinist stench.

In reality, one of the causes of Khrushchev's fall lay, perhaps, in his inability to transform the machinery of the state created under Stalin, the *system* of political power to which Togliatti alluded, which ended up by pulverizing him.

That system has not been transformed, has not been democratized, and even has kept many of its aspects of coercion in its relations with the socialist states of Eastern Europe, as was made brutally evident by the military occupation of Czechoslovakia.

The massive and annihilating repressions of Stalin's days have disappeared. Khrushchev, deposed, died in bed at home. There has been progress, stained by forms of oppression and repression in certain areas, especially in culture. But we still do not find ourselves looking at a state which can be considered a workers' democracy.

This affects the credibility of our party more, very much more, than if a dictatorship of the proletariat really existed in the USSR. If *bourgeois democracies* have a lot of the formal in them, so does the *workers' democracy* achieved up to now by communists.

But today in the communist workers' movement, in the progressive movement, these questions are raised more or less openly, according to specific cases and not by the "influence of bourgeois propaganda," as conformists are accustomed to saying, but because the evidence of reality is interposed.

And are we communists, who consider ourselves (and justly so) to be a force of the vanguard, going to be the last to admit that evidence, to face reality?

To do that is, moreover, the only way to give service to the cause of socialism, as much in countries which have suppressed capitalistic property as in those which keep it.

The type of state which has developed in the Soviet Union, which is no longer a capitalistic state since it does not defend private property, but neither is it the state which Lenin dreamed of, with workers directly exercising power—how can we place it in the Marxist conception of the state? Lenin said that the state in the first phase of socialism would keep many of the characteristics of the bourgeois right. But the state we are talking about has gone past, in that respect, Lenin's predictions. It has not only kept characteristics of the bourgeois right, but has stooped to deformations and degenerations which in other times we could imagine only in imperialist states.

* * *

THE WORLD ENVIRONMENT AND ITS INFLUENCE ON THE STATE

* * *

[S]*tating the struggle for socialism in terms of world confrontation between two systems—in practice, between two powers or groups of powers—is not for us.* First, because the socialism achieved up to now, still in a very primary state, is not yet a luminous example which can decide the victory in terms of an ideological confrontation—I am referring to the developed capitalist countries to which we can propose that model—and secondly, because a military confrontation would be suicide for both sides.

We must take for granted that the workers' and international communist movement is not homogenous, that diverse tendencies do exist. I am simplifying here, but there exists one tendency—propagandized by Soviet comrades—which tries to keep the movement adhered to a series of dogmas that can mean a propagandistic glorification of the type of system achieved in the USSR but that, except in rare cases, does not help communist parties become parties which govern or even direct their countries. There also exists a Chinese tendency, very difficult to define since, up to now, it has been manifested almost exclusively by an attitude of closed hostility toward the Soviet Union and, in practice, devalues the role and the independence of the international workers' movement.

And there is—again, I am simplifying—a new tendency, growing principally in advanced capitalistic countries, which stays faithful to the principles of Marxism, which treats *in a critical way* the conquests of the revolutionary movement up to today, which tries to incorporate the analysis and elaboration of structural, economic, social, and cultural changes into the achievements of theory, and which uses democratic paths and independence to elaborate its own strategy.

Among all these heterogeneous and diverse tendencies, it is the national factor which is most influential, as is logical. In this stage of distension and cooperation, national forms of class struggle—and not the collaboration of the classes—are placed on the first level; political maturation and achievements in theory influence on a greater or lesser scale parties which possess their own long and rich experience in the struggle of the classes.

Here are found the bases for a simultaneous coincidence and contradiction—a coincidence which springs from a social regime, which is non-capitalist, in which the material bases for the development of socialism exist; contradiction with a type of state which, by its characteristics, tends to place itself not only above its own society, but above the societies of other countries; a type of state which tends toward power because of a series of objective and subjective factors, some of whose causes I have pointed out.

The progress of the socialist movement in developed capitalist countries can help society and Soviet communists to overcome that type of state, to take steps forward in their transformation into an authentic state of a workers' democracy. That is a historical necessity which would do great good for the cause of socialism in the entire world and would destroy much of bourgeois propaganda at its roots. For that reason, it is even more lamentable that in 1968 the Czech comrades were not permitted to continue their experiment.

INDEX